TENSIONS IN THE MIDDLE EAST

TENSIONS

in the

Middle

East

EDITED BY PHILIP W. THAYER

INTRODUCTION

BY

CHARLES MALIK

BALTIMORE

THE JOHNS HOPKINS PRESS

Foreword

DURING THE LAST WEEK of August, 1957, the School of
Advanced International Studies of The Johns Hopkins University sponsored in Washington a four-day conference on
"Tensions in the Middle East." Like similar gatherings held
in previous years, the conference was designed to provide a
forum for expressions of opinion on recent developments in
an area of great significance to the free world. Those present
at the sessions, numbering more than three hundred, included
members of the faculties of American and foreign universities,
government officials concerned with the Middle East, and
representatives of business firms with interests in the region.
The conference was opened with an address of welcome by
President Milton Eisenhower of The Johns Hopkins University and closed with a summary of impressions by Ernest
K. Lindley of Newsweek magazine.

Prior to the summer of 1957, mounting tensions had produced in the Middle East an increasingly delicate and potentially explosive situation, which was commanding the
anxious attention of capitals throughout the world. Recurring
incidents in Cyprus, the Suez affair, and the position of Israel,
all contributed to make it seem highly desirable to explore
the pertinent backgrounds of a number of the problems in
the Middle East as objectively as possible and with the greatest authority that could be enlisted for the task. In planning
the conference, therefore, thirteen topics that it was felt might
contribute most constructively to the ends in view were selected for discussion. A number of these were concerned with
basic considerations, others with economic and social factors,
and still others with specific situations. Papers on these topics
were presented by outstanding authorities on the points under
consideration, and each paper was followed by a commentary

v

prepared by a scholar of equal eminence in the field. This volume contains the papers and commentaries thus submitted to the conference. Although it is fully appreciated that the result does not by any means constitute an exhaustive treatment of the Middle Eastern problem, the School of Advanced International Studies hopes that the work of these scholars may lead to a better understanding of some of the most important issues involved.

In the work of the conference and in the preparation of the materials for publication, my grateful thanks are due to all those who took part in the proceedings, to the officers of The Johns Hopkins Press, and to the members of the School staff. It is their labor and co-operation that have made the result possible.

Washington, D. C.   PHILIP W. THAYER
October 15, 1957   Dean, School of Advanced
                                     International Studies

Contents

vii

Introduction

EXPERTS IN THE DIVERSE ISSUES of the Middle East have contributed their views to this volume. I wish to say a word about the situation in general.

Five matters appear to me to dominate the situation. First, there is the Palestine question. Although new factors have complicated the Middle Eastern scene in general, the Palestine question remains very much at the center of things. We are no nearer a solution today than we were five or ten years ago. The basic elements of the problem are now fairly clear. The Arabs do not recognize any right to a Jewish state in Palestine. About a million of the original inhabitants of Palestine were displaced from their country and have been living for ten years as refugees in neighboring lands, where they have been looked after for the most part by United Nations agencies. This army of refugees is at the base of many social and political problems troubling the Middle East today. Far from softening issues, the passage of time is hardening hearts. In contrast to the situation five or ten years ago, today great-power politics mightily determines the whole question. There is the phenomenon of what might be termed "competitive extremism" with respect to this problem as between governments and governments, and governments and peoples, in the Middle East. The United Nations Emergency Force, by inserting itself between Egypt and Israel, appears to have stabilized the situation militarily in the south. But there is no over-all political improvement at all. Jerusalem remains a focus of great potential danger, and the apparent quiet along the armistice lines between Israel on the one hand and Jordan, Syria, and Lebanon on the other is most deceptive. As matters stand and without costly sacrifices on the part of Israel, including substantial territorial concessions, I see no immediate solution to this problem. From the point of view of regional and world peace (in the sense of mere absence of armed clashes), the utmost that can be hoped for now is to keep on preventing, through diplomacy and the United Nations, the actual outbreak of hostilities between Arab and Israeli. He who can now hope for more must be wiser or more sanguine than I am.

A second dominating matter is the diversity of political relationships emerging among the states of the Middle East. There are the Baghdad Pact states in the north—Turkey, Iraq, Iran, and Pakistan. This arrangement is not without its internal strains, but as long as the Cold War persists it will remain a defensive anti-Communist pact friendly to and co-operating with the West. There is the Egyptian-Syrian alliance in the south. Ideologically, this alliance bases itself upon Arab nationalism, with some leaning towards the East, both the Asian East and the Communist East; economically, militarily, and politically there are closer ties between this alliance and the Communist world than between it and the West. Then there are Saudi Arabia, Jordan, and Lebanon, which belong neither to the Baghdad Pact nor to the Egyptian-Syrian alliance, but which have a very loose and informal understanding among them based on opposing international communism in their own lands and on co-operating with the United States in diverse ways. This mosaic of formal and informal arrangements is of course partly a function of the Cold War. Committees of the Arab League still meet, but as an effective organ for the co-ordination of political effort among the Arab states, the Arab League has practically ceased to exist. How this diversity of political relationships among the states of the Middle East will develop depends for the most part upon political developments in each of the countries concerned, the wisdom of the leaders, the awakening of the peoples, and the bearing of the Cold War upon the area.

The third factor governing the Middle Eastern scene is the strategic and economic importance of the region. (It must be noted here in passing that all these "factors" interdetermine one another. Thus strategy and economics determine great-power interest, and all three complicate the Palestine issue;

similar functional linkages can be worked out between any two or more of these five factors. These factors then are not extraneous elements extraneously bearing upon the region; they are in fact so many diverse modes of being of one and the same thing—the Middle East. They are of the nature of dimensions through which or angles from which the Middle East can be viewed.) The strategy and economics of the Middle East have been widely discussed, both in this volume and elsewhere. Western strategists affirm that the Middle East is vital to the defense of the West; and the Soviet Union never tires of reminding the world that the Middle East is its immediate neighbor. In fact, the Soviet Union through its Caucasian and adjacent regions regards itself as a Middle Eastern power. The problem of bases and of the neutralization of the Middle East thus takes on the greatest importance. In any fundamental defense planning anywhere in the world, the Middle East must figure prominently. And for peaceful transportation of men and goods the Middle East is, through its waterways and airfields, which join three continents, probably the most important communications center in the world. The economic importance of the Middle East arises partly from this central location, partly from the fact that it is a huge market for manufactured goods, but chiefly from the fact that European industry depends and will depend at least for some time to come upon the oil resources of the area. There is plenty of oil in Arabia and around the Persian Gulf. The strategic and economic importance of the Middle East at once focuses the eyes of the world upon it and turns its eyes upon the world. This means that as long as the world is in conflict, this conflict will inevitably reflect itself in the Middle East. International interest is of the essence of the Middle East, and the Middle East can never abduct itself away from the world.

There is, fourth, the phenomenon of the rise of the masses. This embraces the phenomena of Middle Eastern nationalism, of the gradual rise in the standard of living of the masses and therefore of their self-articulation, of the clamor for social and economic justice, and of the demand for a more equitable distribution of the wealth accruing from the oil resources of

the region. This complex massive awakening is a novel factor
in the history of the Middle East. In former ages there was
God, there was his immediate representative, and there were
his subjects, and these had simply to conform; today the ruler
more and more has to conform to the will of his subjects. The
people are beginning to count. Where there is no strong government resting upon stable social and political institutions
and traditions to start with, and until the masses become more
enlightened and therefore more independent and critical in
their thinking, the conformation of government to people
must mean a considerable catering to their whims and imag-
inations. This is the ideal soil for the development of demagogy. The passage from medievalism to democracy appears to
entail demagogy as a necessary first stage. How to guide, lead,
and inspire the rising masses of the Middle East—socially,
politically, and above all intellectually and spiritually—will tax
the highest available statesmanship, and not only in the Middle
East.

Last, there is the changing configuration of the interest and
influence of the great powers in the Middle East. There is a
relative decline in European influence and a corresponding
increase in Soviet and American influence. These two giants
face each other today for the first time directly across the
Middle East. The direct or indirect presence of America—
through its commerce, its economic interests, its educational
and other institutions, the trickle of Middle Eastern emigration
that found its way to its shores, and its European friends and
allies—was always there; but what is distinctly novel is the
prominence of the Russian presence. In its positive aspect this
is not more than five years old. Negatively, the Middle East
has always been living under the shadow of the Russian col-
ossus, as witness the well-known historical discomfiture of
Turkey and Iran. But the actual political and ideological penetration of the Middle East by international communism is a
very recent phenomenon. Far-reaching economic, political,
and military arrangements have been concluded for the first
time in history between Russia and some countries in the
Middle East. Communist literature is more widely spread than

ever before, and some countries witness a marked anti-Western reaction. The recent technological successes of the Soviet Union have helped to enhance this anti-Western pro-Soviet general feeling. The whole intellectual climate in some countries forbids even the whisper of a criticism of the Communist world. There is thus an alliance between communism and nationalism. Two related questions arise: Is "peaceful coexistence" or "peaceful competition" between communism and the West possible in the Middle East? And is neutralism with respect to communism and the West (namely, equal and balanced dealing with or indifference to communism and the West) possible in the Middle East? These two questions raise matters of the profoundest significance. They deserve a whole separate responsible investigation by themselves. He will win in the present crucial struggle who shows in the long run a more genuine respect for the legitimate political, economic, and cultural aspiration of the Middle Eastern peoples and a deeper concern for their intellectual and spiritual needs. He will win who shows in truth greater strength of character and mind and determination. If the West desires to hold its own, it must have much greater faith in its own ultimate values and in their genuine universality, and on the basis of this faith it must come forward with bold and dynamic plans, to the end that the peoples of the Middle East be freed from the insidious danger of regarding any new ideology as their only way of salvation. I believe the Western resources of wisdom, depth, diplomacy, and love are not yet exhausted in meeting this great historic requirement.

Will the desert, both in its physical and its existential sense, be overcome in the Middle East? Will the masses be liberated from their dark and blind cravings? Will social responsibility —a genuine respect and concern for others—really flourish in the Middle East? Will there be peace with justice and freedom in this central region of the world? Will the state of the world itself permit such peace with justice and freedom? Will the patience and power of reason shed their wonderful blessings upon these ancient peoples? Will civilization and culture and depth come once again to their own in this cradle of all

civilization and all culture and all depth? Will the great positive cumulative heritage of the West, from Pythagoras and
Pericles to Pasteur and Lincoln, with its infinite universal
riches and its priceless view of nature, man, and God, shine
soon with vigor and conviction and glory, not only in and for
the West, but in and for the whole world? These are some of
the ultimate issues facing us all in the next fifty years.

Beirut, Lebanon
December 30, 1957   Charles Malik

Basic Considerations

I

The United States and the Middle East

ROBERT STRAUSZ-HUPÉ

Director, Foreign Policy Research Institute,
University of Pennsylvania

I

IN UNITED STATES FOREIGN POLICY, the term *Middle East* connotes a complex of related problems in strategy, diplomacy, and international economics rather than a geographical region. Once upon a time, when Britain stood at Suez and at the Khyber Pass, the Middle East was bounded by the Levant to the west and by British India to the east, with the Caspian Sea to the north and the Arabian Sea to the south. This "Middle East," albeit a geographical illusion, accommodated nicely a number of regional concerns of British policy, just as the "Near East," composed of the Balkan Peninsula, Turkey, and the Levant, served as a convenient compartment for another set of British problems. One of the consequences of World War II was the decline of European power and the emergence of a Middle East that belies its parentage in geographical terminology even more outrageously than did its prewar predecessor, yet accords happily with the political and strategic realities of our times. For the United States, the Middle East ranges from Athens to Teheran and from Ankara to Cairo. Now the meaning of the term is more forthrightly functional than ever before. The Middle East is the southeastern flank of NATO, the world of Arab nationalism, the greatest oil reserve of the West, the slender link to the United States' alliance system in Southeast Asia—and the premier theater of the Cold War. Today's Middle East is what the collapse of European empires and the rise of American and Russian power have made it.

Viewed in this light, the overarching fact about the Middle East is its place in Soviet strategy: it is the area along the periphery of the Communist bloc where Soviet maneuverability is least restricted by local countervailing forces and by Western defense arrangements and where the Communist strategy of disruption carries the highest premium in terms of Western embarrassment. Nowhere has Soviet policy inflicted upon the West, at relatively small cost, more painful injuries than in the Middle East; nowhere are the future prospects of Soviet policy brighter than on the West's most sensitive and troublesome flank, the Middle East. It is the Soviet challenge that has shaped American foreign policy east of Athens. Here, as elsewhere, American policy has been reactive rather than activist.

Even without the Soviet challenge, the United States still might have been drawn into the affairs of the area. Yet American initiative would have been confined to a number of local and highly selective issues, and even in these the United States would have confined itself to its traditional roles of moderator, offering its good offices before the bar of world opinion and counselling the proper legal procedure; of trader, seeking markets and sound investments; and of generous mentor, endowing schools and spreading the blessings of universal, secular education. The United States can still play these roles and, indeed, does play them. It has been forced, however, into another unaccustomed and perilous part, that of the strategic ringmaster of the Middle East.

Ambiguous as may have been the stand of the United States on not a few issues of the Middle East, in matters affecting the area's strategic security American policy has been about as consistent as that of Britain at the zenith of her power. The Truman Doctrine and the Eisenhower Doctrine, together with the attendant deployment of force, asserted the predominant interest of the United States in the Middle East and placed American policy in straight succession to British diplomacy in the nineteenth century, designed to preserve the integrity of the Ottoman Empire and to bar Russia from the Persian Gulf. True, the advances in the technology of war, the rise of nationalism, and the spread of new ideologies have wrought many changes, but none of these factors has altered the strategic equation.

The Middle East remains the keystone of the Western arc that spans Eurasia. If this keystone were knocked out, the Western defensive system, over which the United States now presides, would be changed beyond recognition. There would be a yawning gap between the free world's Atlantic and Asian alliances; Soviet power would be entrenched along the eastern shores of the Mediterranean and along the Persian Gulf and would press upon Africa and envelop the Indian subcontinent. Although these developments would not exhaust the consequences of a Western withdrawal from the Middle East, they would suffice to bring about a decisive change in the world balance of power. Conceivably, the West could establish a new perimeter of defense in Central Africa and its remaining island possessions in the Indian Ocean. Conceivably, too, the nuclear stalemate (if it does exist) has diminished the value of Middle Eastern bases and, in general, has lessened the relevancy of strategic considerations, since, so we are told, war has become unthinkable anyhow. Thus far, however, the United States has been reluctant to sever its strategic attachment to the Middle East, obsolete as it might be in the light of technological as well as of more elevated considerations.

The Middle East, like all debated grounds, is fertile soil for conflict. Strategic involvement has fostered American intimacy with virtually every contested issue of the area. This intimacy not only has strained the resources of American diplomacy but also has sorely tested those basic assumptions that formed the approach of the American people to the facts of international life. Although the rationale of American foreign policy is no enigma, its application has given rise to baffling controversies over not a few venerable principles that

Americans view as trusted guides to policy. The Middle East has confronted the United States with a series of painful dilemmas, essentially moral ones: how to reconcile diverse "rights" to national self-determination with one another; how to reconcile diverse "rights" of national self-determination with the claims of America's allies; how to square the United States' obligations to the United Nations with the United States' diverse stated positions vis-à-vis allies, neutrals, and enemies; and, finally, how not to compromise the ideals of democracy by condoning, here and now, the usually undemocratic practices of local rulers. In brief, the United States has become enmeshed in a series of contradictions, some of its own making and some contrived by others, that invariably fall to the lot of the paramount power in the ancient East.

II

In the Middle East, the United States is confronted by four principal conflicts: first, the struggle with the Soviet Union for strategic control of the entire area; second, the contest among Western interests deriving largely from the liquidation of empires; third, the rivalry of the Arab states over the leadership of the Arab world; and fourth, the Arab-Israeli conflict. To each of these conflicts the United States is a party. Each conflict feeds upon the other, and any Middle Eastern settlement, if it is to endure and accord with American interests, must be based upon solutions to these four major problems.

The position that the Soviet Union now occupies in the Middle East is a novel one. When the United States was confronted after World War II with the expansionism of the Soviet Union, it did not anticipate that the Soviet Union would become a party to the affairs of the Middle East. It is debatable that Britain could have retained her control of the Suez Canal even had American diplomacy not pressured Britain into evacuating her Egyptian bases. It is likely that Britain's straitened circumstances and public opinion would have compelled any government, Labour or Conservative, to withdraw from Suez and to terminate an increasingly costly military occupation in the midst of a hostile Arab population. Since Britain would have had to withdraw from Egypt sooner or later, and since American foreign policy seems to have hastened Britain's timing, it is all the more surprising that the United States failed to discern that the eclipse of British power would create a political vacuum, that this vacuum would have to be filled, and that were it not filled speedily, the Soviet Union would seek to fill it and thus to turn the Mediterranean flank of NATO. It can now be seen that the cloak of NATO was cut too skimpily and thus exposed the tenderest part of the alliance's anatomy.

It is impossible to blink the historic fact that the Soviets have succeeded, far beyond the boldest expectations of the czars, to penetrate into the Middle East and to exploit, albeit forty years after the event, the fragmentation of the Ottoman Empire. It is unlikely that the Soviets could have accomplished this feat had the West gauged correctly the growing dynamism of the Arab masses. Long before Russian armaments and technicians flowed into Egypt and Syria, the Communists set out patiently to win over and to train carefully selected groups of Arab white-collar workers and intellectuals. The primary objective of the Communist effort was not so much to build elaborate party cadres as to supply the leadership of the heretofore inarticulate masses of Arab workers and peasants. By contrast, the West, in its effort to make friends, succeeded only too well. The favored few accepted the benefits of Western education, embraced Western values more or less sincerely—and became alienated from the mass of their own people.

It is here that we must seek the basic reason for the Western failure to build a secure rampart against communism as well as against Russian imperialist penetration in the Middle East. Obviously, the United States cannot be burdened with the past mistakes of those European imperial powers that until the end of World War II dominated the Middle East. Yet the decline of these European powers has placed the social and economic as well as the political and strategic problems of the area at the doorstep of the United States. It is no accident that the one and only country of the Middle East that stands as a reliable bulwark against Soviet penetration is Turkey. The Kemalist Revolution not only transformed Turkey into a modern state, but also created the rudiments of a social order that can accommodate itself to modern economic development. The task is as yet far from completed, and Turkey is plagued by many growing pains. Yet Turkey has furnished an example that the Middle Eastern countries, most of whom once were Turkey's vassals, can seek to emulate. The model of Israel is, for most of the Arab states, out of reach economically, even if it were a much more attractive one emotionally than it now is and promises to be in the foreseeable future. Thus, by necessity, the Middle Eastern policy of the United States, insofar as it seeks to shore up local powers of resistance against Soviet penetration, must pivot on Turkey. Incidentally, this consideration, aside from others, should dictate United States foreign policy towards the Cyprus question.

The United States has fallen heir to a number of issues that divide the peoples of the Middle East and has helped to create several new ones that complicate its relationships with several of its traditional friends in Europe.

The promulgation of the Eisenhower Doctrine, although it marks a new phase in the Middle Eastern policy of the United States, leaves unsettled many problems that led to the crisis in 1956 and, ultimately, to the United States' blanket commitment to the security of the entire area. Among these, the most pressing is still that of the reconciliation of the policy of the United States on the one hand and of the policies of Great Britain and France on the other. In retrospect, it now appears that the Suez debacle can be traced to the failure of the Western allies to view the Middle East as what it is in fact: the eastern and most exposed flank of the North Atlantic alliance. The machinery for joint consultation, developed under NATO, did not extend to the Levant, nor did the Baghdad Pact, which the United States did not join, provide an alternative machinery of co-ordination.

It is difficult to assess the rationale that guided, in the Middle East, the unilateral policies of the United States. Three reasons have been given by responsible American officials as having prompted the stand taken by the United States on the Suez imbroglio: first, the deference of the United States to the principles of the United Nations and to world opinion; second, the threat of a world war, had the Suez crisis not been resolved peacefully; and third, the need for maintaining the good will of the Afro-Asian bloc in order to preserve the United States' stake in Asia and, incidentally, the integrity of the British Commonwealth.

It should be noted that these three alleged motivations are not consistent with one another politically or ethically. The first derives its ethos from principles of the United Nations Charter, the second from an estimate of Soviet intentions, and the third from expediency.

Although certain provisions of the United Nations Charter and the subsequent resolutions of the General Assembly supported the United States' case against Anglo-French-Israeli "aggression," Britain and France, too, have rested their case against Egypt on the spirit and stipulations of the United Nations Charter. In fairness to all, it must be conceded that, up until now, the controversy has not been adjudged by the one authority that conceivably might be qualified to do so, the International Court of Justice. As regards world opinion, it did not become articulate until after the United States and the Soviet Union had come down on the same side of the issue. Would the Soviet Union have gone to war in order to stop the Anglo-French-Israeli intervention at Suez? Although the Middle East was rife with rumors of menacing deployments of Soviet power, there is, in the public domain, no convincing evidence showing that the Soviets would have gone to war. To the contrary, the events in Europe and the subsequent evolution of Soviet domestic politics go far to discredit estimates regarding the alleged bellicose intentions of the Soviets in the Middle East. Would Afro-Asian public opinion

have turned against the West and, specifically, against the
United States had the United States not taken its stand in
the United Nations against Britain, France, and Israel? This
is unlikely, for a homogeneous Afro-Asian opinion does not
exist. It can be argued that a smart riposte against Nasser
would have reassured the West's Asian allies and sobered
some of Asia's mischievous neutralists. Indeed, the promulgation of the Eisenhower Doctrine and the deployment of
United States forces in the wake of the Jordan crisis produced
precisely these effects.

Although other events have superseded the Suez crisis, its
consequences still disturb the relations of the United States
to its oldest European allies and to Israel, a state which the
world regards as an American creation. There are other Middle Eastern issues that divide the United States and its Western allies. To some extent, such lesser controversies as, for
example, American-British rivalry over the exploitation of
Middle Eastern oil reserves might yield to negotiation and
compromise, particularly since the rival interests are mostly
represented by proxy, and the two respective governments do
not confront one another directly. Perhaps the most important item on the Western agenda of unfinished business in
the Middle East is Egypt's support of the Algerian rebels.
There can be no doubt that the Soviet Union, by supplying
modern arms to Egypt, supports indirectly the Algerian rebellion against France, for the obsolete weapons discarded by
Egypt find their way into the hands of the Algerian guerrillas.
This example, although but one among many others, illustrates the close correspondence of the strategic complex, the
Middle East, with the strategic complex, NATO.

The increasing urgency of the Cyprus problem derives from
the Suez crisis. Through Cyprus, the Middle East reaches
deep into the affairs of NATO. The three parties to the
Cyprus conflict, Great Britain, Greece, and Turkey, are members of NATO. Up until the outbreak of guerrilla warfare on
Cyprus, the mutual relationships of the three countries had
been about as friendly as they had ever been in history. The
aggravation of the Cyprus problem began with the evacua-

tion by Britain of the Suez Canal zone and the transfer of part of the Suez garrison to Cyprus. Greco-Turkish relations worsened with the initiation of EOKA terrorist activities, directed in part against the British garrison and in part against the Turkish minority on the island, and with the hardening of the official Greek position on *enosis*, i.e., the union of Cyprus with Greece. The fiasco at Suez, although it did not alter the strategic importance of Cyprus in the scheme of Britain's Mediterranean defenses, weakened Britain's determination to finance the garrisoning of the island and to fight a diplomatic rear-guard action against her old ally, Greece. If British public opinion has grown weary of the struggle, the Turks have grown more intransigent in their opposition to *enosis*. Turkey would accept either of two alternatives: the preservation of the status quo or partition of the island, the northern half to go to Turkey, and the southern half to be ceded to Greece. It is unlikely that the present deadlock can be broken except by the collective initiative of NATO, since Turkey's attitude virtually rules out the acceptance of United Nations arbitration. The Council of NATO remains the one international forum that can come to grips with the Cyprus question and hope to strike a tolerable compromise. It is unlikely that this formal approach—the sublimation of the Cyprus problem by NATO intervention—will, by itself, lead to the settlement of the Cyprus problem. The United States, by virtue of its leading role in NATO and in the Middle East, must take the diplomatic lead in order to break the present deadlock and must furnish the guarantees that will make any settlement acceptable to the contesting parties, strategically, politically, and economically.

Those who, in 1918, hailed the "Arab awakening" as the harbinger of Arab unity, envisaged one Arab state comprising an *Arabia Deserta* and the Fertile Crescent. The fragmentation of the Arab world into a number of small and weak states and the subsequent rise of Israel, have turned the Middle East into another Balkan. Only Turkey, Iran, and Egypt are historic states. The other Middle Eastern states owe their existence to diplomatic legerdemain or to the fortunes of tribal warfare. Gratifying as is the present coalition of the Arab monarchs, the kings of Jordan, Iraq, and Saudi Arabia, against the two revolutionary republics, Egypt and Syria, it is as unlikely to endure as were the many previous alignments and realignments of Arab politics. Whatever may have been the achievements and transgressions of Nasserism in Egypt, it responded to a real craving for leadership in the Arab world. Egypt's defeat in the Sinai Peninsula and Nasser's abortive attempt to subvert Jordan probably marked the end of Egypt's role as spokesman of the Arab world, so sensitive to changes in the distribution of power. So pressing is the need for regional integration, especially in the area of economic development, that the present rulers of the Arab peoples cannot resist indefinitely the Arab masses' aspirations to unity.

The emergence of Israel has been the greatest challenge to Arab unity. The Arab states have failed to meet it and, by this token, have forfeited, in the mind of their own peoples, their right to existence. On the other hand, Israel herself is now the greatest obstacle to the ordering of the Middle East on a regional basis, which would allow the co-operative exploitation of the region's resources, especially as regards irrigation, land reclamation, and power resources. The realignment of the Arab kingdoms under the protective umbrella of the Eisenhower Doctrine has given the Middle East a breathing spell in which to reappraise the problem of Palestine and sublimate it into a regional solution. Bilateral settlements are still precluded by mutual suspicion and intransigence. The flow of immigration, at its present pace, into Israel is bound to create demographic problems, which, if history can furnish precedents, have always led to political frictions and, ultimately, to war. Similarly, the manipulation of the Palestinian refugee problem by the Arab host countries tends to aggravate a situation that, under the best of circumstances, will remain explosive for a long time to come. The real problem of the Middle East is how to divert the gaze of its harassed peoples from a series of problems that, taken one by one, are insoluble, and to turn their attention to co-operative undertakings that will redound to their mutual benefit and channel their energies into the economic transformation of the region as a whole.

III

A United States program for the Middle East should aim at the following objectives:

1. The United States should concentrate its efforts in the Middle East on those areas where its political, economic, and strategic objectives converge. This, admittedly, is easier said than done. It so happens, for example, that because of the distribution of the oil reserves and the location of American air bases in the Arab world, the United States will be committed for a long time to come to the support of the monarchical principle in the persons of Idris, Hussein, Faisal, and Saud. The most advanced Arab nationalism, the greatest Communist penetration, and the highest degree of Soviet diplomatic support all converge in the two revolutionary Arab republics, Egypt and Syria, that do not play host to Western bases, that reject all Western-oriented security arrangements, and that, although they are "oil have-nots," control the major oil transit routes to the West. Only the moderate republic of Lebanon sides with the West. Unless a drastic change should occur in the Egyptian and Syrian regimes within the next year or two, the position of the United States in the Middle East during the next decade will hinge upon the ability of the Arab kings to hold the line against the forces of republican nationalism. So far as the Arab masses are concerned, the outcome of this struggle may very well turn on the issue of social reform. Social reform demands a forward-looking mentality and adequate technical resources. It is not a foregone conclusion that republics must necessarily prove superior to kingdoms on this score, especially if the kingdoms are backed by the economic power of the West.

2. The intellectuals, the bureaucrats, the petty bourgeoisie, and the masses of the Arab world want their countries to emulate the successes, the abundance, and the technical

wizardry of the United States. They may be impressed with
the magnitude of the Soviet developmental achievements
within the last quarter of a century, but it is still the image
of American society, with its casual, luxurious freedom for
the average individual, that fascinates them. They admire
what Hollywood has shown them; they crave what they admire. As they undergo the process of socio-economic transformation, they suffer feelings of guilt for abandoning or
diluting their traditional culture, and they seek escape by
criticizing American techno-cultural "imperialism."

Opportunities now exist in the Middle East for the United
States to help create a managerial class that would, in the
long run, exert a stabilizing influence upon the area because
its members would have a vested interest in the existing
political order. Thus, for example, in planning for the economic development of the Middle East, a high priority should
be given to a program under which adequate housing can be
made available to the rising group of technicians. One approach, which, incidentally, would create a more favorable
climate for private investment, would be the extension by
American companies to their Arab employees of loans at low
interest rates for the construction of homes. This would be
one of the least costly methods of promoting an important
class of people committed to the concept of private ownership. While striving to create a new intellectual and political
elite, along with a new middle class of managers and technicians, the United States must seek to avoid an error on
which Western policy has come to grief. Heretofore, the
West has never been able to win over the upper and middle
classes of the Middle East without alienating them from the
masses. The Arab masses are more important today in Middle
Eastern politics than ever before, as Nasser has amply demonstrated. True, their importance may wane, if and when a
sizeable middle class emerges. But if the United States exercises its economic power toward the development of a middle
class, it must avoid the appearance of supporting privilege.
Through education, it should strive to create a popular mentality favorable to the evolution of an "open society," in which

all men and women may aspire to improve their socio-economic status.

3. Western economists have frequently called attention to the "take-off point" for economic development—that stage in the economic progress of a country when it commands sufficient numbers of technically trained people, sufficient amounts of savings, and sufficient economic data to launch itself upon a program of accelerated economic growth. This economic take-off point, however, must be preceded by a psychological take-off point, which is only reached when a country possesses an elite that is ethically formed and prepared to lead the people in the direction of social and economic progress. It is not possible to create such an elite, properly motivated toward the common social good, in the absence of an ethical climate, based upon a system of values. Modern economic development virtually demands the acceptance of a Western value system. Thus, the whole problem is thrown back into the lap of American society. It is reduced to the problem of the character formation of those whose task is to train the Arab elite. If the American who is assigned to a foreign mission is properly motivated, he will be capable of helping to create an elite in the underdeveloped areas that brings to its task technical competence as well as devotion to the common good. Thus far, American society, with its orientation toward the profit motive and the pleasure potentialities of an economy of abundance, has not shown itself as capable as the devotees of the "Marxist myth" to contribute to the formation of a dedicated elite in the economic no man's land that lies between them.

4. American aid should be channeled into developments that satisfy concretely the aspirations and wants of the recipient peoples. For example, the United States should identify itself dramatically with local efforts to regulate the water supply and make it readily available to the village economy. Next in importance as regards the economic development of the Middle East is a program of road construction and improved communications. The United States is admirably fitted to supply the requisite skills and equipment.

5. It is possible that the Arabs, having been defeated twice by Israel, may settle down to a fairly long period of military and diplomatic preparation before bringing the Israeli issue again to a head. In the meanwhile, other factors may be brought into play and gradually ease Arab-Israeli tensions. The first step toward pacification must be the settlement of the refugee problem, to which Israel must contribute her share, not merely by making financial assistance available for rehabilitation projects, but also by accepting a sizeable contingent of refugees for repatriation inside Israel. If this cannot be done during the current year, because of the increased number of Jewish refugees from eastern Europe and North Africa, perhaps it can be done next year. If Israel can thus participate in the solution of the Palestinian refugee problem, due consideration being given to Israel's internal security, it would then be politically easier for the pro-Western monarchs—Hussein, Faisal, and Saud—to absorb the great bulk of the Palestinian refugees into their respective countries. This would remove one of the most infectious sores from the Middle East, deprive Nasser and the extreme Arab nationalists of an argument that has proved highly effective in their efforts to keep the Israeli issue alive and to gain Western support, and furnish the Arab countries with what they need most, namely, trained manpower, for many of the Palestinian refugees are highly educated and skilled people.

6. The Cyprus controversy, since it embitters the relations among three NATO partners, is one of the most serious problems confronting the United States in the Middle East area. The United States should not support *enosis* with Greece, for this would alienate Turkey, which is, from a strategic point of view, a more valuable ally of the United States than is Greece. An American policy decision in favor either of *enosis* or of self-determination for Cyprus might be fraught with two consequences: the eventual loss of a NATO base in the eastern Mediterranean and the development of anti-NATO or anti-American sentiments within Turkey. Probably the best solution for the Cyprus problem would be some form of local autonomy under NATO supervision, with Great Britain,

Greece, Turkey, and the United States playing a joint tutelary role. It would be of great psychological value for NATO to undertake such a political experiment. For Cyprus, if placed under NATO supervision before external intervention renders a moderate solution impossible, might accommodate an invaluable pilot project in the evolution of a new federative approach to the political problems confronting the West and the Middle East alike.

In the Middle East, as elsewhere, the nation-state has lost its *raison d'etre*. It can no longer singly defend its people against the military threats from without or meet the demands of modern economic development within. It has become an obstacle to human progress. In the Middle East, as elsewhere, the spirit of the times calls for supranational formations. In the long run, United States policy in the Middle East will be judged by the contribution it will have made to the political and economic integration of the region.

Commentary

J. C. HUREWITZ
Associate Professor of Government,
Columbia University

PROFESSOR STRAUSZ-HUPÉ has presented an essay on "The United States and the Middle East" that is both original and stimulating. Still, he could hardly have intended that we accept his every observation without question. I am thinking especially of his offhand dismissal of the Middle East as an identifiable geographic region. I do not regard myself in any sense as a traditionalist, and I rather favor being tarred with the innovator's brush. Yet you and I are bound to challenge the cavalier relegation to the scrap heap of a concept that, to the area specialist at least, not only means bread and butter but also admits of geographic definition, variable though it may be. The Middle East, it is true, is a vague and ever-changing geographic designation. But without entering further into what may become a semantic dispute, I should like at this stage merely to make known my reservation.

Let me establish at the very outset that I do not take issue with the basic thesis of Professor Strausz-Hupé that the Middle East is today the region along the Soviet periphery most exposed to Russian machination, that conditions at the present time favor their purposes and not ours, and that in this sense we have become heirs of the United Kingdom as the primary custodian of Western interests in the Middle East. Yet despite this area of agreement, I do find fault with some of the testimony that he adduces in support of the major thesis. At several crucial points, therefore, my analysis of cause and effect and of the interplay of forces, my diagnosis of the ailment, and my prognosis of the recovery markedly diverge from or wholly contradict those of my colleague.

Professor Strausz-Hupé tends to generalize on an area that, more often than not, defies generalization. The Middle East— which for my purposes embraces non-Soviet southwestern Asia to the eastern borders of Iran and adjacent northeastern Africa to the western borders of Libya and the southern borders of Sudan—is a disparate region, noted chiefly for its diversity and disunity. The forms of government range from patriarchal principalities and absolute monarchies on the Islamic pattern through constitutional monarchies and republics to at least one full-fledged military dictatorship. The motley array of forms as thus categorized conceals varying experiences, mostly unhappy, with Western political practices. What is more, perhaps nowhere else in the world have religious, linguistic, and ethnic minorities been able to survive as distinct communities to the same degree as in the Middle East. An extreme illustration is Lebanon, which is a country of nothing but minorities. At the other end of the Middle East demographic spectrum lies Turkey, which has become a relatively homogeneous country.

This is not the place to enter into a detailed description of Middle East disparities. Suffice it to say that in the Middle East one land's meat is another land's poison. This becomes readily apparent when one considers the problems of economic and social development in the Arab area. Egypt, with a population density in the small inhabited zone of more than fifteen hundred per square rural mile, suffers from extreme population pressure. Iraq and Syria, however, may be classified for purposes of economic and social planning as underpopulated countries. Clearly then it would be misleading to apply a single system of measurement and appraisal to the three Arab countries, let alone to the Middle East as a whole. In these circumstances generalizations as a rule must relate to forces far below the surface, as I shall attempt to demonstrate.

The caution on oversimplification, I might add, should be heeded at times in consideration of Western policies and activities. My colleague contends that "British diplomacy in the nineteenth century" was "designed to preserve the integrity of the Ottoman Empire and to bar Russia from the Persian Gulf." It might be said that the United Kingdom from 1798 to 1806 and again from 1840 to 1878 aimed at safeguarding the territorial domain of the Ottoman sultan. But surely Britain's policy changed substantially after the occupation of Cyprus in 1878 and of Egypt four years later. Those very acts largely negated the earlier policy. Analogously, no one would discount the intensity of Britain's fear of Russia's forward policy in Iran and in Central Asia in the 1830's and again in the more than half a century after the outbreak of the Crimean War. Surely, Whitehall was no less anxious in this period about Russian expansionism at the Turkish Straits. Nor did Russia alone spur England's competitive instincts, for in the Ottoman Empire—the Turkish Straits and the Caucasus apart—the rivalry with France took precedence throughout most of the nineteenth century, only to be replaced by rivalry with Germany in the last decade before World War I. I merely wish to call attention to the fact that Britain's Middle East policies in the nineteenth century as in the twentieth were framed in response to constantly shifting pressures from

a wide variety of sources both in Europe and in the Middle
East. Still, I do subscribe to the theory that similar geopolitical factors have been at work on Russia under the Soviets
as under the czars and that in this respect the United States
has inherited from Britain the mantle of primary responsibility for defense of the Middle East against Russian aggression.

In turning from the general to the specific, I sharply disagree
with the suggestion that the Kremlin's diplomatic triumph
in Egypt in the past two years may be attributed in any significant measure to the prior effective Communist penetration
into and build-up of support among "carefully selected groups
of Arab white-collar workers and intellectuals." The fact is
that the effectiveness of recent Soviet policy in Egypt may be
ascribed chiefly to the co-operation of the military junta,
whose actions are motivated, not by Communist or pro-Soviet,
but by nationalist, considerations. Nor can it be said that
Egypt's military defeat in Sinai in the fall of 1956 and its
diplomatic defeat in Jordan in the spring of 1957 have "probably marked the end of Egypt's role as spokesman of the Arab
world."

Any appreciation of Nasser's growing popularity in the Arab
world after the summer of 1955 would have to take into account Egypt's geographic and cultural centrality in the Arab
world. From Cairo have come newspapers, periodicals, and
books to mold the thinking and the sentiments of the literate
segments of society throughout the Arab East. The illiterate
urban masses have fallen under the influence of Egypt's motion picture industry, which has found a ready market in
every town where Arabic is spoken. To al-Azhar Seminary and
to Cairo University have flocked students from the far corners
of the Arab world, later returning to their native lands to
take up religious or lay teaching posts and to practice the
various professions. Nor may we overlook numbers, for in
Egypt are concentrated nearly one-third of the total Arab population of the world. Little wonder that the Arab states acquiesced in Egypt's demand for recognition of its primacy in the
negotiations that led to the creation of the Arab League, in

1945. From the very outset the Egyptian government was prone to treat the Arab League as an extension of the foreign ministry at Cairo. To this practice the military junta has added that of handling the Arab collective security scheme as an extension of the Egyptian army. The Arab policy of the military regime at Cairo has not basically differed from that of the dynasty that it overthrew, although under Colonel Nasser's leadership the policy has been executed with far more telling effect. This has been emphasized daily by the pervasive agitational impact on the Arab East of Radio Cairo, or more accurately of the so-called unofficial Voice of the Arabs station. It seems clear enough that Egypt's capacity to influence the course of international politics in the Arab East has hardly been suppressed. At best it may be said that the shock of the double failure in Sinai and Jordan has temporarily checked Egyptian initiative.

One of the constants in the Arab-Israel zone has been the unifying effect upon the Arab countries of hostility to Israel. Regardless of how the Arab governments may differ on many issues, they can always find a common purpose in their contempt of the state that emerged in their midst against their firmly expressed wishes. This has been dramatically exhibited in the recent co-operation of Jordan and Saudi Arabia with Egypt on the question of Aqaba at a time when Jordan was fighting for its very political existence, which was being undermined by Egyptian subversion, and King Saud had otherwise broken with Colonel Nasser over Egyptian efforts to weaken the monarch's hold in his kingdom.

It may hardly be assumed that republican nationalism in the Arab East automatically represents devotion to the cause of social reform. The present regime in Egypt launched its career on such a program. But it did not take very long for the young military leaders to be deflected from their original dedication to social change by the very massive social and economic problems that they faced. The population pressure in Egypt is so great that, even if the Aswan Dam, completed on schedule, returned the fullest measure of benefits anticipated by the drafters of the project, the Egyptians could at best look forward only to maintaining their present living standards. In the face of such depressing prospects, the military leaders moved naturally in the direction of militarism and adventure in external politics. Colonel Nasser and his colleagues would doubtless resent being told that in their preoccupation with building a strong military establishment they are essentially following in the footsteps of the founder of the late Egyptian dynasty that they brought to a bloodless end, for even a superficial examination of Mohammed Ali's record would clearly indicate the close parallelism.

It would be difficult to substantiate the claim that Israel is "the greatest obstacle" to areawide planning for the co-operative development of Middle East resources, "especially as regards irrigation, land reclamation, and power resources." No one will deny, of course, that Arab-Israeli tensions have frustrated even the most ingenious negotiations, such as those of Ambassador Eric Johnston, who for the first time fused automation and diplomacy in an effort to circumvent the Arabs' steadfast refusal to have direct dealings with Israel. But as regards land settlement and irrigation, the Arab-Israeli dispute affects only those districts served by the Yarmuk-Jordan river system, a very small fragment of the Middle East. In almost every political dispute affecting international rivers in the Middle East, from the Nile to the Indus, the countries involved have refused to work together in the common interest for the rational exploitation of the water resources.

Yet I would also venture to suggest that these political problems are less serious in the long run than the human problems. The technical planning and construction of large-scale river-harnessing schemes can easily be accomplished by any Middle Eastern state simply by requesting the assistance of one of the United Nations specialized agencies or of the United States or latterly even of the U.S.S.R. It is when such projects pass from the technical stage to the social that the really knotty problems set in. Development entails far more than the mere construction of dams, irrigation canals, hydroelectric and sanitary water plants, and installations for scientific sewage disposal. In many Middle Eastern countries there is injected the additional problem of persuading the wealthy landowners, who often constitute an oligarchy that controls the government and who resist the proposed social innovations, if for no other reason than their fear of losing their positions of political dominance. But of even greater significance is the problem of convincing the peasants that the change of agricultural methods, and at times also of farm land, will serve their best interest. They must then be carefully trained and provided with the necessary implements. New credit facilities that are geared to the peasants' ability to pay must also be furnished. In my view, these are factors of far greater moment in retarding river development than interstate disputes, although I do not wish in any way to suggest that the tensions among the emergent states of southwestern Asia and northeastern Africa are imaginary. They are real and stubborn enough to merit the closest attention.

One of the gravest handicaps that we face in trying to win friends and influence governments in the Middle East is the inadequacy of the American image. In the eyes of all Asians and Africans, the United States achievements do not constitute a realistic goal. Surely for the peasant of Iran or Egypt or the refugee in Jordan or even the factory worker in Turkey or Israel, the level of American material civilization lies far beyond reach. We should be well advised, therefore, in our attempt to explain the United States to the Middle East, not to lay primary stress on our material accomplishments. On this ground we can only lose the psychological war with the U.S.S.R., which can focus on the transformation of Russia in the past half century from a relatively backward society to the second most powerful and industrialized country in the world.

In any evaluation of United States policy on the Middle East one must ineluctably consider certain basic realities. We are newcomers to political and strategic responsibility in that region. As recently as a decade ago we still thought of the Middle East primarily as a British preserve. Even to this day most Americans show little awareness of the nature and scope of United States commitments in the area. United States action—in a majority of instances it might even be more ap-

propriate to say inaction—contributed, it is true, to the aggravation of Middle Eastern disputes. But we can hardly be
accused of having created the tensions in the area. These are
a legacy of an earlier period, when American interests and
activity were largely cultural. But whether or not the disputes
in the Middle East were of our own creation, we have sought
since the end of World War II, more particularly since the
enunciation of the Truman Doctrine, to assist the peoples of
the area and our allies to settle their differences. Yet our
mediatory services could at best be characterized as sluggish
and largely unimaginative. For we have steadfastly refused to
take the initiative in the postwar Middle East in any zone or
situation of tension until the issue has become so critical that
we could no longer dodge the responsibility. It might be observed, in fact, that while some powers in the Middle East
were born with initiative and others achieved initiative, we
had initiative thrust upon us.

Our sluggishness in dealing with Middle East affairs may
be attributed in part to the fact that we were caught, in the
most delicate problems, between the pressures of our allies
and those of the Middle Eastern states. In the circumstances
of the Cold War it seemed urgent that the United States and
its transatlantic allies should continue to have access to the
military bases that proved so decisive in World War II. To
these were added after 1947 the oil resources of the Middle
East that had acquired a significance in Western economic
and military planning that far transcended even the wildest
imagination of the most enthusiastic oilman in 1945. For
these reasons the earlier postwar steps of the United States
aimed above all to integrate the Middle East into the Western collective security system. As long as Britain remained in
control of its major bases, particularly the massive installations
in the Suez Canal zone, this kind of planning was useful.
When Britain, France, and the United States issued on May
25, 1950, their common declaration of intent to preserve the
territorial status quo and to prevent an arms race in the Arab-
Israel area, the Western powers proved able to realize their
purposes for more than five years. What gave the tripartite

declaration its vigor was the combination of moral support from the United States and the continued presence in the region of substantial British garrisons.

Still the United States experienced constant pressure from the Middle Eastern lands concerned to help throw "the imperialist rascals" out. This confronted the United States, as Professor Strausz-Hupé has cogently observed, with one of its most "painful dilemmas," for the United States has steadfastly eschewed any imperialist ambitions in the Middle East and has been by tradition basically sympathetic to the principle of national self-determination wherever it manifested itself. A cursory examination of political developments in the past decade and a half in Syria, Lebanon, Libya, and the Sudan would reveal that our record in the Middle East in this respect is not one that need cause us any serious misgivings in nationalist circles. We have always been quick to acknowledge such claims to self-determination, even when they related to economic matters, as in the case of Iran's nationalization of the Anglo-Iranian Oil Company in 1951, and to persuade our transatlantic allies to do the same. Even in Palestine in 1948 the element of self-determination was not absent; here our problem was compounded by the conflicting claims of Arabs and Jews to the same territory. In Egypt the contest focused on Britain's surviving military rights under a preferential alliance, which the local nationalists were convinced infringed upon their country's sovereignty. In this instance we brought increasing pressure to bear on Britain until in 1954 it finally agreed to surrender the base in the Suez Canal zone without our having procured concrete assurances in advance of Egypt's co-operation with the purposes of the Western collective security system.

One need hardly wonder, in the circumstances, that our political objectives in the Middle East should have remained ambiguous and largely undefined for so long. Under the Eisenhower Doctrine we seem to have served notice on the U.S.S.R., as on the Middle Eastern states, that we favor the present political map of the region and have every determination to preserve it against a sudden change that is in any way either inspired by the U.S.S.R. or helpful to its purposes. Yet it might frankly be asked whether our lonely and unilateral declaration for freezing the status quo in the Middle East as a whole can by itself produce the results that we seek. I am inclined to feel, for reasons that I shall explore presently, that we still have a long and arduous way to go before the Eisenhower Doctrine is translated into a workable policy.

In a negative sense we have been anxious, as is evident through the attempted application to the Middle East of our containment strategy, to exclude the U.S.S.R. from positions that would enable it to meddle in the internal affairs of the region. But now that the Russians have scored their diplomatic breakthrough to the very strategic heart of the Middle East without firing a single shot and without the aid of strong local Communist groups, containment no longer makes any sense. Is it realistic for us to contemplate the hermetic resealing of the region against all Soviet activity in the area? This would necessitate our own intervention in the internal affairs of Egypt and Syria, overturning the present regimes, and endeavoring to install governments that are more reliable from our viewpoint. But even if these ends were attainable, we are hardly likely to seek them. Indeed, as we demonstrated to the world last fall, we were fully prepared to humiliate our major Western allies and weaken the very structure of NATO in deflecting Britain and France from such a course. If this is manifestly not the kind of policy that we may be expected to pursue, what is our alternative? Can we expect to coexist peacefully with the Russians in the Middle East, given their avowed plans to convert the world to communism and their unavowed, yet unmistakable, habit of reducing their immediate small neighbors to submission? I merely take this one example to illustrate that, even in relation to the U.S.S.R., which after all was the overriding anxiety that led to the framing of the Eisenhower Doctrine, we have no clear political strategy in the Middle East. Ought we then to be astonished at the failure of our political tactics to hold the Soviet Union in check in the region?

What complicates the American conduct of meaningful

diplomacy in the Middle East, particularly in the Arab-Israel zone, are the inherent forces making for instability. Many factors after 1953 accentuated the stresses and strains and intensified the mutual fears between the Arab states and Israel. Among other effects, the decay of the British position, particularly the withdrawal from the Suez base and the termination of the Jordan alliance, lifted restraints that earlier had been interposed between the Arabs and the Israelis along the major part of the armistice lines. This drained further vitality from the armistice system that had been brought into being only as a temporary measure and that therefore had already become pallid. The United States, meanwhile, turned in 1953 to a policy of cultivating Arab trust by "friendly impartiality" in the Arab-Israel area. The new program, as it unfolded, seemed to stress military aid as a means of neutralizing the movement toward neutrality in certain Arab states. Iraq was won over in 1954, as part also of the larger effort to reinforce the northern tier. Egypt, however, turned down the terms for American arms—either by grant or for cash—and then became the implacable enemy of the Baghdad Pact, into which the northern tier blossomed in 1955. Stalin's successors, for their part, seized the ready-made opportunities to turn on the charm in the Arab East by a policy of "friendly partiality." Russia unreservedly endorsed Arab charges against Israel at the United Nations, aided the Arab states in propaganda campaigns against British and French (and American) "imperialism," abetted the leaders of Egypt and Syria in their espousal of "positive neutrality," and offered these two lands weapons of recent design at post-Christmas prices.

The changing alignment of the outside powers and their altered policies threw into a complete imbalance the unstable equilibrium between the Arab states and Israel and even among the Arab states themselves. This was unfortunate for the West, since Israel and Egypt, the countries most adversely affected, were the two most capable of producing an international crisis of primary magnitude. Israel's determination to survive by a policy of preserving a substantial military lead over its hostile neighbors and the thrust of Egyptian

expansionism in the Arab East are themes too well known
to require repeating here.

The instability arising from the sharpened American-
Soviet competition, Israel's hypersensitive vigilance, and
Egypt's bid for supremacy have been rendered more acute by
turmoil in the domestic politics of most Middle Eastern lands.
This in part is a normal concomitant of establishing the machinery of government and fixing the political process in the
early years of emergent independence. But even more it is
the product of doubts and disillusionment that derive from
the breakdown of experiments in political Westernization.
But even in those states where parliamentary institutions have
not been introduced, such as Saudi Arabia or the principalities
in the Persian Gulf, the impact of Western communications
and Western industry and the provision of unprecedented
revenues have led to the partial Westernization of government. This of necessity has weakened time-honored values and
undermined traditional institutions. The nationalists in the
saddle almost everywhere in the Middle East seek as their
political goal nation-statehood on the Western model. This
in turn demands of the population loyalties wider than any
that existed in the past in an area that has long been noted
for social atomism. With the breakdown of the traditional
forms of social integration and immobility has come not immediate national integration, but political and social confusion, and the realization of nation-statehood remains as distant as ever before.

Meanwhile, the population in the Middle East has been
expanding at an unprecedented rate. It has become at least
one-fifth larger than it was in 1945. The demographic explosion has not yet been accompanied by a comparable expansion of economic opportunities and production, so that
in the oil-poor lands there has, if anything, been a relative
decline in living standards. Nor do the prospects for the future
seem especially bright, despite the fact that since 1950 most
of the countries of the Middle East have succumbed to the
development craze. There is hardly an independent state in
the area that has not launched development projects of vary-

ing size and ambition. The schemes for planned social and economic change can only further unsettle Middle Eastern societies.

The meaning for American foreign policy of the political, social, and economic ferment is essentially this: we must recognize that the elements producing instability in the Middle East are likely to endure for the remainder of the twentieth century. Some unstabilizing forces are fundamentally benign. The efforts to modernize the Middle East societies and polities are certainly salutary in the long run, even though we must recognize that in the short run they complicate the framing and conduct of American policy. The most that we may expect is to control those unstabilizing forces that are malignant or threaten to become so. Chief among them, of course, is the spirit of militarism. We should encourage every action that will help instill self-confidence into the peoples of the Middle East, especially in their relations with one another, without catering to their natural impulse to build up military establishments that their economies and societies cannot sustain. For better or for worse, we must live with the ferment and turmoil, both benign and malignant. But we must cease running after the will-o'-the-wisp and begin positing our policies on attainable—if limited—goals.

II

Strategic Military Importance of the Middle East

VICE-ADMIRAL RUTHVEN E. LIBBY, USN
Deputy Chief of Naval Operations (Plans and Policy)

HISTORY, AS WELL AS the international climate of today, recognizes the Middle East as a focal point of world politics and military strategy. An understanding of those factors that give the Middle East its very special strategic value is necessary if we are to appreciate the problems of strategy and policy that currently face the United States in that part of the world. I believe that we all accept the fact that the Middle East is of great strategic importance to the free world. Yet it must be obvious to us that this area would have little or no military importance were it not for the interplay of other forces—political, economic, psychological—among the dominant political groupings of the world, the pressures exerted upon the Middle East by these external forces, and the reactions thereto on the part of the Middle East.

Conflict in the Middle East has paralleled the story of mankind. No area on the earth's surface so continually has been the scene of conflict among men and nations. At one time or another the Middle East of the Arab states, or even the greater Middle East stretching from Morocco to Afghanistan, has been overrun by invading armies. The armies of the Hittites, Greeks, the Romans, the Arabs, the Crusaders, the Mongols and the Turks all left their various imprints upon the East. The imposition of Ottoman influence over a several centuries marked the first time since the heyday of Islam and the Arabs that the Middle East fell completely under the yoke of a single power. In view of current Soviet efforts to expand their influence in the area, it might be well for us to remember that Ottoman control over the Middle East was broken only as a joint result of a gradual disintegration of the Ottoman Empire, the sick man of Europe, and the successful conclusion of World War I. The U.S.S.R. shows no signs of becoming the sick man of Europe in the foreseeable future.

Throughout the last century, and even before, the interests of the great powers of Europe—Russia, England, France, and later Germany—all clashed in the Middle East. In World War I, as the armies of General Sir Edmund Allenby rolled up the Turkish carpet in Arabia, Britain, France, and czarist Russia were slicing up the corpse of the not quite defunct Ottoman Empire. This dismemberment, eventually known as the Sykes-Picot Agreement, initially envisaged a Russian czar as vice-president in charge of the Turkish Straits and Constantinople and as proprietor of much of the hinterland. Collapse of the czarist empire as a result of the war blocked Russian expansion into the Middle East at that time. However, this represented no more than a temporary cessation of Russian expansionism—a breathing spell for the new masters in Moscow.

World War II once more focused world attention on Africa and the Middle East, and here again the same powers locked in the struggle. During the twilight of Soviet-German relations shortly prior to the outbreak of hostilities between these strange bedfellows, Moscow gave positive evidence of a willingness to deal with Hitler—provided that, among other things, "the area south of Batum and Baku in the general direction of the Persian Gulf is recognized as the center of aspirations of the Soviet Union."

Hitler later made his own bid for the Middle East. Had he understood better the employment of sea power, and had he listened with more attention to the pleas of Rommel, a German-Japanese link-up in the vicinity of India might have been possible, and the course of World War II far different.

Since the end of World War II the Russian bear has been busy fattening up on a diet of satellites and buffer states. He has gained a militarily powerful ally in Communist China and politically helpful associates among the neutralist states. Events of the last few years have shown beyond the shadow of a doubt that Moscow is once more moving in the Middle East and means business.

The Kremlin of Khrushchev and Bulganin is all too well oriented in the direction of the Middle East; unfortunately, the stakes are higher today and the aims of the Soviets are more far-reaching than those of their predecessors.

The events of today, the clash of great powers in the Middle East, and the conflict among the Middle Eastern nations themselves simply serve to emphasize the lessons of history and the importance of what might otherwise appear to be a rather unimposing piece of real estate.

It is obvious from the history of this ancient land that men have sensed its strategic importance since the days of the Old Testament. What were the factors involved? Why the continuing struggle?

Essentially, although the strategic importance of the Middle East has changed in form over the centuries, it still derives from three fundamental factors: position, resources, and people. These are the factors that, in the broader sense, are recognized and contested for by the participants in the three-way strategic tug-of-war among the Soviet bloc, the West and the nations allied with the West in opposition to communism, and the hazy world of neutralism. The comparatively weak nations of the Middle East are inexorably caught up in the struggle; it is small wonder that the Middle East itself is in turmoil.

e Position

ed as it is, the Middle East serves as a link between Asia, and Africa; between the Atlantic Ocean, the nean Sea, and the gulfs and oceans to the east of

Suez. It can equally well serve as a barrier between these continents and oceans. The military and economic requirements for secure communications among Europe, Australasia, and Africa are obvious. Further, with the continued development of the industrial complex of western Europe, with the economic growth of the heavily populated countries of southern Asia, with an ever-increasing need for the movement of goods and services among the three continents, with a continuing expansion of world demands for petroleum, and with a growing requirement for the strategic resources of Africa, the Middle East, by virtue of its unique position, will assume even greater importance. The Suez Canal by itself is merely one segment of the entire transportation complex; while extremely important, it hardly can be considered vital to world communications. In fact, under conditions of war, it is most doubtful that the canal could be kept open. Even with the canal closed, slower but effective communications between West and East would still be possible if the physical and political security of the Middle East were assured. Without such assurance, however, the threat to Africa would be immediate, and the security of the sea lines of communication around the Cape of Good Hope would be endangered. Loss of the Middle East, either through the extension of Soviet political influence or the subjugation of the area by Soviet arms, would mean the parting of the most essential link in free world communications. Aligned with and friendly to the West, the Middle East ties the free world together. In the hands of the Soviets, the Middle East could be the nuclear pellet that could blow the world apart.

The Mediterranean Sea is the most magnificent interior traffic network on the face of the earth. It directly serves the three continents of Europe, Asia, and Africa. Indirectly it serves more remote parts of the world; the Americas, southern Asia, the Far East, and the lands down under. Control of the Mediterranean is essential to the security of Africa, to the protection of the European flank and the right flank of NATO, and to the support of the northern tier. The vitally important Turkish Straits can be denied to hostile naval forces only as long as Greece and Turkey are capable of resisting aggression, either military or political. It follows that successful resistance on the part of Greece and Turkey will depend in large part upon the degree of Western control of the Mediterranean and the ability of the United States to maintain forces in and around that sea ready, willing, and able to support these friendly nations in time of emergency.

From the point of view of the military strategist, the land defenses of the Middle East logically are predicated upon the successive defense of two major terrain features: first, the line of the Caucasus and the Elburz; and second, the Taurus-Zagros Massif extending from Turkey to the Persian Gulf. This latter position is by far the stronger. Should it be breached, Soviet air forces would be able to operate from bomber bases in Iraq, and penetration of the remaining barriers between Iraq and the coast of the Mediterranean would be simplified. Once the Mediterranean littoral fell to hostile forces, our position in the eastern Mediterranean would become untenable. The Turkish flank would be turned, and Turkey, as a positive military factor, would be out of the picture. As Western influence waned, the Soviets would make corresponding gains, first in the area of the Persian Gulf and then across the Suez and into Africa.

The possibility of Soviet military expansion that I have described is unpleasant to contemplate. As a matter of fact, given the willingness and determination of the United States to resist such aggression, and given the relative strengths of the great powers as they are today, such a military operation is beyond Soviet capabilities. However, Soviet capabilities for political penetration of the Middle East on an equal scale is a different matter. Think for a moment of the open invitation to such political penetration that would exist should the deterrent military power of the United States be withdrawn from the area, or should the United States let the small and weak nations of the Middle East feel that they face the encroaching pressures of the U.S.S.R. alone and without friends.

The Resources

The petroleum reserves of the Middle East are the second factor in the over-all strategic importance of the area. They already represent about three-fourths of the free world's known reserves, and the petroleum industry has little more than scratched the total area of exploration possibilities.

In 1955 western Europe consumed on the order of 2.2 million barrels of oil per day. For almost ten years petroleum demand in western Europe has been increasing at about 15 per cent a year. Every indication is that, for the foreseeable future, the increase in demand for petroleum energy in western Europe will continue at about 10 per cent per year. What does this mean in terms of barrels of oil? If we project free Europe's increasing demands at 10 per cent a year, and similarly project the corresponding domestic production, we find that in 1967 western Europe will need to import something on the order of 6.5 million barrels per day—and most of this will have to come from the Middle East. This means that in ten years western Europe will have to import from the Middle East nearly 5 million barrels per day more than was being imported immediately prior to the closure of the Suez Canal. Furthermore, the problem of providing Europe with petroleum consists of much more than the mere availability of crude oil. We still have to move the oil. By 1961 the Suez Canal, unless greatly enlarged, will be operating close to its saturation point. At that time the situation as concerns western Europe's petroleum will look something like this: utilizing to the fullest both the capacity of the canal and the capacities of all presently existing pipelines, Europe will require the means to transport some 3 million barrels a day over and above the capability of the entire existing transportation complex.

The People

The third factor of strategic importance is people. There are about 45 million Arabs in the Middle East, mostly Mos-

lem. If we expand the area to include the Arab states of North
Africa, as well as Turkey and the other non-Arabic Moslem
states to the east, we have a total Moslem population of over
200 million.

The vast majority of these people face a lifetime of poverty,
disease, and ignorance. The social structure, except in Israel
and in certain urban areas of the other states, is largely of a
feudal or semifeudal nature. Governments, while generally
trying to improve the lot of their people, nevertheless are
handicapped in their efforts by such factors as the resistance
of dissident land-owning elements, chronic political instability, corrupt officials, tottering economies, dangerous external
pressures, and a volatile, easily swayed, and almost illiterate
populace.

For better or for worse, we must realize that the collective
will of these people will, in the long run, determine the future
of their countries. Today, however, the voice of the people too
often is confused with the preconditioned muttering of the
mob. While the appeal of nationalism or Pan-Arabism to the
people of the Middle East is to be expected, the emotional
impact of nationalism is such as to make the people vulnerable
to exploitation by rabble-rousers of every conviction. The
Communists are past masters at the exploitation of human
emotions, and there is no doubt that Soviet leaders realize
fully the importance of people in the development of a strategic appreciation.

It is necessary, therefore, that the West come to understand
these people of the Arab world and of Islam—to understand
why this xenophobic form of nationalism permeates much
of the Middle East. At the risk of oversimplifying the subject,
I would relate it to the harsh impact on the Middle East of
Western civilization, the advent of rapid means of communication, and the logical corollary of an awakening of old
prides in race and nation. Through these influences, the peoples of the Middle East have come to realize that there is a
better way of life—and to want it. They have learned that in
some nations men are truly free—free not only in the sense of
being members of a free society, or of being politically inde-

pendent, but free also of the scourge of poverty, free to shape their own future, free to share in the economic benefits of the state. Lacking these freedoms, men will turn to any "ism," however empty of truth, in their search for light and hope, and in the belief that, for them, any change would be an improvement.

Nationalism is to many of these people a cure-all for their ills. In the Middle East it is invariably associated with anti-colonialism. It takes many forms, varying from the moderate and enlightened brand of nationalism represented by Prime Minister Bourguiba of Tunisia to the horrible excesses of the National Liberation Front (FLN) massacre in Algeria last June. Nationalism represents a power that cannot be opposed successfully by force. It may be guided by wisdom in the direction of enlightened independence. It will make the folly of oppression destroy itself. Independence before a nation is ready is dangerous; independence too late can be disastrous.

Along with the extremes of nationalism and Pan-Arabism so evident throughout the Middle East, there are basic political differences among the Middle Eastern states themselves that further add to the over-all instability of the area. At the moment there is grave tension between the two camps in the Arab world, with the leftist-oriented governments of Egypt and Syria on the one hand, and Iraq, Saudi Arabia, Jordan, and Lebanon on the other. The struggle of nationalism continues in Algeria, where France is combatting some thousands of terrorists (as the French put it) or the military forces of the National Liberation Front (as the Arabs put it) with almost 400 thousand troops. Although both of these issues are extremely serious, and are reflected not only in the internal, but also in the external relations of the area, neither of them poses so vital an issue in the Middle East as does the Arab-Israeli dispute. Over this bitter controversy there has been continuing bloodshed ever since the war of 1948. Both parties have taken adamant stands. As far as peace is concerned, the Arab position in general has been that United Nations resolutions concerning the Partition Plan of 1947, the return of or compensation for the Arab refugees, and the internationaliza-

tion of Jerusalem first must be implemented before consideration is given to negotiation of a peace. The Israeli position
has been to call for direct negotiations without agreeing in advance to any elements of a settlement.

The Arabs feel that Israel has usurped land that had been
Arab for some 1,300 years prior to 1948. The Israelis feel that
their right to Palestine was divinely vested in the Hebrew
race. If reason ever is to prevail, a reappraisal of the pertinent
United Nations resolutions in light of the situation existing
in 1957 may be in order. The dispute is so surcharged with
emotion and prejudice that the possibility of a settlement is
remote. Nevertheless, if a solution is to come, it is essential
that the facts of life be accepted and faced calmly and objectively, and that peace be sought on a basis of compromise
by both parties.

We have examined the basic factors upon which the strategic importance of the Middle East rests, as well as the major
internal problems of the area. Now let us look at the relative
positions of the Soviet Union and the United States in the
Middle East today. As I have said, the history of Russian desire to expand into the Middle East is an old story, and the
current efforts of the Soviet Union in furtherance of historical
precedent are obvious. Is there today a particular objective of
Soviet expansion in the Middle East?

Essentially, there are three great industrial-economic power
groupings in the world: American, western European, and
that of the Soviet Union. Of these three groupings, the
United States and the Soviet Union represent by far the most
powerful elements and are in fact the hard core of each of the
opposing camps they represent. Examined in isolation, these
opposing powers are of nearly equal strengths. Western Europe, with its population of 200 million and its complex industrial plant, is the factor that retains the balance of power
for the West. Barring recourse to the catastrophe of thermo-
nuclear war, the economic-industrial balance of power will remain with the West only as long as western Europe and the
United States remain allies.

It is obvious that splitting western Europe from the United States, with western Europe adopting either a neutralist or pro-Soviet position, would enormously enhance the power position of the U.S.S.R. What more logical move is open to the Soviet Union than to use the Middle East as the lever with which to accomplish this separation?

Western Europe has had one taste of what it means to have the flow of Middle Eastern oil stopped. The extension of Soviet influence over Syria and Egypt is a clear warning to the West that the vital flow of petroleum can be stopped again at the whim of the Kremlin. This threat in itself, particularly if accompanied by occasional stoppages of various durations, could have a most disruptive effect upon the industry of western Europe. It could be used, carrot-and-stick fashion, to force the normal flow of world petroleum production and transportation into abnormal, complicated, and wasteful patterns.

It is not likely that western Europe would completely lose access to Middle Eastern oil. The U.S.S.R. would hardly care to destroy the largest natural market for this petroleum, for to do so would call down the wrath of the Arab upon his Russian tutor. Europe will be able to purchase its requirements from Soviet-controlled sources in the Middle East—at Soviet prices—expressed in terms of political concessions. If Europe demurs, the continuing threat of a sudden oil shortage, perhaps without warning and in the dead of winter, would always be a handy whip for the Russians if they felt that Europe needed urging.

United States objectives in the Middle East certainly are not predicated upon political domination of the area or even upon the denial of legitimate interests of other states. Nevertheless our objectives in the Middle East must insure the protection of the national interests of this country. In broad terms these objectives may be stated as follows:

1. To insure to the free world the unrestricted utilization of the resources, strategic positions, and transit rights of the Middle East;

2. To deny to the Communists the resources and strategic positions of the Middle East;

3. To support the establishment and continuation of free, independent, and stable states in the Middle East, friendly to the United States and to the West, ready and willing to resist the encroachments of communism of their own free will.

The future relations of the United States with the countries of the Middle East and the corresponding attainment of United States objectives will depend, to a great extent, upon the wisdom and courage with which we handle Middle Eastern problems in the next few years. It is no simple problem. To solve it, it is essential that we view world reaction to events in the Middle East and Middle Eastern reaction to the pressures exerted from without clearly and in accurate perspective. We must recognize that the U.S.S.R. has been adroit in convincing the Arab nationalists that the aims and objectives of the U.S.S.R. in the Middle East parallel their own. We must understand that an implacable enemy will do his utmost to thwart our efforts to develop the stable Middle East that is so vital to the attainment of our objectives in the area.

Actually, our preoccupation with the major threat posed to the free world by the Soviet bloc militates against the adoption of some of the policies best designed to serve our interests in the Middle East. We have a tendency to become preoccupied with the problems of a so-called bipolar world to the extent that we tend to overlook other world problems. We should realize that in most instances the small nations of the Middle East face a multipolar world and live in a multipolar world. Where we see but one major threat, they see many. Their fear includes a fear of the neighbor next door. This fact becomes evident when we try to bring several small nations into common alignment against the forces of international communism. Then, to our surprise, we find that local dangers, viewed in local perspective, often appear more threatening than the distant menace of the U.S.S.R.

It is always difficult to keep a coalition of nations welded together in common cause; and it is harder in peacetime than in war. This natural phenomenon offers widespread opportunity to the Communist. He can apply his pressures, light or heavy, subtle or obvious, wherever the application best suits his purpose. Since moral values and international ethics have no part in Communist techniques, we can expect the most ruthless exploitation of the people and the governments of the Middle East by the Communists. They will shift the focus of attention in the Middle East now here, now there, seeking always to create conditions of instability and animosity toward the West in an effort to divert the attention of the Middle East away from the basic aim of the U.S.S.R.—political domination of the crossroads of the world.

In the next few years the Western alliance will face a period more critical than any which has tested it before. The encroachment of communism in the Middle East must be stopped and rolled back, or it will accelerate. If Moscow becomes the dominating influence in the Middle East, North Africa and Europe will be outflanked and the U.S.S.R. will control Middle Eastern petroleum and could well be in a position to force fatal political concessions from western Europe. The Americas could be isolated.

The American doctrine clearly points up the strategic importance this country attaches to the Middle East. That policy statement is a reaffirmation of willingness on the part of the United States to meet its responsibilities to itself and to the world—a promise that the United States does not intend to have the Middle East lost to the free world.

The doctrine, however, represents only a basic statement of policy. The implementing strategy itself must be developed. It must be planned in full understanding of the many complicating factors. It must further the national interests of this country. It must not be emasculated by the voices of dissident minority groups. It must not be a strategy designed to placate all factions at once, for such a strategy is doomed to failure. Finally, it must be implemented, boldly and firmly, for a strategy that is not carried through is no strategy at all.

In summary, we know what our objectives are and who our enemy is; we have the essential broad policy guidance; it is now up to us, as Americans, to accept our full share of our national responsibilities and get on with the job in the Middle East.

Commentary

PAUL H. NITZE
President, Foreign Service Educational Foundation

I

ADMIRAL LIBBY in the initial section of his essay suggests that the military importance of the Middle East arises, and historically has in the past arisen, from the political, psychological, and economic pressures exerted upon the Middle East by the external world and from the reactions thereto on the part of the Middle East.

It seems to me that two separate lines of analysis are opened up by this suggestion. One line of analysis goes to the question of the general relationship between military strategy and political policy. The other line of analysis goes to the question of the relationship between a particular geographic area, such as the Middle East, and the outside world.

Let us begin with the first line of analysis. In general, I would support Admiral Libby's implication that military strategy derives its significance from political policy. But in this context the words "political policy" have a special meaning and include economic, psychological, diplomatic, and also strictly military considerations under the general heading "political." In other words, strategy with respect to a particular group of means, in this instance military means, can quite properly be said to derive its significance from broad policy considerations that include the totality of factors bearing on the situation and not just a single and isolated set of factors. It should be borne in mind, however, that "political policy," in this sense, is compounded of a number of different factors, one of which is the military factor.

In considering then what our over-all political policy should be toward any area, in this instance the Middle East, we must still look at the strictly military considerations with all honesty and seriousness. Military questions should not just be swept under the rug because their significance derives from broad political considerations. Political policy should never be dominated by military considerations alone, but it can rarely ignore them.

Now let us move to the second line of analysis. It is true that in the past and today both political and military influences from outside the Middle East have been and are important to the situation within the Middle East. The influence of the political and military power of the U.S.S.R. looms over the area. The Eisenhower Doctrine is but a formal statement reflecting United States political and military influence and responsibility toward the Middle East. That influence and responsibility may in large measure be a response to the collapse of British and French influence and the growing threat that, unbalanced by other forces, Russian power would dominate the area.

But to a considerable extent the political situation and the military problem in the Middle East have independent origins within the area itself. They are certainly affected by, and react to, outside influences, but it would seem to me to be a mistake to minimize in our analysis the internal indigenous content of both the political problem of the Middle East and its military counterparts.

II

This brings me to a discussion of the military analysis suggested by Admiral Libby's essay.

Admiral Libby emphasizes the importance of the lines of communication across the Middle East, including the Suez Canal, and particularly stresses the significance of the Mediterranean as a link connecting Europe, Asia, and Africa. He emphasizes the significance of control of the Mediterranean littoral and states that the land defense of this area is logically predicated upon successive defense of two major terrain features: first, the line of the Caucasus and the Elburz; and second, the Taurus-Zagros Massif extending from Turkey to the Persian Gulf.

A number of assumptions would seem to be implicit in this statement of the Middle East strategic situation. The first assumption is that our principal military concern is with the contingency of a major war involving both the United States and the U.S.S.R. The second assumption is that the line of the Taurus-Zagros Massif has not already been outflanked by Soviet penetration prior to the outbreak of such a major war.

The current situation in Syria raises serious doubts as to the validity of both of these assumptions.

In the past we have looked upon the Middle Eastern theater as being distinguished from both the European and the Far Eastern theaters by one important circumstance. This was the absence in the area of any Communist satellite that could be used by the Soviet leaders as a pawn or front for military aggression while leaving Russia overtly uncommitted. It appeared that in the Middle East Communist overt military aggression would have to come from Russia herself. In that event the general deterrents to overt Russian military aggression could be expected to operate. The defense of the area against Communist military aggression could therefore be considered as being a mere facet of our over-all general war strategy. Issues of possible military aggression by one non-Communist Middle Eastern state against another could be handled through United Nations procedures and need present no great military problem even though the resulting political and economic issues might be very tense indeed.

Today all that looks quite different. Syria may now have crossed the divide into Communist control. The Communists have planned carefully. The appearance of full legality has been preserved. President Kuwatly apparently signed the appointment of General Bizri as Chief of Staff before leaving Syria for Egypt. Conscious of the thinness of Communist control in other analogous situations where Communists seized power, as in Azerbaijan and Guatemala, where the appearance of even the slightest counterforce revealed that those in charge amounted to only a hundred or so people, the Communists have brought forth charges of an American counterplot to discourage and discredit in advance any organization of an opposition. The Russians have been careful to indicate the unity of their support for their Syrian policy by having every member of the Praesidium sign the August 8 statement of Soviet Middle East policies.

One gets the impression that the Soviet leaders are fully conscious of the significance of the move they are making, have taken careful thought of every possible reaction others might make to this move, and have tried, as well as careful planning may make possible, to narrow the possibilities of that reaction. It remains to be seen how successful their forward planning has been. But there can be little doubt as to the significance of the move, provided they succeed in fully consolidating the position.

Assuming such consolidation, one will then have to consider the military situation in the Middle East as being fully comparable to that in the Far East.

Let us assume that such consolidation is successful, that the purge of all possible opposition elements goes forward under cover of an alleged United States plot, that the port of Latakia is deepened and developed, that eight major airfields are constructed in Syria, that stores of weapons and supplies are moved to Syria and stockpiled, and that the Syrian government becomes a wholly supine tool of Soviet policy. It has certainly leaned to the Soviet side for some time past. But leaning to one side does not seem to be a very stable position and evidently was not considered by the Communists to be a firm enough position on which to build anything of lasting strategic significance. If one makes all these assumptions, how does the military situation in the Middle East look?

Obviously Syria is a small country in comparison with Turkey, Iran, or Egypt. Its population is something over 3,-500,000. As I understand it, the Syrian army does not amount to much today. But we have seen what Israel has been able to do with a much smaller population and with a truly miserable geographic situation. National morale, training, and equipment can do much with very little.

In a global war, fought with nuclear weapons, I would doubt that the positions the Russians could develop in Syria would be of much significance. A single port, a limited number of airfields, and five or six brigades could hardly be expected to stand up long against modern weapons.

But in the more likely contingency of limited military engagements, or of political maneuvering influenced by threats of limited military action, such a position could be of the utmost significance. It could enable the Russians to escape from the position they were formerly in, in which any military move on their side would involve action by Russia herself and therefore a high probability of initiating World War III. Granted, in the past they have threatened to send Russian volunteers to Egypt and have talked about the vulnerability of England and France to rocket attack. But they have always been careful to preserve lines of retreat for themselves so that the full faith and credit of Russia itself would not be irrevocably committed. Assuming consolidation of their position in Syria, they are now in a much better position to maneuver, to threaten, and even, if necessary, to attack, while preserving a high degree of security for Russia itself.

III

At one point Admiral Libby indicates that he is about to discuss the relative positions of the Soviets and the United States in the Middle East today. I anticipated that at this point he might draw up a balance of the relative military assets and liabilities of the two sides. But instead he turns immediately to the importance of the Middle East to Europe, with which I am in full agreement, and finally to the general objectives of our policy toward the Middle East. The concluding section is more in the nature of a statement of hope and an exhortation to unity in support of policies to be developed than a statement of policy as such. Perhaps it would be foolhardy to attempt to do more. But not having access to classified information and occupying no position of responsibility with the government, I may be under greater temptation to be foolhardy than most.

It would seem to me that one might consider first the relative capabilities of the two sides to fight a global and unrestricted war. It is my view that it should be the objective of policy not to have to fight such a war. But relative capabilities to do so are the background against which the more likely developments of local political and military conflict are going to be played out. It is my view that technologically, geographically, and with regard to resources, the Western world has very great relative advantages over the U.S.S.R., provided we continue to make the necessary physical effort, and provided we maintain our alliance system in good working order. For the purposes of this discussion it seems to me we can assume the continuance for at least the intermediate future of a relative superiority for the Western world in global war capabilities. It is when we consider relative capabilities to manage the more likely limited military threats without resort to global war that the comparison becomes more difficult. Turkey, Iraq and Iran, Lebanon, Jordan, and Saudi Arabia certainly represent vastly greater potential strength than do Syria and Egypt. It would seem open to doubt that Colonel Nasser is really happy with what appears to be happening in Syria. If Nasser were to see the light and were prepared to follow a course designed to preserve his independence, I should think that we should do all in our power to help him and let bygones be bygones. In that event Syria would become an annoying, but not necessarily critical, thorn in the Middle Eastern side. The relations between Israel and the Arab states and the drive for greater Arab unity would still present extremely serious problems. But even these problems might at last become more manageable before the overt and present threat of a Soviet satellite state in the middle of the Middle East. If the Middle East could manage its own internal problems, we could continue to balance off the threat of Russian pressure from the north.

The major danger arises if the Middle Eastern nations cannot manage their affairs with one another. If Jews and Arabs start fighting each other, or if left-wing Arabs start fighting right-wing Arabs, there is a risk that either Russia or the United States will be sucked into the developing contest. If one is sucked in, it is quite probable that the other will be sucked in too.

Let us assume for a minute that such a thing has happened, that both Russia and the United States have become militarily involved in the Middle East. What then are the relative military positions?

Russia is much closer to the Middle East than we are. Hanson Baldwin, in an article in *Foreign Affairs*, refers again to the geopolitical concept of Russia occupying the "heartland" and the United States and its allies being concerned with the defense of the "rimland." [1] In a speech last spring Admiral Arleigh A. Burke gave it as his opinion that operations by sea gave us a great logistical advantage over the U.S.S.R. with respect to possible military operations in the Middle East. Undoubtedly it is access by sea that makes the defense of the rimland possible. But when one adds considerations of air power and the availability of near-by bases, the equations do not appear to me to be quite as favorable as Admiral Burke seemed to imply. One's doubts become particularly strong if one assumes that the Soviets have succeeded in consolidating their position in Syria and that the use of nuclear weapons is deemed to be unwise and inappropriate except in a general war directly involving both the U.S.S.R. and the United States. I recognize that some people would not agree with this last assumption that nuclear weapons should be ruled out in considering the equations of limited war. It is possible that they are right and that those who, along with me, hold the opposite view are wrong. But one thing does seem to me to be evident: if we fail to take the measures necessary to maintain the military security of the Middle East without having to rely upon nuclear weapons because we have in the back of our minds that in the last analysis we can restore the situa-

[1] Hanson Baldwin, "Strategy of the Middle East," *Foreign Affairs*, XXXV (1957), 655-65.

tion through the use of such weapons, and then in the final development of affairs we find that the use of such weapons would be politically or militarily unwise, we may find that we have needlessly sacrificed the security, not just of the Middle East, but of the world.

And, finally, what should we be doing about all this? I should think that one range of meaures would be designed to maximize the possibility that those political elements in Syria still wanting independence may be able to temporize, restrain, and eventually throw off the descending Russian yoke. I should think another group of measures would be directed toward making it as easy as possible for Egypt to work out an accommodation with the other independent Arab states and with the West that would also recognize Israel's continued right to security as a nation. I should think a third group of measures could be designed to increase the capability of Turkey, Iran, Iraq, and other independent Middle Eastern states to meet the increased threat posed by a possible Soviet-dominated Syria in their midst. And, finally, I should think a group of measures could be worked out to increase the assurance that the United States can balance off Russian power by assuring (a) that Russia cannot use nuclear weapons without sure disaster to herself, (b) that Russia cannot intervene locally in the Middle East with nonnuclear weapons without every prospect of being defeated, and (c) that aggression by satellite can also be contained and defeated without resort to nuclear weapons. Hanson Baldwin in his *Foreign Affairs* article suggests some of the specific measures that might be included in this latter group. In total it seems to me that quite a lot needs to be done.

III

The Middle East in World Affairs

BERNARD LEWIS

Professor of the History of the
Near and Middle East, University of London

THE MIDDLE EAST TODAY consists of a series of sovereign national states, almost none of which, in their present form, have any roots in the past. Some, like Turkey and Persia, are the metropolitan remnants of bygone empires, in which the former ruling peoples are feeling their way toward a national instead of an imperial identity and existence. Others are new creations, fashioned from the debris of empires, with frontiers drawn not by history and geography, but by statesmen on maps. These new political entities were long irrelevant and unreal to the peoples who lived under them. The territorial and linguistic nation and the nation-state are both alien to the Moslem Middle East, where men's basic loyalties were determined not by language or fatherland, but by religion. Loyalty to a place was known, but it was to a village or a quarter, not a country; loyalty to one's kin was ancient and potent, but it was to the family or the tribe, not to the ethnic nation. The ultimate loyalty, the measure by which a man distinguished between brother and stranger, was religion, and political allegiance belonged to the dynastic sovereign of the Islamic state.

Today this has changed. The sense of Turkish, Persian, and Arab national identity is very strong, at least among those classes that have received a modern education or have been affected by modern ideas. Even the more specifically European sentiment of patriotism, love of country in the political sense, has made some headway. In Turkey the Kemalist government and its successors discouraged Pan-Turkish and Pan-Islamic tendencies, loyalty and politics by race or faith, and instead tried, with considerable success, to foster in the Turkish people a sense of communion with the country they inhabit. Egypt is a country well defined by both history and geography and has now been the center of a separate, modern state for a century and a half—long enough for a sense of separate territorial nationality to emerge. Iran, distinguished from its neighbors by both language and religion, has always had a strong sense of cultural identity and has, moreover, long been the seat of a sovereign and separate state. Israel, transplanted from overseas, has refashioned a unity of faith and destiny into a more or less European form of political loyalty and organization. Even in the Fertile Crescent the new states are beginning to take root in the loyalties and sentiments of their peoples and at times manifest a strong desire for separate survival. This is especially so where their politics coincide with ancient distinctions and rivalries, as for example between the eastern and western slopes of Lebanon or between the rulers of the Nile and of the Tigris-Euphrates valleys.

These forms and these allegiances are, however, new. Even where they are taking root they are still tender, immature, and precarious. They do not yet correspond to the feelings and loyalties of the great mass of the population; they cannot adequately express the instinctive and spontaneous responses even of the educated elite to the challenges of internal and international affairs. They cannot therefore provide us with a key to the understanding of those movements and policies in the Middle East that are due not to the calculations of groups or individuals, but to a real upsurge of popular sentiment and emotion.

To achieve some understanding of Middle Eastern attitudes in world affairs at the present time, we must view the Middle East not as countries, not even as nations, but as a civilization. It is unfortunate that we have formed the habit of calling the area the Near East or Middle East. The first of these

names is diplomatic in origin; the second, strategic. Both are
colorless geographical expressions that fail to express or even
suggest a civilization, as real and distinctive an entity as Europe, India, or China, and very much more so than Africa or
Asia.

We may define the area historically as that of the great
Islamic empires of the caliphs and their successors, and of the
classical Islamic civilization that grew up under their aegis.
Its early, formative period ended before the Crusades. Its final
flowering took place under the Turkish and Persian empires,
which, from the sixteenth to the early twentieth centuries,
divided what we call the Near and Middle East between them.
Essentially, it was a civilization of three peoples and of three
languages—Arabic, Persian, and Turkish. Its territorial core
was Northeast Africa and Southwest Asia. In this sense the
Middle East does not stop at the Soviet border, as in the
rather artificial diplomatic and military usage, but includes
extensive areas in Transcaucasia and Central Asia, which, from
the Middle Ages until the Russian conquest, were under Arab,
Persian, or Turkish rule and which are still inhabited by Per-
sian- or Turkish-speaking Moslems.

Of those parts of the Middle East that are under Soviet
rule there is little that can be said now. Our governments
have for some reason followed the Soviet lead in excluding
them from the consideration of Middle Eastern affairs, and
in any case, despite a common background, their recent and
present situation differs so much from that of the sovereign
states of the Middle East that it is difficult to consider them
together. I shall therefore confine my remarks to those parts of
the Middle East that lie south of the Soviet border.

Now that the fog of battle and the mists of diplomacy are
clearing from the Middle Eastern scene, it is becoming apparent that certain fundamental changes have taken place.
One of these has been the decline of British power. The turning point came in July, 1954, when, a few weeks after the
Eisenhower-Churchill conversations in Washington, Britain
and Egypt reached agreement for the evacuation by the British of the Suez Canal zone. Great expectations were placed in

that agreement. At the time, the hope was widely entertained and still more widely expressed that, with the removal of the final Egyptian grievance against the West, real friendship and co-operation would at last become possible.

For those who held them, those hopes have been disappointed. The general situation in the Middle East, far from improving, deteriorated rapidly. The Egypt-Israel border, after a period of comparative calm, became and has remained the chief battlefield of Israeli-Arab conflict. The removal of the last specifically Egyptian grievance left the Egyptians free to take up the larger causes of those whom they call their Arab and African brothers. And finally, although the term power vacuum may be objectionable, the fact remains that the withdrawal of British influence has been preceded, accompanied, and followed by the growth of the influence of other powers.

It may be useful at this point to review, briefly and schematically, the chief phases in the development of great-power influence in the Middle East. After the victory of 1918, Great Britain and France were in exclusive control of the area, unchallenged except by one another. In the 1930's and 1940's Britain and France drew together to meet and, ultimately, defeat the attempt of the Axis powers to oust them from the area. Since then, first France and then—with a change in the casting, but not in the script—Great Britain have been eliminated from most of their positions of power and influence, leaving the center of the arena to a new set of contestants.

It would, however, be a misleading simplification to describe the present Middle Eastern situation only in terms of American-Russian rivalry. For one thing, Britain and France, though reduced in stature, can still call on certain reserves of good will and esteem in the Middle East. These, after reaching their lowest point at the time of the Suez incident, have begun to recover, and may be expected to grow still further as the Middle Eastern peoples come to realize that their protests against domination and tutelage, power politics, spheres of influence, and the rest must be delivered to new addresses.

Moreover, there are other heirs to Britain's Middle Eastern policy. Britain's direct interest in the Middle East dates from the late eighteenth century and was a consequence of the establishment of British paramountcy in India. It was after the end of that paramountcy that British interest in the Middle East began to dwindle, and it was not long before both the successor governments to the British raj in India began to pick up the pieces of its foreign policy on the North-West Frontier, the Indian Ocean, the Persian Gulf, and the Red Sea—on the land and sea approaches to India, that is—and to fashion new Middle Eastern policies of their own. Their task is, of course, greatly complicated by the fact that there are now not one but two governments in the subcontinent and that neither of them possesses the military resources for an independent great-power policy. Both, however, possess in their dealings with the Middle East certain advantages that Britain and other Western powers could never have, and it would be a grave error to underestimate the role of either Pakistan or India in the Middle East—or to forget that their policies rest on genuine national and geopolitical interests.

Another Asian contestant is China, which in recent years has for the first time begun to evolve a world-wide and not merely a Far Eastern foreign policy and has already shown many signs of an active and growing interest in the Middle East. It may be noted that Colonel Nasser's dalliance with Moscow was preceded and perhaps prepared by his meeting with Chou En-lai at Bandung.

But what of the Middle East itself—of this group of sovereign states and peoples who are no longer content, in a common phrase, to be the objects of history, but wish to become its subjects? Middle Eastern statesmen insist vehemently that there is no such thing as a power vacuum, that the Middle Eastern peoples must be masters of their own fate, and that they are not concerned with the rivalries of great-power blocs. There can be no doubting the sincerity of their wishes in this, but, as the great Arabic writer Hariri says: "You are in one valley and I am in another valley and what a difference there is between the wisher and the wish." [1] In fact no Middle

[1] *The Assemblies of Hariri* (Assembly XXXIV [al-Zabidiyya]), ed. F. Steingass (London, 1897), p. 282.

Eastern state, nor any conceivable combination of Middle Eastern states, could in present circumstances play an active and wholly independent role in Middle East affairs—as can easily be seen in the maneuvers, in the last few years, of pro-Westerners, anti-Westerners (a more accurate description than pro-Communists), and the adherents of the a-plague-on-both-your-houses school.

A crucial question is: What are the relative strengths of the three schools? There are governments and politicians, groups and individuals, of all three tendencies, and some which seem to fluctuate between them. But of one thing there can be no doubt—it is the anti-Western policy that commands the widest, readiest, and strongest support in most of the countries of the Middle East. This was most strikingly demonstrated in September, 1955, when the Czech-Egyptian arms deal was announced. Far more significant than the arms deal itself was the wave of almost ecstatic joy with which the news of it was received all over the Arab world. The Syrian, Lebanese, and Jordanian chambers of deputies at once voted resolutions of congratulations to Colonel Nasser, and almost the entire Arab press greeted the news with exultation and delight.

This reaction was due, not to any special love for the Soviet bloc, nor to any desire to see its influence extended in the Arab world, but to a lively appreciation of the quality of Colonel Nasser's act as a slap in the face for the West. The Colonel's slap, and the red-faced, agitated, and ineffectual Western response to it, gave dramatic expression to a mood and a wish that unite many people in the Middle East—the mood of revulsion from the West, and the wish to spite and humiliate it. There are many statesmen and even a few governments in the Arab world who believe that the long-term interests of their countries and peoples require co-operation with the West, help from the West. They can, however, only pursue such policies by disregarding or suppressing popular feeling. It is the policy of rejection and insult that arouses immediate and spontaneous enthusiasm among the mass of the people.

What is the reason for this anti-Western feeling?

There is no lack of answers to this question. First, there is the long list of specific political grievances, beginning with the Palestine question and including such other items as Algeria, Suez, and the rest. Then there are the economic and social dislocations resulting from the impact of Westernization in its various forms. These are, in the long run, far more important than the political grievances as a source of restlessness and resentment. By their nature, however, they are not easy to formulate and discuss on a political level, at any rate in countries that have no tradition of such discussion; nor can the blame for them readily be thrown on nameable and recognizable culprits. It is, therefore, the political grievances that are most to the fore, both as an outlet and as a focus for anti-Western feeling. Sometimes, indeed, it is difficult to tell whether a particular grievance is an irritant or a safety valve.

In discussing the relative importance of these various political grievances, Middle Easterners will naturally give primacy to those in which they themselves are directly concerned. Westerners, on the other hand, incline to the view that if those grievances that are directed against *other* Westerners could only be met, their own more reasonable requirements would find easy acceptance—and there is always someone ready to serve an interest or a prejudice by encouraging this belief. Variants of this view have been put before many different audiences in the past and have been argued, asserted, suggested, or hinted, according to the ductility of the evidence and the skill of the advocate. A current form of this interpretation, which enjoys a measure of popularity in some quarters today, is that were it not for the existence and persistence of the Israelis, the incompetence and greed of the French, and the duplicity and rapacity of the British, there could be an idyllic marriage of American interests and Arab nationalism, in which the latter would be firm and independent against all others, but gracefully acquiescent in American requirements. In that happy day there would be bases for the military, treaties for the diplomats, concessions for the businessmen, converts for the missionaries, and a general glow of mutual friendship and good will.

A pretty picture—but of an apocalyptic rather than a historical quality. The events of the last few years have shown that the removal of particular grievances produces no real alleviation, since the general upsurge of anti-Western feeling soon finds other outlets and expressions. They have shown, too, that though anti-Western feeling was directed chiefly against Britain and France, it was to no small extent in their capacity as leaders of the Western world. Today they are no longer the exclusive targets of hostility; soon they may no longer even be the chief targets.

Why should this be so? Why should the United States, which has never annexed or occupied an inch of territory in the Middle East, which on the contrary has shown a generosity without precedent in history towards the states of the Middle East, be included in this generalized hostility to the West?

We shall be better able to understand this situation if we view the present discontents of the Middle East not as a conflict between states or nations, but as a clash between civilizations. The "great debate," as Gibbon called it, between Islam and Christendom has been going on since the Arab Moslem conquerors first swept westward into Christian Syria, North Africa, and Spain. It continued with the Christian counter-offensive of the Crusades and its failure, the thrust of the Turks into Europe, and their hard-fought retreat and withdrawal. For the past century and a half Middle Eastern Islam has been subjected to the impact and domination of the West—political, economic, and cultural domination even where, as in most of the Middle East, there was no direct rule. This impact has shattered traditional patterns of thought and behavior, of political and social loyalty and organization, beyond repair, and has posed to the peoples of the Middle East an immense problem of readjustment, both in their dealings with the outside world and in their own internal affairs.

The change brought great benefits and will no doubt bring others in the course of time; but it would be a piece of myopic self-conceit on our part to deny that it has also done great damage and is the chief cause of the political and social form-

lessness, instability, and irresponsibility that bedevil the public life of the Middle East. In our own day the crisis has come
to a head, and the anger that it engenders is directed outward, against the West—the millennial adversary and also the
place in which these devastating changes had their origin.

In the twilight world of popular myths and images, the
West is the source of all evil—and the West is a single whole,
the parochial subdivisions of which are hardly more important than are those of the Middle East for the average West-
erner. And in this mood of hostility, which we must concede
has cause, if not justification, those who pander to anti-
Western feeling will be able to count on a ready and fervent
response, while those who seek to co-operate with the West
will have to circumvent popular opposition by guile, stealth,
or force. To many Americans it must have seemed incon-
gruous, if not uncongenial, that their government should
support a king against an elected parliament, but the outward
forms of Middle Eastern political life should not mislead us
into equating them with their Western originals. In the Middle Eastern poker game there is nothing inconsistent in a
good republican's playing a hand of three kings—and hoping
that no one else will play the aces.

The only people who have ever succeeded in ruling the
Middle East for any length of time, the Turks, had their own
views on these matters. In a Turkish manual of statecraft,
written in the middle of the seventeenth century, the author,
Huseyn Hezarfenn, advises the sovereign to use fear as well
as law to maintain his authority:

> If the fear of punishment were to pass away from people's
> hearts, the evildoers would become more numerous and more
> arrogant. The right thing is that there should be fear among the
> bad and trust among the good people. Permanent fear and
> permanent trust are both harmful. While the people are be-
> tween fear and hope, let the Sultanate be well-ordered and let
> the Sultan be generous.[2]

[2] *Hezarfen Hüseyin Efendi'nin Osmanlı Devlet Teşkilâtına dair Mülaha-
zaları*, ed. Robert Anhegger, *Türkiyat Mecmuası* X (Istanbul, 1951–1953),
p. 376.

Between the Sixth Fleet and the Eisenhower Doctrine, as it were, let the United States be both firm and munificent.

In what has gone before I have tried to raise the conflicts of the Middle East from the level of a quarrel between states to that of a clash between civilizations. But civilizations can have no foreign policies, and governments must. The question therefore remains: What action should the Western states take in the present Middle Eastern situation? My own answer would be: As little as possible. The peoples of the Middle East are going through a crisis of transition, which we helped to precipitate, but which they alone can resolve. The United Nations has the limited but overtaxing duty of keeping the peace or at least of curbing the appetites of violence. We of the West can also do something to help, on nonpolitical levels, but should beware of proposing solutions that, however good, are discredited by the very fact of our having suggested them. The West must, of course, safeguard its minimum interests, which I leave to others to define; it may also give some material help—though without hope of much political return. Apart from that, let us watch and wait, do little and say less, and hope that in time the peoples of the Middle East may find their own way back to stability and health.

But, of course, the great dilemma of such a policy of "masterly inactivity" is how to leave the Middle East alone and at the same time insure that others also will leave it alone. The point was well made by Mr. Laqueur in his book on *Communism and Nationalism in the Middle East:*

> It is quite true, as an Indonesian prime minister stated in Delhi recently to great applause, Asian affairs are no longer settled in London and Paris. What remains to be seen is whether the new rulers of the Middle East and South-east Asia will be able in the future to prevent Asian affairs from being decided in Moscow and Peking.[3]

[3] W. Z. Laqueur, *Communism and Nationalism in the Middle East* (New York, 1956), p. 281.

Western rule in Asia has indeed gone, and a distinguished Indian scholar was right in speaking of the end of "the Vasco da Gama era" in Asian history. It would be both tragic and ironic if it were to be succeeded by a Khrushchev and Bulganin era, which some future historian might also date from a voyage of exploration to the East.

Commentary

C. GROVE HAINES
Professor of Diplomatic History,
School of Advanced International Studies

MR. LEWIS HAS VIEWED the present discontents of the Middle East as a clash between civilizations and has thereby thrown into bold relief the fundamental elements of the crisis over Middle Eastern affairs. There is nothing that I could usefully add in elaboration of this theme. But it may be of interest to examine the problem from another vantage point —from the more restricted one of international diplomacy.

We have been cautioned that it is a misleading simplification to describe the present Middle Eastern situation in terms of American-Russian rivalry. Quite rightly it has been pointed out that beyond these two giants there are to be found other powers that are actively interested and influential in Middle Eastern affairs. While acknowledging and accepting this, I think something can be gained from an examination of the role of the Middle East in the larger struggle between the Communist and Occidental worlds in which, admittedly, the Soviet Union and the United States are the leading, though not the sole, adversaries.

Considered in the restricted context of current international diplomacy, the role of the Middle East is disproportionate to its inherent strength. At the moment, the importance of the Middle East to the great contestants lies mainly in its usefulness as an instrument to withhold from or insure to western Europe the oil resources upon which Europe so largely depends, in the political impact of its nationalistic strivings upon the ancient great powers of Europe as well as upon the uncommitted areas of the world, and in its strategic significance relative to Western global defense. This is merely restating what has been so ably expressed by Mr. Lewis—that the Middle East itself, whether we refer to individual states or to the collective grouping of all of them, is not very consequential as an active, independent element in international politics, but is rather a dependent and malleable one exposed to and responding to the competing influences of the great powers on the outside. Its political weakness, combined with its great riches in oil and its strategic location, invites the exertion of influence and makes it inescapably an area of major contention. As recent experience has seemed to demonstrate, the contest for the Middle East—to which the commotions and discontents in the Middle East are often corollary—has become and is likely to remain for a long time one of the most significant in the struggle between the Soviet-influenced world and the Occidental powers.

Indeed, it would be difficult to exaggerate the importance of the Middle East in this contest. Lying athwart the main lines of communication between western Europe and the East, it can secure or deny to the West the junction of rimland defensive arrangements against the Soviet Union. It can stand as a barrier against easy Soviet penetration of the African continent or it can provide the highway for such penetration. The security of western Europe depends upon it in the measure by which that security is contingent upon control of the Mediterranean. Its fate may well determine the fate of India and hence the fate of the other remaining Asiatic states that have been seeking to shape their destinies according to the non-Communist pattern.

Today and for some decades to come, as far as one can judge, the oil of the Middle East, like the strategic location of the Middle East, will remain one of the most important factors in world politics. Nearly two-thirds of presently known potential reserves are located there, and while neither the Soviet Union nor the United States needs to depend upon their availability, the fact of the matter is that they are vitally important on a long-term basis to the economy and hence to the defense of western Europe. Eighty per cent of Europe's oil imports now come from fields in the Middle East, and it is expected that this dependence will increase rather than diminish in the foreseeable future. In time of crisis, the oil fields of the Western Hemisphere may be drawn upon by Europe to replace those of the Middle East, but they cannot be an effective or efficient substitute for the long run. What this means, when described in terms of current world politics, is that the strength and efficiency of the Western alliance is in no small measure dependent upon the accessibility or inaccessibility of Middle Eastern oil.

During the decade immediately following World War II, in spite of local upheavals and occasional Soviet gestures in regard to Turkey and Iran, neither the flow of oil nor the political orientation of the area appeared to be seriously jeopardized. The reason was not that the Western powers had found a common policy suited to the requirements of the area and to their own security, but that the Soviet Union was not prepared to exploit the opportunities that were taking shape, certainly in part as the result of its extensive activities there, to favor a Soviet initiative. This was a decade of rapidly spreading anti-Western Arab nationalism kept constantly inflamed by the unresolved problem of Israel and encouraged by the weakening power and prestige of France and Great Britain, whose influence had long been dominant in the area. Although ancient rivalries and disagreements continued to keep the governments of the area apart, the rank and file found in the Israeli question and in anti-Westernism a common bond, and the pressures that they were more and more able to generate both against the Western powers and local regimes were well suited to Soviet manipulations.

In 1955 the Soviet Union seized the initiative, and the

current crisis can be said to be largely the product of the manner in which this initiative was employed, and is still employed, for the accomplishment of Soviet foreign-policy objectives. It is undeniable that Moscow enjoys great advantages for the exercise of this initiative: geographical proximity; an historical reputation in the area of being less sullied than the other imperial powers; and, above all, the championship of the anti-Western cause. At the same time, the turbulence of the area has been ideally suited to those forms of infiltration and penetration in which Soviet leadership is particularly skilled. Consequently, although forces of resistance, both internal and external, have lately rallied, the fact is that the Soviets are still capable of calling the tune in the Middle East.

Without doubt, the Soviet Union would be glad to see the Middle East Sovietized, but this evidently is not an immediate objective for which all is to be risked. On the contrary, Moscow's Middle Eastern policy has been keyed to other and more important foreign policy objectives and can be properly assessed only when examined within this larger framework.

The Western alliance—Europe and the Atlantic powers—is the principal adversary of the Soviet Union, and its weakening or dissolution is naturally and logically the great desideratum of Soviet policy. The Middle East, if properly manipulated and influenced, whether Sovietized or not, if kept in a state of tension and unrest, if encouraged in its natural hostility toward the Western powers, can contribute in no small measure to the achievement of this larger goal. Soviet policy in the Middle East has in the last few years been shaped mainly in these terms and has enjoyed a considerable measure of success.

The beginning of the current crisis over the Middle East may be traced to the autumn of 1955 and the announcement of the shipment of Czech arms to Egypt. This was not an isolated gesture, made simply in response to the Baghdad Pact, but was closely co-ordinated with policy toward Europe and the Western alliance as a whole.

During the preceding two years, following Stalin's death, there had been some significant shifts in the European scene, which, on balance, were probably less advantageous to Moscow than to the West. The period of relaxation had resulted concretely in a Korean truce and a negotiated French withdrawal from Indochina, but it brought the contending powers no nearer together on such crucial issues as German unification, West German participation in NATO, or disarmament. It is true that the European Defense Community, in which so many Europeans and Americans had placed great store and to which the Soviet Union had registered the strongest opposition, failed to materialize, but there was substituted for it immediately the London-Paris agreements that ended the allied occupation of Germany, established the Western European Union, and provided for the rearmament of West Germany as well as its admission to NATO. The Soviet response to the ratification of these agreements in 1955 included, among other things, the denunciation of its treaties with Britain and France, the establishment of a military union of the satellites under the Warsaw Pact, the negotiation of the Four Power treaty of May, 1955, restoring sovereignty to a neutralized Austrian state, the restoration of contact with Yugoslavia, and an energetic campaign of penetration in the Middle East, combined with military assistance to Egypt.

Whatever other motivations there were for an active policy in the Middle East, there can be no doubt that the Soviet Union calculated upon embarrassing and weakening the Western allies. Britain had agreed the previous year to abandon Suez and was now engrossed in Cyprus; France, while extricating itself from embarrassments in Tunis and Morocco, was caught in the toils of an Algerian revolution that enjoyed both sympathy and support from the Arab world. Hotting up the fires could not fail to weaken Western defenses by maintaining a heavy drain upon forces that otherwise would be available to NATO and, at the same time, was calculated to sow discord between the two chief European powers and the United States, which never ceased to be embarrassed by their so-called colonial or imperialist policies.

The alignment of the Soviet Union with Arab anti-Western nationalists and, in particular, with Nasser in the face of

Franco-British weakness and American irresolution emboldened Nasser to defy the Western powers openly. Of all the elements that entered into the decision to nationalize the Suez Canal Company and thus to precipitate one of the most serious crises since World War II, the assurance of Soviet support was certainly the most important.

The Suez crisis will be fully dealt with later, so there is no need here of entering into details. But it is desirable to make note of those consequences that were of most significance for the West. It came near to shattering the Atlantic alliance, exposed the shortcomings of the consultative mechanisms through which policies were to be co-ordinated, and momentarily gravely weakened the defense posture of NATO. It precipitated a fuel crisis in Europe, particularly in France and Britain, where resort had to be made to rationing, and revealed in the most dramatic way how the shutting off of Middle Eastern oil reserves can in our day imperil the European economy and, in the larger sense, the Western defense establishment. It left behind a heritage of bitterness among the greater allies that, although now fortunately blunted, will nevertheless long remain. French and British prestige was further shaken severely and their inability, individually or jointly, to pursue an independent policy was demonstrated for all the world to see. In the Middle East itself, from which France had previously been eliminated, British influence suffered irreparable losses, even though it was far from extinguished. And, most notably perhaps, Soviet prestige was enhanced in the area, and the opportunities for the exertion of its influence were improved.

One of the paradoxical consequences of this crisis was to give fresh impetus to the European integration movement. In a very important sense, this was the result of French bitterness toward the United States and of a widespread sense of European impotence before the two great contending powers following Franco-British humiliation at Suez. As Guy Mollet, then French Premier, put it in a public press interview in Paris on February 8, 1957:

For each of our countries, Europe offers the only opportunity for real independence. Beside those colossi, which the Soviet Union and the United States are, what European country can claim to make its own views prevail? Before an America sometimes too impulsive, sometimes too slow to understand changes, and a Soviet Union which is the cause of disquietude and at times is still menacing, a united Europe will become a world force, not neutral but independent, will have a great part to play and will enable our peoples to make their contribution to the peace.[1]

As Charles Malik, Foreign Minister of Lebanon, wrote recently, with the Suez crisis the United States entered "the history of the Near East." We need not review the reasons for remaining on the outer fringe previously, whether wisely or unwisely, but we should make note of the fact that the circumstances surrounding this crisis and its development made it imperative that the United States assume its leadership as the first among the Western powers. This cannot now be abandoned, however great the burdens and perils may be. In substance, here, as in so many other parts of the world, the major protagonists must stand face to face and resolve the issues at hand.

I have dwelt upon the repercussions of the Suez crisis because they offer the clearest concrete evidence of the place that the Middle East holds in the East-West struggle. The developing situation in Syria may present an even more dramatic demonstration, for a Syrian satellite will clearly establish Soviet power on the Mediterranean, encompass our safest NATO ally on north and south, immobilize the most important oil pipe lines, and expose Iraq, Israel, and Saudi Arabia to serious menace.

The stakes in the Middle East are very large indeed, and in the interest of the West as a whole it is mandatory that ceaseless, constructive, energetic efforts be made to keep it from sliding further and faster into the Soviet camp. What this means precisely is that the United States must shoulder the greatest part of the burden, for alone among the Western

[1] *Corriere della Sera*, February 9, 1957.

powers it enjoys at least a measure of respect in the area and
the power and prestige that are essential to the exertion of
influence.

Like Mr. Lewis, I would prefer to leave the question of
what the policy of the United States should be to others, but,
unlike him, I would suggest that that policy cannot really be
one of "masterly inactivity." As things now stand, this could
very well be a policy of abdication that would leave festering
sores unhealed, that would earn us no respect, and that would
only expose the Middle East to further penetration and domination by the Soviet Union. Having said this, I think I may
usefully repeat what Mr. Lewis has phrased so well: that it
will be no easy task to shape and develop a policy that will be
productive of the desired results, for the United States, like
the other Western powers, is held in mistrust because it is
of the West and, more especially, because of its ties with
Israel. Yet judicious exercise of our power and influence
locally and firmness before the Soviet Union in general may
in time reduce the handicaps and keep the Middle East in
the non-Communist sphere, for all that this will mean to the
security and well-being of the West, no less than of the Middle East itself.

IV

Problems of
Arab Political Behavior

ELIE SALEM
Assistant Professor of Middle East Studies,
School of Advanced International Studies

THE SPONSORSHIP of this conference by an academic institution influences our presentation in two ways—the one
negative, the other positive. The negative restrains us from
indulging in controversial and ephemeral subjects, while the
positive channels our efforts in the exploration of the truth,
hidden behind the picture of conflict and tension in the
Middle East.[1] A sheer exposition of the current events is
hardly worth undertaking at a time when the facts are known
and are comprehensively reported by radio, press, and television. The most condensed synopsis of present Middle Eastern
problems would include the Palestine conflict, the Arab refugees, violent nationalism, North African rebellion, Suez, conflict with the British in southern and eastern Arabia, the crisis
in the Arab League, the problems of alignment, the Communist exploitations, and others. These, I admit, are most
urgent problems worthy of wise scrutiny and treatment; in
fact, they constitute the center of attention in the eyes not
only of the Middle Eastern peoples, but of the whole world.

On the other hand, the Arabs are suffering from deep and
chronic enigmas that seem to play subterranean roles beneath

[1] The term *Near East* as originally used here by Dr. Salem is synonymous
with the *Middle East* of other authors of this book and consequently has
been changed for the sake of consistency.

68

this whole panorama of trouble and discord. The disturbing thing is that these deeper enigmas not only are ignored by politicians and reporters, but they are almost unknown. Of the few thinkers who have made an attempt to tackle them, and then only superficially, it is significant to note that the majority have been non-Arabs. In unravelling some of these problems, I hope to attain a measure of truth that will be used as a steppingstone for the furthering of a good end. The good we are seeking is the general welfare of the peoples of the Middle East, this being the professed objective not only of the American government, but of all well-meaning peoples in the world.

Now that I have established my theme, above and beyond the staggering details of present political turbulence in the Middle East, I shall proceed to analyze some of these problems that have, for a long time, impeded our political life in the Middle East. These should be regarded not as elements of despair, but as new challenges worthy of the deepest attention and respect. The starting point in mutual understanding between the West and the Middle East is to know the parties as they are, i.e., to inquire into their history, character, and nature. My part is humble; it is limited to the inquiry into why the Arabs manifest seemingly awkward political behavior, why they are not in full control of their socio-political life. Though I appreciate the difficulties introduced by foreign powers into the Middle Eastern political scene, I shall not delve into them here, for my interest is concentrated on the Arab problem as it arises internally. The exterior phenomena are observed only to the extent to which they are directly related to the inner Arab attitudes. These attitudes, I must emphasize, are deeply rooted in Arab culture. Their understanding, therefore, necessitates the investigation of the factors that have, for centuries past, determined Arab political character.

On closer scrutiny the difficulties seem to be due not so much to an inappropriate political philosophy as to a lack of real interest in it. The tragic dearth of an organized tradition in political theory puts the Arabs in a relatively awkward position vis-à-vis the modern political ideas and institutions that they have adopted from the West in the past half century. It is an easy matter to borrow the Code Napoléon, to translate Swiss laws into Arabic, and to introduce a constitutional framework of government worthy of the most advanced democracies. The test is whether Arabs are capable of enforcing these laws and of managing these foreign administrative systems. To function properly, the constitutional and representative governments under which we live in the Middle East must presuppose a long and mature experience in democracy, public service, rule of law, responsibility, and social co-operation. These basic requisites are never imported; they must be lived, nurtured, and developed on native soil.

Whereas these principles were not seriously entertained in Arab society, and perhaps because of this fact, we find a relative prevalence of excessive individualism and narrow allegiances. The Arab's greatest weakness in political behavior has been his incompetence to reach to the whole. Unlike the Greek, he is not known to be in love with political ideas and theoretical speculations along the line of state, justice, citizen, right, etc. The abundant political literature handed down to us by Arabic writers in the classical period consists primarily of detailed legal expositions and of historical descriptions. A thorough investigation of these writings reveals the absence of free adventurous thinking (i.e., the courage to examine the state in isolation from Sunna and Sharia), of analysis, and therefore of universal relevance. It is true that a certain portion of freedom existed in the political reflections of a few men like ibn-Sina and al-Farabi, but it yielded no significant results. The reason for that is twofold: (a) these thinkers incorporated Greek political ideas without digestion and in effect reiterated them in Arabic, knowing full well the impossibility of applying them to their political institutions; (b) the intellectuals (i.e., then the religious leaders and teachers) have always distrusted the intrusion of foreign secular ideas. Not only were the intermediaries, therefore, not highly qualified, but the reception itself was very poor. Perhaps the deepest question that suggests itself in this context is why Greek learning, while activating Arab philosophy, logic, science, and theology, failed to create a similar connected and coherent chain of reaction along lines of theoretical political speculation. The scanty philosophical writings on the polity by Arab thinkers, though colored haphazardly with Greek concepts, were never given the ground to mature and gain recognition. Greece's rich political heritage had therefore no tangible impact on the attitude of the Arabs. The deep metaphysical inquiries made by the Greeks with reference to the state and its purpose (which was defined as the good) were not *really* raised by the Arabs.

The Arab looks at the world and sees individuals and objects and identifies them as such. The totality, namely, the civil entity, has rarely interested him. His concern is more with the immediate and the practical. This attitude explains in part, but only in part, why Arab political writers tended to ignore the state and concentrated their voluminous writings on the caliph. The allegiance of the Arab is personal, and the domination of the personal over the public interest is at the basis of the Arab political problem. If lack of tradition in free theoretical reflections in matters of state is a serious cause of present political confusion in the Arab world, then the presence of simplicity would constitute another factor, in the same manner as the other side of the coin. Unlike the former, this is a positive element constantly operating in the Arab mind and directing it into all types of vistas with childlike innocence. The Arabs have always taken pride in their simplicity; indeed, the very democracy that Arab writers insist was the form of government of early Moslems was just that—simplicity. But democracy, in essence, has nothing to do with being kind, simple, humane, and socially accessible in the Bedouin style.

It is the record of history that most Arab rulers since the Umayyad period with notable exceptions have not treated their subjects in accordance with the high ideals of the Moslem religion. The argument may be raised that in the West the kings lived a no less corrupt life, and their behavior therefore can be justified by the spirit of the age in which they lived. One point should be clarified. In the West there were political writers who, through independent reasoning, were able to discern the excesses in their rulers and to restrain them through guidance, and at times through violence. There was always the intellectual element, which tempered the licentiousness of kings and princes. Government in America and western Europe is greatly influenced by the writings of political philosophers like Locke, Mill, Montesquieu, and Rousseau. In the Arab world the balance is lacking. Government power was too strong for the scanty intellectual tradition in political speculation. Though hundreds of books exist on political history and the legal aspects of the caliphate, there is not one single authentic book in Arabic on political philosophy. This is a serious matter, especially in a land whose people have consistently suffered injustices. Not only in the Arab world, but in the whole of Asia, the people are unfamiliar with natural rights and with the theory of government that holds the state responsible for the protection and promotion of these rights. Since the people as such are often passive, the fault cannot be attributed to them, but to their intellectual leadership.

Arab society, even prior to Islam, found leadership in wrong quarters—the poets. The poet was not only the custodian of the aesthetic, but the fount of knowledge and wisdom as well. To compose beautiful poetry was the highest type of achievement. Unfortunately, this tradition survived with negligible modification. The association between the rulers and the poets is a long-established one in our Arab society. The Arab ruler always had a poet and the majority of Arab poets thrived on praise generously supplied to their patrons in return for money. The tendency toward the poetic is perhaps the most dangerous element in our civilization. Poetry, the product of imagination, does not necessarily cater to seriousness, hardness, and objective truth, and it often is nonrational. Nevertheless, the poetic element is still dominant in Arab life. Every important political gathering is often addressed and stirred by a poet. A few years ago the Arab Medical Conference met in Cairo. Its plenary session was opened by a poet. The general attitude of Arab leaders to the Palestine question was poetic, i.e., pretension without knowledge, promises without preparation.

Essentially tied with the poetic is the attitude of rest and carelessness, manifested in the wasting of time, official time, in storytelling and the relating of anecdotes. A *Thousand and One Nights* does not, without significance, claim Baghdad as its stage. It is also interesting to recall that this annal almost always involved the ruler. For a person schooled in the doctrine of efficiency and achievement, nothing is more shocking than to witness this exhibition of irrelevant detail. The emphasis on titles and form is equally subject to criticism. In the past the Arabs expected their government officials to be well founded in the forms and manners of the language. A good official wrote eloquently and poetically. He was supposed to be an artist in the manner of addressing and flattering his superiors. A grammatical mistake, as much as inefficiency, marked his value. Many officials felt insulted if a simple and clear document was attributed to them. They preferred complicated language, full of riddles and obscure expressions. It is astounding how much of this frivolity is still revered in government circles, not only in written form, but in the highly ceremonial relations among officials. When an administrator writes a note to another, he uses titles and adjectives that, if omitted, would greatly reduce its size, thereby saving time and money. The Arab language is alleged to be the cause of this evil. The language lends itself to poetry, color, praise, and the like and is extremely rich. Its magic drives the writer away from precision. There is a profound connection between language and the operation of the mind, and when the latter is not thoroughly disciplined in logic, the former tends to dominate.

The Arab mind, under the impress of language, therefore tends to operate in a peculiar manner that lends itself to imagination. Involvement with form and external arrangement are manifestations of the above. In World War I the British, through Sir Henry McMahon, approached Sherif Husein of Mecca to win his support against the Ottoman government and for effect attempted the Arab style:

To the excellent and well-born Sayyed, the descendant of
Sharifs, the Crown of the Proud, Scion of Muhammad's Tree
and Branch of Quraishite Trunk, him of the Exalted Presence
and of the Lofty Rank, Sayyed son of Sayyed, Sharif son of
Sharif, the Venerable, Honoured Sayyed, His Excellency the
Sharif Husain, Lord of the Many, Amir of Mecca the Blessed,
the Codestar of the Faithful and the Cynosure of all devout
Believers, may His Blessings descend upon the people in their
multitudes.[2]

In this instance, I must admit, the result was disappointing.

In many of the Arab states today, where the call to modern-
ity is vociferous, titles are prohibited by law; nevertheless,
they are still used. It is not really the letter that counts, but
the mentality behind it. It is easy for the Egyptian government to outlaw the usage of titles in official correspondence.
The real test lies in whether the minds of men are converted
to a new way of life that scorns this practice. The Egyptian
fellah still refers to his superiors as beys and pashas, and it
will take decades of proper education to persuade the average
man of the Arab world, who has been a negligible entity since
history was written, that he is really equal to the pasha in the
eyes of the law. It will take an equal amount of training in
democratic principles under freely elected institutions to convince the citizen that by political status he is equal if not
superior to his administrators, whether mudir (director) or
mutasarrif (governor). To be truly convinced that government is the servant of the people and that the citizen can
approach the latter and demand without fear and humiliation
that his right be granted is indeed a great attainment.

The greatest weakness in Arab administration is the absence
of enlightened civic responsibility.

No topic is more worthy of investigation and research than
this one. At the moment I shall venture only to suggest two
explanations, the one legal, the other social. Islamic law, unlike Western law, is religious and by necessity, therefore,
streams upward, above and beyond the political jurisdiction.
The allegiance that it nurtures is religious, not secular. West-

[2] George Antonius, *The Arab Awakening* (Beirut, 1955), p. 167.

ern law, with the exception of the common law, is derived
from Roman law as compiled under Justinian. As it is fully
secular, it was natural for it to promote, throughout its development, a reverence for civic responsibility. In this distinction lies the basic difference between Islamic law and Western
law. The second explanation lies in the kin-group substratum
of Arab society. A glance at the law of inheritance in Islam
or at town administration in the classical period is enough to
reveal the preponderant position of the family and blood relations. It should be admitted, however, that under the impact
of Western influence rapid transformations are taking place
in this area. In the gradual broadening of political horizons
these inner conflicts and narrow loyalties will eventually be
resolved.

The promotion of enlightened democratic attitudes invites the condemnation of obsolete institutions and the construction of new vigorous ones in their place. In our society
no attitude is more deserving of the deathblow than that of
charity. Though the institution of charity (or waqf) was commendable when propagated by the Prophet, it no longer can
be tolerated as a political principle. The concept of charity
implies the presence of second-class citizens. The modern
state abhors charity and thrives on responsibility. It is the
duty of the government to give shelter to the poor and food
to the hungry. Modern civilization rejects the belief that the
life of the poor depends upon the goodness of heart of the
rich.

In an age when the lower classes are slowly seeing the light
and gradually assuming a revolutionary bent against the old
institutions, charity has no place. Unless right replaces charity,
the theoretical foundations of government in the Arab world
will remain faulty. It is not merely charity as manifested in
waqf that is criticized here. The argument delves deeper into
the charitable attitude that permeates the government. When
an average citizen approaches a government official, he feels
that he is approaching a man a hundred grades higher than
he is; he is afraid and hesitant. In making his request, the
citizen pleads with the official to expedite his business and

to do it as a personal favor. He usually expects complication and delay and constant reminders from influential friends and politicos. And it often happens that when an official does your work for you, he makes you feel that he was charitable to you. Right and duty are democratic features. They have to wait until democracy has matured in the minds of our people. There is still a large gap between the government and the people and a much larger one between constitutional provisions and actual operation.

How to inculcate the spirit of public service and responsibility at all levels of administration is a serious question. Schooling and training are certainly helpful, and they will eventually give results. Meanwhile it is obvious that bureaucracy has no miraculous solutions. The need for educated and efficient administrators cannot be overemphasized, for without them the ship of state will sail aimlessly and dangerously. The difficulty of the Arab governments in this respect is twofold: first, the absence of an adequate number of educated and trained citizens to fill the important posts in the administration; and second, the reluctance of the educated few to accept government employment at the present scale of salaries. Arab governments do not enjoy a high prestige, which in itself would be sufficient to attract competent young men to the civil service. It is also doubtful whether Arab governmental budgets can be substantially increased to provide for higher salaries at a time when more than half of the ordinary budget is spent on salaries. The lack of human resources leaves the student of Arab governments in a sober mood, knowing that the most revolutionary of laws cannot achieve, without due consideration to time, patience, and serious preparation, the real reform that the enlightened mind seeks.

So far we have not really reached the crux of our inquiry. The "why" is still unanswered and is left insistent.

The Arabs believe that man's destiny is in the hands of God. "Why fight the inevitable?" is the typical attitude of the Arab. The crucial weakness in his thinking is the conviction that somehow, in God's infinite wisdom, things will resolve themselves.

There is a lack of belief in the capacity of reason to create, achieve, share, or even destroy man. In relegating all acts of creation to God, man is relieved of responsibility. The need for understanding man, therefore, his purpose, and his responsibility in promoting his personality, is most imperative in the Arab world; for without this understanding there is no hope for the modulation of the human problem. If the state is to undertake this function, it first must be governed by men who appreciate these values and who are in turn courageous enough to embark on radically new plans. They must be sincerely convinced of the seriousness of the task and of their accountability to the people and to history. Since we, the Arabs, are not steeped in democratic heritage, it is natural for our leaders not to comprehend fully their role in service; and many of our leaders are not really convinced that they are the servants of the people. It will be some time before this political philosophy is actually believed and followed. For our world has had the misfortune of breeding masses who were always so poor, so ignorant, so reduced, so crushed by nature, religion, and society as to accept their lot without question. For the Arab world, indeed for the whole of Asia and Africa, the problem of the masses constitutes the deepest and most challenging problem of government.

A society of masses and lords cannot withstand the compulsions of the twentieth century unless the lords are already conscious of the potential volcanoes that may erupt under them at any time. When they are aware of these possibilities, they might be led, willingly or unwillingly, to break the tradition of history in Asia and the Middle East and to establish a government whose role is to elevate the total dignity of the citizens. Under the influence of communism, that wonderful devil that scares away ghosts, and under the impact of the consistent Western challenge of the past two centuries, the Arab masses are awakening and demanding new rights. Their voice is loud and confused, yet it emerges with force and potential. Every significant political decision in the Arab world today is taken with the masses in mind. Their power for good and evil is incalculable. It is the trust of enlightened leadership to channel it to constructive ends. Until this gigantic question is tackled effectively, there can be no talk about progress, freedom, and stability.

Arab apathy in political and social life is certainly a dangerous thing worthy of investigation, for in it lies the essence of the crisis. The Arab's suffering is material and concrete and is the most eloquent witness to the cruelty of nature and man. The problem of "man" is the fount from which all the major conflicts in Arab life flow. This theme must be pondered again and again before the other problem, that of nature is considered. The most pressing function of the Arab intellectuals who really care for the construction of a better state founded on reason and dedicated to the promotion of fundamental and inalienable human rights is to start now, before it is too late, to disentangle first their rulers and then their people from the restrictions of self-imposed theology, which prevent them from life in the world. Life in the world is subject to reason, science, daring, curiosity, and openness. Nothing is more alien to its calling than poetry, imagination, and myths. If man is the master of the earth, then he must deal with its infinite possibilities with mastery and command. It is the nature of the earth to be subjected and exploited by man in the process of elevating himself, materially, intellectually, and spiritually. Reason is the means through which this mastery is attained. This rational interpretation, I hesitate to say, is not readily accepted by the Asians, of whom we Arabs are part. The Asians respect nature and approach it cautiously. They fear it, and they do not fully understand it. Victory, however, presupposes understanding. With the renewal of learning among the Arabs and the consequent expansion of vision and horizons a new system is being molded. It is still too early to predict its impact on sociopolitical development.

The searcher for the undercurrents in the Arab soul is immediately faced with the problem of nature. The Arab mind is stamped to all eternity by the impress of the desert. Despair and lack of initiative are the fruits of its womb. For centuries the Arabs fought against the desert, and the desert always won. At present we are witnessing a unique opportunity to subdue the desert once and for all. It will be a race between time and consciousness, a most interesting race to behold. Not to respond fully to the challenge of nature is shameful, but there are certain cases in which not much can be done. The heat of the desert, the scarcity of water, and the dearth of industrial material are enough to cause despair. Egypt's agriculture is perhaps the most efficient in the world, and yet its people live in tragic misery. A survey of Arab material conditions, in spite of newly found oil in certain parts of the Arab world, shows the urgent need of the Arabs for substantial economic aid. Balanced men are rarely found in economic misery, and stable political institutions are often the fruits not only of solid men, but also of solid economics.

After this candid vivisection of the Arab soul, we find ourselves face to face with a multiplicity of inner conflicts, which, in their jostling, shape the attitude of the Arabs toward themselves and the whole world. The ultimate goal is to resolve these tensions into settlement and rest. It is my contention here that our deepest crisis is internal; it is more serious than Suez or Algeria. To digest their problems, or perhaps to heal their wounds—the wounds received throughout a merciless history—the Arab people need peace. Peace provides the opportunity to concentrate on the real issues and to seek their solutions through free communion with the more advanced societies. Regretfully this peace has not been insured, either by the West or by the East. In creating the Palestine problem and the colonial issue, the West must be held responsible for wittingly or unwittingly arousing the suspicion of the Arabs and for diverting their thinking from the deeply embedded problems that gnaw their souls to the immediate and the ephemeral. The selfish and merciless exploitation by the Communists today of the desperate and confused Arab mind is saddening indeed.

With the new American policy that seeks to defend the rights and liberties of the peoples of the Middle East against alien threat and subversion we have a refreshing approach potentially laden with promise and opportunity. We firmly believe that there is enough wisdom, love, and vision in the

West, namely, in the United States, to promote trust and friendship between two well-meaning peoples. Without these cordial relations it is difficult, if not impossible, for the Arabs to treat conclusively the inner problems briefly alluded to in this paper.

Commentary

HAROLD B. MINOR

Chairman of the Board of Directors,
American Friends of the Middle East, Inc.

MR. ELIE SALEM, in his essay "Problems of Arab Political Behavior," deliberately turns his back on pressing Middle Eastern questions and upon the political relationships between the Arab world and the Western powers. He seeks, rather, to throw light upon these problems and relationships by delving into the Arab mind. He addresses himself to the "deep and chronic enigmas that seem to play subterranean roles beneath this whole panorama of trouble and discord," in the interest of truth and of the furtherance of understanding between the Arabs and the West. He stresses the Arab tendency toward excessive individualism and narrow allegiances, which restrict the Arab's ability to see the whole or to give proper support to the state. He enumerates qualities in the Arab mind that have retarded the development of a high sense of civic responsibility. He observes a dangerous tendency of the Arabs to relieve themselves of responsibility on the grounds that things are caused, and will resolve themselves, through God's infinite wisdom. But he insists that under the profound impact of Western culture and the more recent influence of communism, the masses are awakening and demanding, in voices loud but still confused, new rights and dignity. In his opinion the harassing and urgent problems of the area may find solution only through enlightened leadership based on these principles. The crisis, therefore, is internal, although he clearly does not exculpate the Western powers or the Communists for their parts in the creation of problems, exploitation, and misunderstanding. Finally, he expresses the belief that without love, wisdom, and vision on the part of the West it will not be possible for the Arabs to treat these inner conflicts and thus contribute to peace and international amity.

Mr. Salem has, I believe, made a significant contribution by turning his eyes inward to examine, in quiet and thoughtful introspection, qualities in the Arab mind that must be better understood by Western peoples if the foundation itself can be laid upon which the superstructure of policy and peace may be built. An assessment of this kind can come most convincingly from an Arab. It would be presumptuous of me to set myself up as a critic or judge in matters so intimately bound up with the mentality of a foreign people. But I can permit myself, in all modesty, to say that in my opinion Mr. Salem has put his finger on the pulse of the problem. What he has said is but an extension of St. John's injunction: "And ye shall know the truth and the truth shall make you free." Only thus can the Arabs move on to the development of civic responsibility and to a positive contribution to the international order.

Mr. Salem might have pointed up even more the inexorable march of the Arabs toward better government, more responsible leadership, and a more abundant life for the masses. Evidences are seen everywhere of these growing demands by the masses for leaders and governments more responsive to the will and needs of the people. The voice of the masses, long thought nonexistent by Westerners, is heard calling insistently and successfully, and this is reflected in wiser government and in plans designed to benefit the masses through developmental programs. Propaganda, in calling attention to abuses and misguided spending of public funds, has obscured the very real and rapid social and economic progress being made in all parts of the Arab world. This is, perhaps more rapidly than

we know, diverting some of the negative factors mentioned by
Mr. Salem into more constructive and hopeful channels.

It seems to me that Mr. Salem lets the Western powers off
much too lightly in considering their responsibility for creating instability in the Middle East and thus preventing the
kind of atmosphere in which the Arabs might resolve their
inner conflicts. How, for example, can an individual find
peace and inner serenity in a household torn by dissension,
bitterness, and greed. While I would not quarrel with Mr.
Salem's contention that the Arab problem is an internal one,
it might be useful to point out some of the attitudes and
actions of the West that have created an atmosphere not conducive to the resolution of these inner conflicts.

Turmoil in the Middle East results from many factors in
addition to the inner struggles Mr. Salem mentions, and most
of these causes of turmoil derive from the West and from
communism. There are, in fact, four power struggles going
forward in the Middle East: the Arabs against Zionism and
colonialism; Arab against Arab; the West against communism;
and the West against itself. These bitter power struggles have
separated brother from brother, creating an atmosphere of suspicion wherein misunderstanding and false propaganda thrive.
The very fragmentation of the Middle East and the creation of
nonviable states, such as Israel and Jordan, was a primary
Western-caused producer of turmoil. The discovery of oil,
and the struggle of the Western powers to have and to hold it
at all costs, created tension and gave a new economic impetus
in Middle Eastern affairs. The failure of the West to understand and accommodate itself to the potent force of Arab
nationalism has been a major cause of friction. The revolution
of technology, thrust belatedly on the Arab world, played a
part. The teachings of communism and Communist fishing
in the troubled waters of the Middle East in a cynical and
heartless fashion contributed in generous degree to unrest.
Above all, the creation of Israel by the West and its nurture
in excessive degree against the wishes of the Arabs destroyed
any immediate hope of Western leadership in the area. Under the circumstances, it is remarkable that the position of the

West is still relatively tenable in the Arab world and that these inner conflicts have found some degree of resolution in an atmosphere of strife and self-seeking.

Mr. Salem's foray into soul-searching and introspection prompts me to do the same in the hope that, by examining our failures, we may help to point the way to future policy. It has long been my belief that the most essential single need in our Middle Eastern policy is to reassert the American moral leadership that we won there as a result of more than a century of private American, largely missionary, endeavor. The reservoir of good will for the United States, so assiduously built up by private American effort, is dangerously depleted, but to say that it is dry is to indulge in gross exaggeration.

It has struck me, as I have wandered along the byways of American governmental and private endeavor in the Middle East for the past twenty years, that America has not faithfully reflected abroad the true greatness of American democracy and tradition. This is a development, it should be quickly pointed out, of recent times, for in the first hundred or so years of our contact with that part of the world we did in fact reveal and project America at its best. In the great missionary period, when our schools, hospitals, and relief activities represented much of our posture, we won an enviable reputation. Americans were venerated because they stood for the best in American tradition. The business community as it established itself in the Middle East in the last few decades has carried on the missionary tradition in policies of sharing and of respect for the sovereignty and susceptibilities of the foreigners among whom it thrived. It was only when the United States entered the arena of Middle Eastern political life on an official basis that the relationships of this golden private era were subjected to the stresses that are now so evident. Why is this? Is it simply because we have now assumed a leadership role wherein we are forced to make unpopular decisions based on our wider interests? This thesis hardly holds up, because the loss of our hard-earned prestige came during a time when our policy toward the Middle East might be described as "intervention and interest without assumption of responsibility," and not in our present political leadership period.

The reason must be found elsewhere. I am sure we all can agree that an American policy anywhere, to be successful, must be based squarely on an unassailable moral position. But it is not simple to define a moral position nor to be sure that the prescription any one of us may propose is more moral or valid than that of persons holding different views. Similarly, what is regarded as the "American national interest" on any question is open to interpretation. However, there are certain guideposts that may help us. One, I suggest, is simply the golden rule. A second is to make sure that in our search for truth and equity we are not deflected by short-range personal desires, by irritations of the moment, or by the pressures of special interests. It is essential that moral positions not be undermined by policies based solely on expediency. In speaking of expediency, I would be the last to suggest that the moral and spiritual qualities that have made America great are in process of decline. But I am afraid there is evidence that we may have forgotten temporarily some of these principles or relegated them to a secondary status as we have faced staggering problems in a divided world in which we have had to assume a role of leadership that we did not desire and for which we were not fully prepared. Most of these deviations may be attributed to lapses from the high standards that we expect of ourselves and not to intrinsic weaknesses.

It must be admitted that we do have certain characteristics that make difficult the conduct of foreign affairs. For example, the natural dislike of Americans for foreign affairs has prevented proper support and encouragement for the State Department and has frequently caused us to disparage foreign problems and peoples. An example of this immature stance is our method of appointing ambassadors. I refer not so much to the dangerous luxury of the spoils system of political appointment, since this is gradually disappearing, but rather to the holding up to public ridicule and criticism of those who represent the United States abroad. In two recent cases ambassadors were gleefully ridiculed in the Senate and press, although their confirmation was fully expected. It simply does not make sense to undercut our own agents as they go abroad to do our tasks and represent us. Another such quality is an extreme naiveté, which has caused most Americans to capitulate, in matters connected with foreign affairs, to vested interests and allowed vocal and influential minority groups to dominate important segments of foreign affairs, sometimes to the great detriment of our position.

Regarding actual lapses from our own high standards, we have shown at times an alarming lack of humility and understanding in dealing with foreigners. I remember, about fifteen years ago, Professor Frank Tannenbaum of Columbia telling government officials in a lecture in Washington that whether we knew it or not America did in fact have a foreign policy —an unconscious reflection abroad of the kind of relationship that exists among the American states and people. If this is valid, and I think it is, we have not been entirely successful in its projection. For example, what could be more regrettable and harmful than the outbursts of Mayor Wagner and others in New York against King Saud, a sovereign full of good intentions and desirous of strengthening relations with the United States? In giving the impression that we wish to make foreigners over in our own image, we have shown precious little of the Christian virtues of humility and tolerance. Our attitude, on the contrary, has frequently been characterized by conceit and arrogance. Even in the giving of aid, we have sometimes given the impression of having hidden motives or of giving alms without graciousness; for without the giver the gift is bare. In short, we have revealed to some peoples a kind of master-race attitude or what might be called "extraterritorial mentality." Perhaps a better term would be "the illusion of omniscience." Let me hasten to say that I do not believe these deviations are either conscious or permanent. Surely, they must derive from impatience to achieve goals in the face of the serious threat to our peace and security posed by international communism. But they nonetheless are a menace to our relations with Asia and Africa. They show

America certainly not at its best, especially in Asia and Africa, which may hold the balance of power for the future.

We should recognize, it seems to me, that emergent or even established nations cannot be conquered or held by mechanisms of force. They are going to dispose freely of their destinies by their own choice, even if this choice means Russia. We should, therefore, think in moral rather than power terms in order to win the hearts and minds of Asia. It is an anomaly that there are to be found, at one and the same time, in Middle Eastern countries a high regard for Americans as persons and for the United States as a democratic ideal, on the one hand, and an intense dislike of American political and governmental actions on the other. It is touching, in fact, for an American to feel the upsurge of good will and affection so evident on the part of the average private person in the Arab world when they meet on a personal basis. Forgetting the political and other grievances of the moment, individual Arabs are quick to remember the America that the Middle East had come to know and love over a period of generations. But when numbers congregate, these feelings are usually sublimated in the emotional throes of real or imagined grievances against the West and of hurt that a friend could, as they see it, have betrayed them. This anomaly illustrates tellingly, I believe, the point that our strength in the Middle East has derived from a private, missionary position and endures in spite of the vicissitudes and stresses of political actions. It is unfortunate that we sometimes forget the need to win peoples themselves and consequently may deal with an area as if there were no people there.

This tendency to forget peoples is evident when most of us describe the aims we profess and goals we hope to achieve in the Middle East. We say that we must keep the Middle East free of Communist domination, that we must keep the oil and strategic resources available to the free world and prevent their slipping behind the Iron Curtain, and that we should support the political independence and territorial integrity of nations in the area. These are laudable goals with which I have no quarrel. But they stand alone and naked unless they are tied to a basic policy of winning the peoples themselves through simple, human methods that will convince them of our friendship and reliability. I repeat that in this era of the United Nations, of self-determination, and of world public opinion, these nations are going to make their own free choices and dispose of their own destinies as they wish. No mechanisms of power or statement of goals will prevent this from happening. Thus, I should prefer to see, in any statement of American objectives in the Middle East a much higher place given to human considerations than to selfish goals, for in the long run, I am persuaded, these will triumph.

Now when we talk in terms of human considerations, of moral policy, and of such intangibles, do we mean a policy of weakness and drift? Not at all—not any more than we can say that Christianity itself over the centuries and as conceived was less than dynamic or militant. In fact, such policies can be carried out more vigorously and persuasively because they capture the imagination and because they inspire policy-makers and their agents with zeal and a sense of mission.

A perfect example of what I have in mind is the response in Asia and Africa to President Eisenhower's reaction to the invasion of Egypt by Israel, Britain, and France. A great wave of approval and of pro-American feeling was evident throughout Asia and Africa. We were, you might say, given a new and precious opportunity to restore our leadership and influence. Of course, some of this was due to the natural reactions of Arabs seeking support against Israel and to the response of dependent or newly independent peoples to any action appearing to them to restrain so-called colonialism. But I suggest that there was a deeper and more significant reason. This was an almost automatic and instinctive feeling that America had had, in a great crisis when the cards were down, the courage and the vision to make a decision on grounds of morality and justice, even though this entailed real heartache and sacrifice in deciding against allies with whom we have so much in common. Our decision and subsequent actions were popular not only because they were what Asia wished to see, but also because they were taken for the right reasons. It seems to me that a single such action can do more to win and hold a position than doctrines, aid programs, or enunciated policies standing alone.

It may be useful and interesting to examine American policy in the Middle East in the light of the considerations I have touched upon. For my own thinking, I like to divide American policy in the Middle East into three general periods: first, the private and missionary period up to the time between the wars; second, the following period in which the United States intervened, gave free advice, and took actions without acceptance of, or perhaps even a sense of, responsibility; and third, the present period of involvement with full and sober acceptance of responsibility. In the first of these periods, when there was a high degree of spiritual and dedicated private effort, we were eminently successful. In the second period, the decline of the American position in the area was severe. In the third, or present, period there is at least hope that the erosion of the American position in the area may be halted. In the second of these periods we seemed to have been motivated by two impulses, the one to give preference to the state of Israel and the other to gear our actions to an overriding need to restrain international communism. The Arabs have staunchly resisted the first of these and have failed to be greatly affected by the other, in spite of the fact that Islamic society has felt no basic ideological attraction to communism. Imbued, as they were, with the twin phobias of anti-Zionism and anti-colonialism, the Arabs not only failed to understand American policy, but came to believe that United States policy, in supporting (as they saw it) Zionism and the colonial powers, brought a new kind of imperialistic danger to the area. Thus our motives as well as our actions became suspect, even in such matters as aid programs, which certainly sprang from a generous and idealistic impulse. Our policy was doomed to failure not only because it met such stubborn opposition, but more importantly because it was not geared to the needs and wishes of the peoples themselves.

The third period coincides with the present American administration, as many policy-makers in the government and

private citizens began to view with alarm the consequences
for the national security of the dangerous drift of Middle
Eastern countries away from us. There was inaugurated in
this new period a policy of sympathetic impartiality, as between Israel and the Arab countries, wherein questions could
be resolved on their merits and in the light of the American
national interest rather than on the basis of political or other
expediency. But to be successful a policy requires more than
enunciation. It needs not only determined day-to-day application, but also strong popular support. There has been, I think,
such a wide gulf between policy enunciation and application
that we need to examine critically the meaning of this word
impartiality. I suggest that the proof of whether our policy
is truly impartial lies not in policy declarations or even in the
sincere desire of the government to be unbiased, but rather
in the totality of an American attitude toward Israel and the
Arab world. It would indeed be difficult to convince an Arab
that the totality of our position is impartial, when he observes
the overwhelming financial and press support given in the
United States to a small state that he believes to be a threat
to his very existence and that he regards as an outpost of
Western influence. I do not intend to go into the substance
of the Arab-Israeli dispute. I merely wish to make the point
that whatever we may mean by the word *impartiality*, it has
quite a different connotation in the Arab mind, which we are
here endeavoring to evaluate and understand. But, just as Mr.
Salem finds no cause for alarm or despair in assessing the Arab
mind, so, it seems to me, there is no cause for alarm or despair
in considering the trend or direction of American policy toward the Arab world. The policy is now soundly conceived,
and there is a tremendous amount of good will and sincerity
in official circles in its implementation. In addition, the general public is increasingly inclined to look at Middle Eastern
questions in the light of the American national interests and,
being better informed than heretofore, is more able to differentiate between truth and propaganda. Thus the administration should find its hand strengthened in carrying out its
enunciated policies by increasing public support and under-

standing. Far from being in despair at the evolution of policy toward this area, we should be encouraged and hopeful for the future.

Having considered the general American policy in the Middle East in the light of the considerations I have outlined, it may be of interest to examine certain American attitudes toward underlying problems in the area. Perhaps no single factor is causing more unrest and giving policy-makers in the West more concern than Arab nationalism, which has taken on emotional and unreasoning overtones that sometimes baffle the foreign observer. The United States, as it views and works with this problem, is caught in an unenviable dilemma. Policy must reflect not only an inherent American desire to favor nations seeking sovereignty and self-expression, but must also take into account America's world-wide interests and commitments. We are in the position of a circus rider delicately balanced on two horses. All is well as long as the two horses can be persuaded to keep in the position in which we want them; otherwise we will be split down the middle or forced to jump to safety in an undignified and probably disastrous manner. It has seemed to me that the only tenable attitude that we could take with regard to Arab nationalism is one of full sympathy and support, based on feelings deeply embedded in the hearts and minds of Americans, qualities that will endure and prevail over any short-term improvisation. The reconciliation of this intuitive policy with that of other and more global commitments would have been, it seems to me, relatively easy had we made clear to our allies from the beginning that these fundamental and inherent feelings of millions of Americans are so strong as to prevent the carrying out of any policy that denies them. Thus, we should have made it clear that while giving full support to our allies where possible, we would be in fact inhibited from a policy of seemingly supporting our Western allies where such actions clash with our fundamental need to support the desire of peoples for independence and full freedom. What is most difficult now to accomplish in the way of a compromise between so-called colonialism and nationalism would have been much easier had we been more true to our historic ideals.

We now find ourselves in the needless and unfortunate position of appearing as an opponent of Nasser, who has emerged, in the eyes of millions of Arab nationalists, as a symbol and a hero. True, we helped to save Nasser as the result of our courageous stand on Suez. The point I want to make is that, had we been truer to our own ideals, we need never have placed our policy in the jeopardy in which it stands nor have appeared in the minds of many as champions of colonialism against nationalism. To blame Nasser or view him as a Hitler of the Nile is childish. He is the result of something, not the originator. He symbolizes something, and symbols cannot easily be destroyed. I was impressed with the views on Arab nationalism expressed by Mr. John C. Campbell, in the quarterly *Foreign Affairs*. Here is an excerpt:

> The winds of Arab nationalism are blowing strong; Arab nationalism seems to have been captured by Gamal Abdel Nasser; its tone is violently anti-Western; it welcomes the friendly support of the Soviet Union against the hated "colonialists" and "Zionists."
>
> To command these winds to calm down is futile. To make a frontal assault on nationalism, as the British and French did, is fatal.
>
> To appease "Nasserism," as the United States has had cause to discover, gains nothing. The Soviets can bid higher than any Western nation. The only hopeful course is one which frankly accepts Arab aspirations to self-determination, equality and independence, but sets limits to support of extreme claims which deny these rights to others. It is the determination of those limits that is so difficult, for Arab claims and grievances range far and wide. An essential preliminary in any case is the establishment of a certain amount of confidence on the part of the Arabs in American motives, building on the prestige gained by our stand against the recent invasions of Egypt, but maintaining necessary bargaining power in working out specific agreements with them.[1]

[1] John C. Campbell, "From 'Doctrine' to Policy in the Middle East," *Foreign Affairs*, XXXV (1957), 441-53.

It is my opinion that the bonds that unite the Arabs are stronger and more enduring than those that divide them. The fact that the divisive factors are many and are more evident than the unifying factors may well seem to justify and give hope for success of a new policy of divide and rule. If my thesis is correct, such a policy might ultimately result in disaster, for at each succeeding crisis in the Middle East, nations and national leaders will be increasingly forced by public opinion to follow a line acceptable to nationalists whether or not they desire to do so. Thus, governments will become more and more prisoners of the street and not the masters. I suggest, therefore, that any policy of divide and rule is foredoomed to failure as it clashes with the potent and unifying force of emotional nationalism.

Our attitude toward neutralism also requires examination. It has been natural that Americans, faced by a grave danger and carrying an awful load of responsibility, should disparage and resent the idea that any nation can be neutral in this torn and divided world. To us, the issue seems a clear choice between slavery and freedom. But to many nations and millions of Asians, faced with more immediate problems, the choice is not so clear. Some Arabs, for example, fearful of colonialism and Zionism and not as immediately concerned as we with the threat of communism, view our policies in their naked power aspects rather than as policies of friendship for peoples. This attitude of lack of sympathy toward neutralism represents a real break with American tradition and our own historic past. It not only reveals failure to comprehend and weigh the problems of others, but also shows the extent to which we have been guilty of betrayal of our own traditions. That this is changing was made clear by President Eisenhower in a press conference on June 6, 1956, in which the President showed a spirit of understanding of the position and sentiments of so-called neutralist nations. The question is not only a moral issue, but a practical and strategic one as well, since our own national security hinges to some extent on our ability to win neutralist nations on the basis of moral suasion rather than by coercion.

As much as I desire to avoid controversial political issues in this essay, I cannot close without a brief reference to the problem of Arab-Israel relations and the accompanying refugee problem. To ignore it is to fail to consider the very heart of the Middle Eastern question and of the American position there. It was on this issue that the United States engaged most notably in expediency, and it is on this problem, I feel, that we will stand or fall. The most regrettable result of our actions was loss of an American leadership position in the Middle East. Had we retained that leadership, we could have been the friend and fulcrum to help to resolve, in an atmosphere of calm and detachment, the admittedly numerous other pressing problems that face the area. We must, therefore, face the realities of the problem while there is still time, since otherwise the drift toward communism in the Arab world, albeit negative and unwanted by Arabs, may solve the problem for us, to the disaster of both Israel and Western policy. The essence of the question, as I see it, is not whether there is to be an Israel, but rather what kind of an Israel is possible. A small, non-expansionist Israel, depending on its own resources, integrated into Middle Eastern society, will, I am sure, find acceptance and peace. But an Israel in which force is substituted for the great Judaic ideal of love, nurtured by huge donations from abroad, agitated and pushed by Zionism, dedicated to a racial doctrine, based on heavy immigration, and imbued with a messianic complex that Israel is the answer to a nonexistent Jewish problem embracing Jews all over the world is not only untenable, but is a threat to the peace of the world. A continuation of the present situation can only hasten the drift toward communism and ultimate disaster. Time does not permit American policy the luxury of delay or of turning our face from the harsh realities.

In conclusion, I repeat that, in my opinion, our difficulties in the Middle East derive to a considerable extent from a departure from sound, moral principles in favor of drift or expediency. But, I reiterate that there is ample evidence that the government and the people of this country appreciate the need for a policy based squarely on moral considerations and upon the American national interest.

Mr. Salem terminated his essay by expressing his firm belief that there is enough wisdom, love, and vision in the West, particularly in the United States, to promote trust and friendship between two well-meaning peoples. His hope and his dedication are, I am sure, shared by the American people, who, if they have in any way deviated from high principles, have not done so deliberately. There is no question in my mind that the basic qualities of common sense and morality in this country still prevail and that, as the Middle Eastern problem becomes more familiar to the people, decisions and attitudes will reflect this new spirit of comprehension. As stated in the Old Testament, out of suffering comes experience, out of experience comes wisdom, and out of wisdom comes hope. We have had ample suffering with accompanying experience; there is evidence of a wiser policy in this country and thus hope for solutions that will be just, as well as tenable.

Economic and Social Factors

V

The Middle East in
the World Economy

ROBERT D. SETHIAN
*Deputy Director, Near Eastern and African Division,
Bureau of Foreign Commerce, Department of Commerce*

AN OBSERVER OF THE MIDDLE EAST once remarked: "By
the time the majority of the people who influence the course
of events in the Middle East, in and out of the area, concentrate on economic problems rather than political issues, the
Middle East will have become a developed region, smoothly
integrated in the world economy."

The events of the last year have amply re-emphasized the
role of political frictions as impediments to the orderly development of this area's international economic relations. But,
more specifically, they have brought out the close economic
interdependence of the Middle East and the rest of the world.
While attention was focused on Europe's need for petroleum
and the world's need of the Suez Canal, the much broader
bases of this interrelationship were also apparent.

It became apparent, for instance, that when the Middle
East ceased to function as a trade route, repercussions were
felt in a wide variety of spheres, such as industrial dislocations
in Europe, a shipping shortage and higher rates throughout
the world, a decrease of oil royalties and government budgets
in the Middle East itself, exchange shortages in several countries, and a disruption of financial relations in general. While
the crisis was of short duration, it gave enough evidence of the

97

mutuality, not the conflict, of interest that exists between the Middle East and other areas.

In effect, the economy of the Middle East is complementary, not so much within the area itself, but with the rest of the world. The finances, trade, and banking of the countries of the Middle East are related not with one another, but with other areas, particularly western Europe and the United States. In both exports and imports, for instance, intraregional trade is relatively small—perhaps less than 15 per cent of the total trade. By contrast, almost half of the area's trade is with western Europe and another 15 per cent with the United States. In the last two years trade with the Soviet bloc has shown gains, mainly as the result of increased transactions with Iran, Turkey, Syria, and, particularly, Egypt, but it still accounts for less than 10 per cent of the total.

Fundamentally, this pattern is likely to continue, since local export products are competitive with one another and must find markets abroad and since none of the countries in the area is equipped to provide the industrial goods that constitute the bulk of Middle Eastern imports.

This is not to imply a permanent role of the Middle East as a purveyor of primary products against manufactured goods of industrial nations. As the better-equipped of the countries of this area become effectively industrialized, this trade pattern will change, of course, and better-rounded economies will develop—but within certain limits. Given the Middle East's lack of many of the resources essential for heavy industry, it is unrealistic to expect the emergence of a series of "Pittsburghs" in this region. With a very few exceptions, the future of industry in the Middle East seems to be in the fields of light manufacturing and food processing, in both of which vast potentialities exist. That substantial progress is being made in such industries is evidenced by the steady and fairly rapid shift in Middle Eastern imports from consumer goods to capital equipment.

Progress in this direction will tend to increase the interdependence of the Middle East with industrialized countries of the world and will require added exports to pay for imports of capital goods. This has actually been the trend in the last several years, and some of the countries have even developed adverse terms of trade in order to maintain their momentum for industrialization.

It has become an unfortunate practice in taking stock of the development of the Middle East to dwell on the massive difficulties and to conclude that population is rapidly outrunning production. While this is largely true, and both the standard of living of the masses and productivity remain low, the progress actually achieved is often underestimated. This progress, although readily evident, is difficult to describe in statistical terms. Figures are either lacking or inadequate for most countries and, rather than attempt to arrive at an estimate of the total achievement on the basis of inadequate data, it is perhaps best to limit statistical measurement to foreign trade, for which fairly adequate figures are available.

During the last ten years, the foreign trade of the Middle East has advanced at a rate faster than the world's. On an average, the Middle East accounts for some 3 to 4 per cent of the world's trade. Percentages are often elusive, however, and to make this a meaningful measurement, a few comparisons may be helpful. In 1956 the Middle East's share in international trade was roughly one-third as large as that of the United Kingdom, only one and a half per cent less than that of France, half as large as the share of Latin America, and over one-fifth of total United States foreign trade.

The Middle East imports a wide array of products valued at slightly less than 4 per cent of the value of all goods exchanged across international boundaries. In return, it provides the world with petroleum worth over 3 per cent and agricultural products worth almost 2 per cent of the value of all merchandise entering international trade.

But this seemingly comfortable trade position is somewhat deceptive, since two-thirds of the exports consist of petroleum products originating in only a few countries, of which only Iran and Iraq have other resources of significance, and it is precisely in exports other than oil that rapid progress needs to be achieved.

For, barring political upheavals, petroleum exports can undoubtedly be sustained. With over 70 per cent of the world's petroleum resources and only about 20 per cent of present world production, the Middle East can look forward to a growing market for oil exports. Even if major discoveries are made elsewhere and when atomic power becomes adapted to daily use, the rapidly increasing need of more and more countries for energy will probably require all the petroleum that can be produced. The outlook for other mineral resources of the Middle East appears modest, unless explorations, which hitherto have been inadequate, reveal unknown deposits.

Aside from oil, agricultural products (mainly cereals and cotton) constitute between 60 and 80 per cent of the exports of most of the countries of the Middle East. Even in oil-rich Iran and Iraq, petroleum production probably does not exceed 25 per cent of total production. In the last several years the area under cultivation has been substantially expanded and, in good years, crops have attained record levels. But progress in this field is hampered by irregular rainfall, the competition of more efficient producers from abroad, and, especially, low productivity. The irrigation schemes in process or planned in certain countries, together with progress in dry farming methods, will eventually save several sectors of the Middle East from the vagaries of rainfall. By and large, however, conditions reminiscent of the biblical lean and fat years are likely to continue.

Low productivity, on the other hand, may in time be overcome if energetic steps are taken to remove such basic causes as poor farming practices, the lack of proper equipment and organization, inadequate application of labor and capital, deficient handling, transportation and storage facilities, and especially land-tenure systems that offer little incentive. Forward steps in this direction have already been taken in many of the countries of this area, but more rapid advances will be necessary not only to meet competition from more efficient producers elsewhere, but also to provide for the rapidly increasing needs of the local population.

Low productivity has also hindered the development of

industry. The Middle Easterner has a long tradition of trading and displays his skill in international markets daily. But the process of manufacturing requires a different kind of experience—not only technical skills, but also long-range planning of sources of supply, labor, and power all the way to economical methods of financing, efficient factory management, and a study of ultimate markets. Besides, the relatively small and fragmented market of the Middle East makes it difficult to produce efficiently in cases where mass production is the only way of becoming competitive with world producers. With a very few exceptions, therefore, local industry has grown behind tariff protection or exemptions from certain taxes and duties or as government-operated enterprises. Only time will show if these undertakings will be able to become efficient producers past their period of infancy. It is probable that some industries will be given long-range protection in order to utilize local resources and man power, to save foreign exchange, and for purposes of diversification and self-sufficiency.

The development of industry and agriculture in the countries of the Middle East has been substantially helped by governmental programs and policies. Almost every government is devoting a substantial portion of its budget to the construction of basic facilities. While the $1.4 billion of oil royalties that Iraq has scheduled for its 1955–1961 program and the $1.1 billion earmarked by Iran for its 1955–1962 program stand out, the development budgets of the other countries are also impressive. These projects, which are already paving the way for the development of agriculture and industry, will gather momentum in the immediate future. In some of the countries, notably Turkey and Israel, development projects have been supplemented by large loans and grants from the United States and with money borrowed from international lending agencies.

By and large, however, the financing of Middle Eastern agriculture and industry has been undertaken by private enterprise, although in Turkey, Iran, and Iraq direct government participation in industry and other projects has been largely responsible for what has been achieved.

The results have been particularly satisfactory where government action has paved the way for private investment, as for instance, in the development of agriculture and industries in the Adana region of Turkey following construction of roads and a power grid by the government.

The much-debated problems of the relative role of government and the private sector are particularly acute in the Middle Eastern countries, in most of which the private-entrepreneur class is not sufficiently large, real income and, consequently, savings are low, and in some cases a large portion of a country's income accrues to the government. The argument for government responsibility to undertake a co-ordinated development of the resources that are needed most seems particularly pertinent in many countries of this area. It can even be claimed that the government's direct participation in Turkish industry was what gave impetus to the development of private enterprise.

On the other side of the coin, however, there are two governing considerations. The area's need for basic facilities is so great that even the large governmental revenues of, say, the oil-producing countries are barely sufficient. It would, therefore, seem more logical if the governments concentrated on the development of basic facilities, undertaking only those individual projects that are beyond the capacity of the private sector.

There is an even more important consideration for giving private enterprise all the room it can fill. This is the urgent need to encourage the emergence of a large body of entrepreneurs. For, as in other underdeveloped areas, the development of entrepreneurial skills is one of the most important prerequisites for establishing broad bases for the economy. For a good illustration of this point, one might look at Iraq. Oil revenues are wisely being used for development projects that will soon yield tangible results. But it is not clear in what way these projects will directly help create a large body of individual entrepreneurs who, in the last analysis, can alone become a self-generating source of capital, outside of oil revenues.

What has been said of local private enterprise can also apply to private regional and foreign investments. There are few instances of capital moving from one country in the area to another to finance either agriculture or industry, and it is probably safe to say that investments by Middle Easterners outside of the area far outweigh any regional investment. Given favorable conditions, a considerable portion of these expatriate funds might well find their way into constructive ventures in neighboring countries. This would strengthen intraregional economic relations, which, despite the efforts of the Arab League and the Baghdad Pact countries, are still largely neglected by both the private sector and the governments of the area.

As for investment from outside the region, it is readily evident that it could contribute both technical skills and capital in an area where both are scarce. But aside from investment in oil, there has been very little private participation in the Middle East in recent years. In this respect the relationship of the Middle East with the rest of the world stands in sharp contrast to the experience of the past.

In the last century and a half major developments in the Middle East were undertaken by foreign concessionary companies. Not only were public utilities (railroads, ports, power plants) developed in this way, but also mining, industries, and banking. These concessions were granted for very long periods and entailed privileges that, at present, are considered excessive by the people of the Middle East. But for the times, such privileges and guarantees may have been necessary to attract the foreign investor into an area so different from his own environment and presenting certain additional risks. Whether such privileges were necessary or not, the fact remains that these investors contributed capital and skills that were not available locally, and until a few years ago they built most of the basic facilities that existed.

The concessionary era seems to have passed except for very large operations, such as extraction of oil and other minerals. This is in keeping with present nationalist trends throughout the Middle East. But no other institution has replaced the

concession as a means of marshalling foreign capital to contribute to the development of the area. The Middle East is,
therefore, faced with the alternatives either of foregoing the
benefits of foreign capital and skills or of finding ways of encouraging them.

The Middle East seems to be of two minds on this subject—not only as between countries, but also as between the
desire to attract foreign capital, on the one hand, and, on
the other, to control it. A few countries offer somewhat hostile attitudes toward foreign enterprise. But almost every country has, in the last few years, enacted legislation favoring private investments, both local and foreign. Several have specific
laws aimed at encouraging foreign investment. But these regulations are rendered somewhat ineffective in most of the area
by nationalist opposition and the fear of political upheavals.
There is no need to dwell on the character and extent of nationalist opposition to foreign interests in the Middle East.
It may be explained in terms of several unhappy experiences
from the past and the desire of new nations to control their
economic life. The fact remains, nevertheless, that extreme
manifestations of nationalism, hostile attitudes, and political
instability keep away investors who have the choice of invest-
ing their money in more friendly areas where opportunities
are at present particularly attractive. The investor obviously
needs protection for his enterprise and requires confidence.
The host country, for its part, requires that ventures conform
to its own policies. Compromise, of course, is the answer. But
compromise becomes difficult after events like those of last
year.

Several conclusions seem to emerge from this brief review.
The economic interdependence of the Middle East and the
rest of the world is a basic fact of life and will remain an important factor even after the individual countries of the area
develop and regional ties strengthen. Despite political conflicts, this interdependence has increased over the last decade
as a result of the economic progress made by most countries
of the area in their field of specialization. This progress, impressive though it is, has not acquired the necessary propor-

tions to bring about a general rise in living standards. This is because economic development is a painful and slow process involving basic changes in venerated traditions and the adjustment of conflicting interests. But the Middle East has the requisite potentialities, and, in time, its economy will be developed and diversified, and it will find its place in the world economy as one of its important components.

Recalling the events of last year, however, the vital question remains whether this development will come about despite internal and external strife and dislocations, or through what would seem a more rational and speedy course—cooperation.

Commentary

JOHN W. GUNTER
*Deputy Director, Middle East Department,
International Monetary Fund*

MR. SETHIAN HAS GIVEN US a very clear picture of the interdependence of the Middle East and the rest of the world and has placed the problems of the economic development of the area in perspective. I feel that there is very little that I can add to the general picture that he has presented. Consequently, it seems to me that the most useful contribution that I could make would be to attempt an exploration in somewhat more detail of a number of problems that Mr. Sethian has already called to our attention.[1]

It is only too clear that political events in the Middle East have hardly created an atmosphere that is favorable to deal-

[1] This essay is based to a considerable extent on a paper presented to the American Finance Association in Cleveland, December 27, 1956, by Edward M. Bernstein.

ing with the economic problems of the area. As an economist I must, of course, necessarily limit my concern with the political problems of the area. At the same time it often occurs to me that many of the politicians, both within the area and outside, who have as their concern the course of political events, fail to understand the economic potentialities of the Middle East. This failure to comprehend may very well be an important key to why the political problems of the Middle East seem so intractable.

Most people understand the significance of oil production in the Middle East. In 1956 production of crude oil in the Middle East amounted to about 170 million tons. It is generally expected that oil production in the next ten or fifteen years will be trebled or quadrupled. Whereas in 1956 the Middle East received in direct payments from the oil companies an income approaching $1 billion, in not too many years this figure will probably be approaching $3 billion. These figures, moreover, leave out of account the indirect payments that will add at least another 15 per cent. These projections are not based on the capacity of the area to expand petroleum production, but rather on the expected growth in demand for Middle Eastern oil.

These are very large figures, and the impact of this much income can be very large, too. On the assumption of the present pattern of production on a country basis, however, some existing political problems may become more acute, because some Middle Eastern countries benefit in only a limited way from oil production. Some countries may have a larger income from oil than can be absorbed economically on a current basis, while others will have to seek exchange resources in other directions.

While adequate attention may be given to the growth of oil production and its impact on the area, it is not so readily recognized that there could be a similar development in agriculture, which socially, if not economically, would be of greater significance.

This situation suggests that it is important to understand how to achieve a maximum degree of economic development.

For if this problem and the consequences of resolving it could be clearly understood, there would be created a strong incentive for resolving also the more important political problems of the area. The achievement of a maximum rate of economic development is a difficult problem. Economic development is by its nature a very complex process that involves much more than the establishment of a few enterprises using modern methods of production, the construction of a network of modern roads, and a few dams here and there. It also must mean the creation of new attitudes toward production and toward saving and investment.

While governments may find it possible to carry out the construction programs necessary to provide the social capital needed for a modern economy, it is important to recognize that this is fundamentally doing nothing more than providing the framework for economic growth. These development programs will be largely useless unless they result in increased investment in agriculture and industry. It is in this respect that many development programs fall short. They fail to set aside adequate resources for the establishment of credit facilities or ample funds for educational programs in the agricultural community where the proper use of water and fertilizer and improved seeds and tools can make a vast impact on the level of agricultural production. In addition, there must be created conditions that are conducive to the growth of an entrepreneurial group that will carry out the investment in agriculture and industry.

The size of a development program is limited by the resources that are available for investment. These resources can arise in only two ways. They can arise domestically to the extent that current production is not consumed, or they can be imported. It is too often said that the Middle East is a poor area, so that most of its current production must go for consumption, leaving very little from domestic sources that can be used for development. It is concluded, consequently, that the development of the area depends basically on an inflow of capital from the outside.

There is enough truth in this thesis to make it difficult to argue against it. Clearly the Middle East is a poor area, and clearly the extent to which domestic resources can be made available for development is severely limited. Moreover, it is clear that capital inflow has been inadequate in relation to the maximum development of some countries in the area. Yet this thesis in the simple form in which I have stated it, and in which it is so often stated, tends to obscure some important aspects of the process of capital formation and often leads to an improper emphasis.

One aspect of this problem arises from the fact that there are also distinct limitations on how much of a development program can be financed by a capital inflow. It would perhaps also be helpful to understand that the limitations that I shall describe also apply to the financing of development with oil income. In terms of its initial impact, oil income accruing to governments and used as a means of financing has the same consequences as a capital inflow. The share of Middle Eastern governments in the profits from oil operations provides their countries with a claim on external resources in the same way that an inflow of capital provides a claim on external resources. Of course, in other respects oil income cannot be regarded in any sense as a capital inflow, because it is an earned income of the economy, and there is no counterpart in the form of increased foreign liabilities as are involved in the case of the loan from abroad or a direct investment from abroad.

In order to take account of these similarities, I will use the term *external financing* of development to encompass foreign aid and reliance on oil income. *Internal financing* will mean domestic savings available for productive investment, including funds derived from taxation for this purpose.

The reason I have drawn such a careful distinction between external and internal financing is that the economic consequences of the two types of financing are different. External financing increases the amount of investment that a country can undertake, but at the same time it necessitates adjustments within the economy if the volume of external financing to be used to expand investment is relatively large. On the other hand, if the source of the financing is internal, these adjustments are also necessary, but to nowhere near the same degree.

If the major source of financing development arises from domestic savings, the problem of adjustment is not difficult, because additional saving means less consumption. The process of shifting resources from consumption to investment does not involve a higher price-cost structure on an over-all basis. The reduced demand for goods for consumption is replaced by an increased demand for goods for investment, but aggregate demand is unchanged. The goods in particular demand for investment go up in price, while the prices of consumption goods tend to decline.

External financing is obviously necessary to the extent that capital goods must be imported.[2] Moreover, to some extent imported capital goods can be substituted for domestically produced capital goods. In neither of these cases is there a problem of adjustment. If, on the other hand, the additional investment financed from external sources is largely in the form of domestic expenditure, it will be necessary to shift labor and other resources to the investment industries. This will mean that wages will have to be increased and that the prices of domestically produced goods will rise. With a higher cost-price structure there will be a decline in exports and the consumption of domestically produced goods will be partly replaced by imports. Thus external financing requires an expansion of output in the investment-goods industries relative to the export and consumption-goods industries and a corre-

[2] This statement does not allow for the case of increasing imports of capital goods by curtailing other imports or increasing exports. This is deliberate for two reasons. In the first place, such a policy increases the difficulties of diverting domestic resources to the investment-goods industries and adds to cost-price distortions in the economy. This is particularly true if the country applies quantitative import restrictions to reduce imports of consumption goods. In the second place, we are discussing the achievement of the maximum rate of investment, and it would be a rare underdeveloped country that could achieve this objective without relying on external financing at least to the extent of its requirements for capital-goods imports. In this connection also the utilization of accumulated exchange reserves would be regarded as a form of external financing.

sponding expansion of consumption of import goods relative to domestically produced goods. This process of adjustment may be particularly difficult if there is a heavy dependence on external financing, and the difficulty of adjustment will vary considerably from country to country.

A heavy reliance on external financing will also involve reverse problems of adjustment because of cost rigidities as the dependence on external finance declines in the future. To some extent, this is what is happening in Turkey today.

The conclusion to be drawn from all this is not that a country carrying out a development program should not rely on external financing, but rather that it should rely as much as it possibly can on internal financing. The volume of development will not only be larger; it will also be more effective.

The degree to which a country can rely effectively on external financing varies from country to country, depending partly on the extent to which the development program requires (or permits) the import of capital goods, but more importantly on the propensity to import. All underdeveloped countries depend to a considerable extent on the importation of a wide range of consumer goods, but even so there is a considerable variation from country to country. Countries like Iraq, Saudi Arabia, and Jordan can rely more heavily on external financing than countries like Egypt and Iran, because they import a considerably wider range of commodities.

The question may be raised as to whether there are actually some cases of countries in the Middle East that are now depending so heavily on external financing that they are encountering difficult problems of adjustment. This is, in fact, the case at the present time for Iran and Iraq, where the development programs depend virtually 100 per cent on external financing. It has been generally contended that Iran and Iraq can afford very large development programs because they have adequate financing from oil income. On this basis both countries have expanded very greatly the volume of investment expenditures, but at the same time they are running more and more into difficulties of shifting labor and other resources to the investment-goods industries. This is manifest-

ing itself in rising wage rates and prices of domestically produced commodities.

The next question that might be raised is whether the countries in the Middle East, being poor countries, can do much
about diverting a larger part of domestic production to the investment-goods industries. If the answer is affirmative, it will
mean that Middle Eastern countries can not only increase the
rate of investment out of their own resources, but can do so
with relatively minor adjustments of prices and wages. It is
my observation that in the Middle East there is a tendency
to underestimate the amount of savings that can be secured
for the development program even with the present levels of
income. (On the other hand, development plans often over-
estimate the amount of savings that will be forthcoming as income rises.) It would appear that a great deal can be accomplished by increasing the attractiveness of saving in comparison with spending and by developing adequate taxation systems.

The most important aspect of making saving more attractive is the avoidance of inflation. Most people, particularly
small savers, have no satisfactory means of protecting their
savings from a depreciation in value due to inflation. Consequently, an essential condition to the financing of a development program on a sustained basis over a period of years is
the maintenance of monetary and price stability. It is also
possible to offer savers more attractive assets. In general this
undoubtedly means a higher interest-rate structure than now
prevails in most Middle Eastern countries. It also means making it possible for the public to acquire equity shares on attractive terms in the new industries that are being brought
into existence.

There is a tendency in Middle Eastern countries to underestimate the beneficial effects of a higher rate of interest. A
high rate of interest is partly desirable, as I have already suggested, in order to induce the public to increase its savings in
the form of deposits and bonds, rather than in hoards of
precious metals or foreign exchange. In addition, a high rate
of interest will encourage a more economical use of capital,

thus reducing the strain on resources required for development. In most Middle Eastern countries the monetary authorities in dealing with the problems of inflation find it necessary in some degree to maintain credit controls. These credit controls will be more effective if they are based on a high rate of interest that will restrain the demand for credit. From a social point of view a high rate of interest is fully justifiable, for savings have a high value in an underdeveloped country.

Middle Eastern countries can also do a great deal to increase internal financing of development through fiscal policies. Every reduction in public expenditures increases the financing available for development. Moreover, there are few Middle Eastern countries that could not increase the resources available for development through higher taxation. In many developed countries the ratio of central government revenue to the national income is in excess of 20 per cent and in some cases 25 per cent. While it would not be reasonable to expect Middle Eastern countries to tax at this high rate, only Egypt and Israel among the Middle Eastern countries approach the 20-per-cent level and in a number of cases the ratio is less than 10 per cent, as, for example, in Jordan, Lebanon, and Pakistan.

The next question is how rapid can economic development be. Some countries, including Iran and Iraq, have resources capable of quick development. Other countries, such as Syria and Turkey, have provided examples of rapidly expanding agricultural production. Pakistan has shown itself capable of rapid industrialization in some spheres. But in general the Middle East has to run hard to stay in the same place.

Net savings in Middle Eastern countries probably amount in general to about 4 or 5 per cent of national income. This is about what is required to keep the standard of living from declining. An increase in savings to 6 or 7 per cent may be regarded as a major achievement. This may not seem like much of an accomplishment, but such an increase, plus a reasonable degree of reliance on external financing, should be sufficient to overcome economic stagnation.

Development is a continuing process. For example, the

most developed country in the world, the United States, is still one of the most rapidly developing countries. Once development gains momentum it becomes also a progressive process. Not only does it become easier to achieve a higher level of saving, but attitudes toward productive activity are infectious.

The pressures for economic progress in the Middle East are growing. Let us hope that these pressures will be directed along realistic channels so that they will result in a rising standard of economic life for the people of the Middle East. In this, not only the Middle East has an interest, but also the rest of the world.

VI

Technical Assistance in the Middle East

NORMAN BURNS
Deputy Regional Director for the Middle East,
International Co-operation Administration

THE MIDDLE EAST, as defined here, includes Turkey, Iran, Egypt, Iraq, Jordan, Lebanon, Syria, Saudi Arabia, Yemen, territories of the Arabian peninsula, Sudan, and Israel—an area slightly larger than that of the continental United States and with a population of over 100 million persons.[1]

United States technical assistance began in the Middle East in 1951 following presidential approval of the Act for International Development of June 5, 1950, and the appropriation by Congress on September 6, 1950, of $26.9 million in fiscal 1951 to carry out the purposes of the act throughout the world.[2]

The Act for International Development declared it to be the policy of the United States to aid the efforts of the peoples of economically underdeveloped areas to develop their resources and improve their working and living conditions by encouraging the exchange of technical knowledge and skills and the flow of investment capital to countries which provide conditions under which such technical assistance and capital can effectively and constructively contribute to raising standards of living, creating

[1] The views expressed here are those of the author and do not necessarily represent the policy of the agency with which he is associated.

[2] Technical assistance began in Turkey in 1947 under President Truman's Turkey-Greece aid program, which, after April 3, 1948, was administered by ECA.

114

new sources of wealth, increasing productivity and expanding purchasing power. (Sec. 403a)

In passing the act, Congress expressed its philosophy that:

The peoples of the United States and other nations have a common interest in . . . the economic and social progress of all peoples. Such progress can further the secure growth of democratic ways of life, . . . the development of international understanding and good will, and the maintenance of world peace. (Sec. 402)

The United States now has operative Technical Co-operation agreements with six countries in the area, Iran, Iraq, Israel, Jordan, Lebanon, and Turkey. The program in Egypt was suspended in 1956 (except for deliveries of equipment under suppliers' contracts still outstanding) for political reasons. A small program with Saudi Arabia was discontinued several years ago at the instance of the Saudi government. A technical assistance mission is now making a survey of Yemen at the request of the Yemeni government, but a formal agreement has not yet been concluded. Syria, for political reasons, has not entered into any Technical Co-operation agreements with the United States.

Technical Co-operation assistance (sometimes called Point Four assistance) is extended to participant countries in the form of: (a) American technical experts sent to the recipient country to help on specific projects; (b) specialized demonstration equipment and supplies for such projects; and (c) training facilities for nationals of the recipient country, either in their own country or in the United States or elsewhere, in technical fields related to such projects. Such assistance is on a grant basis. Technical Co-operation aid is extended only at the request of the other government, which itself must contribute a share of the cost of the project.

Technical Co-operation assistance is administered by the International Co-operation Administration (ICA), a semi-autonomous agency within the Department of State. The ICA also administers other forms of economic aid, namely Defense Support and Development Assistance. Defense Support is for countries with which the United States has military co-operation agreements. Its purpose is to enable such countries to maintain their economies without deterioration while continuing their military program at an agreed-upon level. Development Assistance is for countries with which the United States does not have military co-operation agreements and is to enable them to carry forward their economic development programs. Defense Support and Development Assistance consist chiefly of commodities and equipment (sometimes accompanied by American experts and local trainees) for: (a) capital works in those countries; and/or (b) essential consumer demands that the country itself cannot meet because of its shortage of foreign exchange. The sale by the recipient government of such consumer goods within the recipient country enables that government to obtain local currency to meet its budget deficit or to cover the local currency costs of its economic development or military programs. Defense Support and Development Assistance may be on either a grant or a loan basis.

In terms of dollars, Technical Co-operation assistance is small relative to the other forms of economic aid. United States government aid to Middle Eastern countries under all programs (including PL 480 surplus agricultural products and Export-Import Bank loans, neither of which is administered by ICA) after World War II through June 30, 1957, totaled nearly $1.9 billion.

United States economic aid of all types to the Middle East in fiscal 1957 totaled $303 million, which was equivalent to about 10 per cent of the total central government expenditures of the recipient countries in that year. Of the $303 million, only $21.9 million consisted of Technical Co-operation assistance.

Types of Technical Co-operation Assistance

Technical Co-operation assistance has been extended to a wide range of activities in the Middle East. An illustrative description of various types of technical-assistance projects follows.

Assistance in health projects has a quick impact. The Minister of Public Health in Iran remarked this year that when the first Point Four American doctors came to Iran in 1951, they found that the peasants, being entirely unfamiliar with vaccination, feared and fled from vaccination needles as instruments of the devil, but that now, if rumors of epidemic arise, they crowd about the Ministry of Health threatening to break windows of the Ministry buildings if denied vaccinations. The Iranian government, which began its program with Point Four doctors, has given eight million vaccinations for smallpox and one and one-half million vaccinations for diphtheria, tetanus, typhoid, and other diseases in the last five years.

The Jordanian government requested assistance in 1950 to start a central public-health laboratory where Jordanian doctors might take specimens for analyses in biochemistry, bacteriology, parasitology, hematology, serology, and histopathology. When this request reached Washington, certain American officials desired to provide not only the laboratory, but also American public-health experts to set up a public-health network in Jordan. The Jordanian government, however, had not requested a complete public-health system and might have become skeptical had we asked them to accept a large number of experts whom they had never requested. Fortunately the temptation to transplant prematurely an American organizational concept into Jordan was resisted, and our aid was confined to their actual request. The laboratory was built and equipped, an American director supervised it in the first years of its existence, a technically well-trained Jordanian staff was recruited, and when the American director departed, a well-qualified Jordanian successor was appointed to carry on the work. The laboratory is now testing over six thousand specimens per month, thus contributing effectively to public health in that country. This laboratory, in turn, has led to many other public-health projects in Jordan. The lesson to be learned from this experience is that technical assistance is most likely to succeed: (a) when confined to a felt need by the recipient country itself; and (b) when it leads to the establishment in the recipient country of a local organizational structure to carry on efficiently after the American experts have gone.

Agricultural demonstration and extension is another field where local receptivity is usually great, provided the American experts are well qualified in their technical speciality and in dealing with people. The story is told of an American livestock expert who in 1951 went to Iran, where, after his first tour of the Iranian cattle experimental stations, the Minister of Agriculture asked for the inevitable report that foreign experts always produce. The Point Four expert replied that he had no report, that he had come to help in any way he could, and that there were excellent people in the Iranian stations already doing a fine job. The Iranian Minister replied in surprise: "This is the first time anyone has come here from abroad without telling us we are doing everything wrong. It's the first time anyone has come without throwing a program at us and telling us to change our ways." [3] Needless to say, with this type of expert, American agricultural extension programs have made considerable progress in Iran. The Iranian government gave twenty million animal vaccinations in 1955 and has made a substantial beginning in upgrading the local cattle strain by producing twenty thousand cows through artificial insemination by crossbreeding of American Brown Swiss bulls with local cows. The Iranian agricultural extension program, initiated with Point Four help, has resulted in the spread of a variety of wheat known as the Shahpassand, which was developed by Iranian experts at Karaj Agricultural College in 1945, and which increases wheat yield by 30 per cent. This variety, heretofore not widely sown, was spread through an arrangement under which farmers might exchange one pound of ordinary wheat seed for one pound of Shahpassand seed.

The agricultural demonstration and experimentation station at Terbol, Lebanon, is based upon sound principles, but

[3] Ferdinand Kuhn, "Point 4 in Iran," *Washington Post*, September 6, 1951.

it has certain limitations. Under the Technical Co-operation program, the United States furnished funds for buildings, equipment, and some technicians for a new 125-acre agricultural and livestock demonstration farm and a 250-acre afforestation tract in the beautiful Bekaa Valley of Lebanon. The Lebanese government contributed the land and some of the building and operating costs. Fifty Holstein bulls and cows were imported for the station and nearby large farms to upgrade the local cattle strain. Various breeds of American poultry were introduced. Experiments were undertaken for the growing of different forage crops, of which Lebanese production is insufficient, and for the scientific feeding of cattle and poultry. Imported cattle scientifically fed produced eight times as much milk as did local cattle with normal local feeding. Crossbred calves, from imported Holstein bulls and local cows, brought higher prices in the local market than did local calves. American chickens, scientifically fed, laid larger eggs, and more eggs, than did local chickens. Thus a promising start has been made at Terbol, but one problem remains. When the project was turned over entirely to the Lebanese government in the spring of 1955, there was inadequate realization of the need for creating a local organizational structure technically qualified to continue the work at its former level of efficiency. It is said that the station has many employees, but not enough qualified technicians to carry on the intensive experimental work desired by the Lebanese government. If true, the remedy would be to obtain appropriate technical personnel as quickly as possible.

Fears have been expressed in some quarters that Point Four agricultural assistance might aggravate for the United States the problem of agricultural surpluses. The fact is that a large proportion of the population of the Middle East exists on 2,000 calories per person per day, or less, as compared with an average consumption in the United States of 3,300 calories per person daily. Until the caloric availability of food in the Middle East and Asia reaches a more satisfactory level, greater agricultural production in those countries will mean simply more food for the local people to eat. This is how they can

improve, in one respect, their present low standard of living.
Technical Co-operation assistance in education, particularly
in agricultural, vocational, and teacher training, has been requested throughout the Middle East. In the last decade, the
Middle Eastern countries have increased their governmental
budget expenditures on education by five fold (allowance being made for price changes during the period), an indication
of the thirst for education. The ICA (then Point Four) arranged with the American University of Beirut in 1951 to
provide training in engineering, agriculture, public administration, public finance, and public health and (later) education
for 128 trainees from the Middle Eastern countries. The contract has been renewed periodically since then, the latest being the three-year renewal of April 30, 1957, to provide training for a minimum of 424 trainees from the Middle Eastern
countries, from Tunisia and Libya on the west to Afghanistan
and Pakistan on the east, in the technical fields noted above,
plus business administration, nurses training, and pharmacy.
Many students apply for these training scholarships, and the
number of trainees has increased steadily since the program
began. The impact of these trainees on the governments, business enterprises, schools, and agricultural life of the Middle
East—which now lacks trained people in these fields—will be
very great in the years ahead.

Various types of technical assistance are being extended to
industry. The general pattern is to establish an industry center, under the joint auspices of the recipient government and
ICA, which will provide technical advice to local government
and private industries on a request basis. The industry center
is staffed not by hiring a large number of technicians, but by
having an ICA-financed contract with a private American
management or technical firm that undertakes to obtain
American experts in any field for particular assignments. In
Iran, an American management firm, the George Fry Associates, works under an ICA contract to supply management
and technical services to factories owned by the Iranian government's Plan Organization. The objective is to improve the
efficiency of the plants and to put them on a paying basis so

that they may be sold to private enterprise in accordance with the announced long-range objective of the Iranian government. The Lebanese government and ICA have set up an Industrial Institute, which, under ICA contract with the American firm of Battelle Memorial Institute, furnishes technical advice on a fee basis to Lebanese industries. In Turkey, plans are under way to establish an Industrial Center, under auspices of the Chambers of Commerce and Industry and with assistance from the Turkish government and ICA, which will furnish technical advice to private and governmental industrial enterprises there.

Regional projects, such as the development of international rivers, often present special difficulty because of political implications. Such projects, if implemented, have major impact. Their capital cost is great—frequently beyond the financial capacity of the local countries to bear without external capital. Technical assistance can set the stage for implementation, but can do little beyond that. The development of the Jordan Valley is a case in point. The Jordan River rises from springs on the slopes of Mount Hermon in Arab territory, flows southward through Israeli territory on both banks, thence through Arab territory into the Dead Sea. The Jordan River waters, now largely wasted, could irrigate up to 125,000 acres in Jordan, 35,000 acres in Syria and Lebanon, and up to 140,000 acres in Israel, in areas now parched for lack of water. An eight-volume engineering study was made in 1954–1955, by the Michael Baker-Harza Engineering Companies, of the Jordan River and its tributaries in Jordan, at a total cost of $2.5 million (of which the ICA contributed $1.1 million, United Nations Relief and Works Agency for Palestine Refugees in the Near East, $1.2 million, and the Jordanian government, $0.2 million). Technical Co-operation has provided a technical basis for an equitable division of the Jordan waters, but political agreement, the requisite for such an allocation, has not yet been reached.

Guiding Principles

Certain lessons have been learned from the seven years of experience with technical assistance in the Middle East that may provide useful directional guides for the future.

First, we have learned that technical assistance, however essential, is not of itself adequate to cope with the economic problems of the underdeveloped countries. At the beginning, there was an optimistic feeling that "our imponderable resources in technical knowledge" (to use the phraseology of President Truman's Point Four address of January, 1949), when "made available" to the underdeveloped countries, would tap the wellsprings of their unutilized resources and bring about a vast upsurge in production. But the underdeveloped countries need capital, in conjunction with technical assistance, to achieve such an upsurge. The underdeveloped countries (except those with oil revenue) live so near the subsistence level that their margin of saving is not adequate to provide the necessary capital to build dams, irrigation works, power plants, roads, public utilities, factories, and schools.

The magnitude of their developmental capital requirement may be illustrated by a few key facts. In the United States, there is cropped annually the equivalent of 2.3 acres per person for the total population of the entire country. In the Middle East, there is cropped annually the equivalent of less than 1 acre per person for the total population of the Middle East. To bring this man-land ratio in the Middle East to a level commensurate with the food requirements of the entire population would require huge investments for irrigation, as there is very little new rain-fed land available for cultivation. The per capita gross national product averages $114 per year in Iran, $296 in Turkey, and $607 in Israel. When one recalls that the Middle East population is increasing at nearly 2 per cent net per year and that the capital-output ratio in the Middle East may be 4 to 1 (i.e., $400 of capital investment to yield $100 of income annually), it becomes apparent that heavy capital investment will be necessary, if production is to increase beyond the population increase to a point where higher standards of living will result for the mass of people.

It is for these reasons that the United States, to further its objective of increasing production in the Middle East, has: (a) extended governmental capital aid in the form of Defense Support, Development Assistance, and Export-Import Bank loans; and (b) encouraged private capital investment, either local or foreign, in productive enterprise.

Second, it has become evident that the essence of the problem is not how to make technical assistance "available" to the underdeveloped countries, but rather how to ensure that, once made available, it will be fully utilized and absorbed in those countries. This is the problem of transfer of technical know-how from one culture to another.

It is far easier to transplant technical knowledge when one understands the cultural pattern—the thought processes, the aspirations and the prejudices—of the recipient country. Language constitutes one barrier to such an understanding, especially since few Point Four experts speak the language of the countries where they work. If the Point Four expert lacks understanding of the other culture, he may find it difficult to obtain acceptance of a new technique, simply because he will not know the best approach with his local colleagues. If he voices disagreement with the methods of his local colleague, even in a way that might be quite acceptable in American terms, this may cause the local man to "lose face" among his own countrymen to a point where he will feel compelled to oppose the Point Four expert simply to save face. The Point Four expert might have achieved positive results had he followed the accepted cultural pattern of the country, by openly praising the local man's work, by asking many questions about how the latter did the job, and then by asking in private for "suggestions" for alternative methods. Americans, intent upon the job itself, are often more or less unaware of these subtle shades of relationship among peoples of older cultures.

The Point Four expert may argue that his proposed new method is time saving—but this may not persuade the local people, who feel no compelling need to save time. Or the

Point Four expert may argue that the new method is technically more efficient—but local people may feel that the old way is good enough for them and that meticulous accuracy is a monotonous affair according to their standard of values. Yet, if the Point Four expert had understood the proper cultural approach, he might have found some way to reach his local partner. The clue may be to appeal to his family pride or to competition with a rival, or to link the new method with something that the local colleague already does very skillfully; or it may be that the development of a feeling of warm friendship with the local colleague will influence the latter to adopt the new method. Or, again, it may be that the proper approach is simply to try out the idea on a small scale so that in time local people will see its merits on a trial and error basis.

The American expert should always try to see the problem through the eyes of the local people as well as through his own eyes. Ideas that are very sound under American conditions may not be equally good in the foreign country, either because local conditions are different or because the local people have a different approach to the problem. Point Four experts should remember that however proficient they may be in their technical speciality, the local people have had long experience in dealing with their local problems—and the foreign expert can be wrong. Therefore, he should approach his task with respect for local practices and with a sense of modesty towards his own qualifications that will go far towards commending him to the hearts and minds of the people with whom he works.

These intercultural difficulties are compounded when technical assistance impinges upon the vested interest of those who stand to gain by perpetuation of the status quo. A Point Four expert whose assignment is to improve the efficiency of a port and customs administration (an actual case in the Middle East) may find himself opposed by those who fear loss of their jobs and perhaps extracurricular emoluments as well, through the adoption of a more efficient system of handling and clearing merchandise. A land-tenure expert whose job is to advise the local government on land-tenure reform may encounter opposition from the landlords even on proposals to establish elementary schools for the children of the tenant farmers or serfs. In such cases patience is necessary, techniques must be discovered that engender the least antagonism in the particular local situation, and even so progress may be achieved only slowly and through a general educational process.

For these reasons the transfer of technical knowledge to another culture ought to be regarded not as an overnight panacea, but as a long-term and continuing educational process.

Given the complexities of the problems that they face, Point Four experts need special qualifications. Technical skill in their respective fields they must have—and usually do. Understanding of the cultural background of the people with whom they deal they should have—but usually do not. When Technical Co-operation began in 1950, it was necessary to recruit a large number of experts for many countries. It was not easy to find experts in the various technical fields who were at the same time familiar with the Middle East or other cultural areas. So the experts were recruited for their technical qualifications and were sent where the job called. There was, in some quarters, a bland assumption that an engineer or an agriculturist could work as effectively in one country as in another, regardless of his knowledge of the people of the country. In some fields, such as bridge-building or well-drilling, this may be true. But in other fields, where the very essence of the job was to work closely with local people—such as agricultural extension, teacher-training, or public administration— a knowledge of the people was essential to achieve results.

In the past, when the expert finished his two-year tour of duty in one country, he was frequently reassigned to a distant country, simply because a vacancy happened to appear there at the moment of his reassignment. So the expert, having come to understand the people of one country, found himself compelled to begin anew in an unfamiliar environment. Many experts resigned, or failed to get reappointment, after their first tour of duty, so that the turnover was very high indeed. The result was that Point Four experts were usually working in countries where they were more or less unfamiliar with the cultural outlook of the people.

ICA is beginning to think of Technical Co-operation in terms of career service, at least in the junior and intermediate grades; and some attention is being paid to regional specialization in recruitment and assignment. Two two-year tours of duty are allowed in a country with possible extensions beyond in exceptional circumstances. There is a feeling in some quarters that ICA should give greater emphasis to regional specialization (not necessarily within each country, but within each large cultural area) in the recruitment, assignment, and training of personnel.[4] It is true, of course, that regional specialization can be pursued to a point where the expert becomes unduly biased towards the local viewpoint—a bias known as "countryitis"—but until now we have erred generally in the opposite direction.

Third, it has become apparent that the acid test of the effectiveness of a Technical Co-operation program is whether or not it leads to the establishment within the recipient country of an organizational pattern to carry on the activity after the Point Four experts have gone home. This is a difficult accomplishment and depends upon an appreciation of the cultural factors described above. Yet the fact remains that if Point Four starts a project, regardless of how efficient or useful it may be, that the local people *do not or cannot* carry on after the American technicians leave, the long-run impact of that project is likely to be limited. The United States will not have achieved its full objective with the dollars invested.

The Point Four goal should be to ensure that local personnel are technically trained to carry on the work themselves, that the activity is institutionalized within the governmental oi private structure of the recipient country, and that it is

[4] See for example Louis J. Kroeger and Associates, *Personnel for the Mutual Security Program*, U. S. Senate Special Committee to Study the Foreign Aid Program, February, 1957 (Chapter IX, especially). Also see Hamilton Fish Armstrong, *Lebanon, Jordan and Iraq*, U. S. Senate Special Committee to Study the Foreign Aid Program, February, 1957, p. 27.

placed under competent local direction before the American experts leave. If scant attention is paid to these matters before the American experts leave—on the theory that the project is a so-called "turn-key" operation that our technicians set up and turn over completely in one gesture to the local government—there is risk that incompetent people may obtain control of the project and impair its ultimate usefulness.

Fourth, experience has demonstrated that many United States governmental procedures are not well adapted to carrying on long-term Technical Co-operation programs. Procedural simplifications would be helpful. At present, Technical Co-operation funds are appropriated by Congress usually sometime *after* July 1 and must be "obligated" (i.e., specifically committed) for particular projects or programs within that fiscal year, i.e., at least 80 per cent before April 30 and the balance before June 30. If these deadlines are not met, however close to a final agreement the project may be, the funds are lost to ICA and the project must be postponed until new funds become available in the next fiscal year, which, in practice, means another long delay. The same procedure applies, also, to Development Assistance funds for capital development.

The result of this system is that in the early months of the fiscal year (before Congress has appropriated money, and for some time thereafter until the appropriation has been tentatively apportioned among the different countries) there is little assurance as to how much money will be available to continue old projects or to begin new ones. Once funds are allocated by country, in the past usually anywhere between November and March, there is a rush to obligate funds before June 30, else they will be lost to the project. Thus, in the later months of the fiscal year there is a feverish rush to obligate funds even though the projects have not been as well planned as they should be. This procedure causes additional complications in carrying out the United States governmental requirement that the recipient country also contribute "a fair share of the cost of the program." The fiscal years of the recipient governments often do not coincide with our fiscal year. The other governments must obtain the approval of their legislatures for budgets to cover their share of the cost of the project. But if the recipient governments do not know until the very last minute (frequently until after their legislature has acted upon their budget) what the United States will contribute, it is difficult for them to plan what they should contribute.

A more orderly procedure for obligating and expanding funds would make for better planning of projects, for more co-ordinated financial contribution by the recipient government, and for more effective use of funds. With these objectives in mind, the Secretary of State, Mr. John Foster Dulles, and the Director of ICA, Mr. John B. Hollister, proposed certain fiscal changes, which are now (August 1, 1957) being considered by Congress, namely that:

(a) Technical Co-operation funds, once appropriated, may be obligated at any time until spent; or alternatively that it be permissible to obligate up to one-fourth of the appropriation for three months after the fiscal year in which they were appropriated; and

(b) A Development Loan Fund be established (which among other things would replace the present Development Assistance aid) with an appropriation that could be obligated for specific projects at any time until spent.

NOTE: (a) The Congress did not make the recommended changes. (b) On September 3, 1957, Congress approved the Mutual Security Appropriations Act 1958, which did set up the Development Loan Fund.

The foregoing fiscal difficulties, together with the complicated process of clearing projects in Washington and slowness in recruiting American experts, have contributed often to long delays in the implementation of projects after the request by the foreign government. Such delays give foreign governments an unfavorable impression of American red tape. There are cases where the Russians have offered aid for economic projects greatly desired by a particular country, and the rapid implementation of their offer, with Russian technicians and equipment, has contrasted in the minds of local people with slower American performance on projects agreed to by us.

Conclusions

To appraise the results of seven years of Technical Co-operation with the Middle East, one should refer to the original basic concept of the program, namely that the exchange of technical information promotes "economic and social progress," which, in turn, furthers the "growth of democratic ways of life" (Sec. 402 of the International Development Act of 1950).

Definitive conclusions cannot be given on these questions, but certain observations are pertinent.

One observation, that anyone may note who has traveled about the Middle East since World War II, is that many new roads, dams, irrigation works, power plants, agricultural experimental farms, schools, hospitals, and houses have been built in recent years. Enrollment in the elementary schools has increased by leaps and bounds. The number of doctors, nurses, teachers, agronomists, engineers, etc. has increased rapidly in the last decade. These developments have been carried out by the Middle Eastern countries chiefly with their own financial resources and personnel, but Point Four experts and United States economic aid have helped in many of these activities.

Agricultural and industrial production has been expanding. The Food and Agriculture Organization, in *State of Food and Agriculture, 1956*, reported for the Middle East a total agricultural production 40 per cent greater, and per capita food production 6 per cent greater, in 1955–1956 than the prewar average. United Nations indices show even sharper increases in industrial consumption of electrical energy and in the output of particular industrial products in the different countries.

Middle Eastern countries, at first dubious of Point Four from their past experience with foreign experts, are now using Point Four technicians in many of their major developmental plans and projects. Despite the intercultural difficulties cited above, Point Four experts have applied themselves to their individual tasks, in the spirit of the Plymouth Pilgrim who said that "all great and honourable actions are accompanied with great difficulties, and must be both enterprised and overcome with answerable courage"—with the result that today the Middle Eastern countries are requesting increasing numbers of Point Four experts in almost all technical fields.

Economic and social progress is taking place in greater or lesser degree in all of the Middle Eastern countries today. This is the result primarily of the efforts of Middle Eastern peoples themselves. The evidence would seem to indicate that Technical Co-operation, in conjunction with other forms of United States economic aid, has contributed significantly to that effort.

Economic development, of course, is not synonymous with democracy. Nor is technical skill indicative of a democratic frame of thought, as we know from the experience of Nazi Germany and Communist Russia. Yet under current conditions in the Middle East and Asia, where unrest and mass poverty fill the people with desires for new solutions to their problems, economic development is a prerequisite to the maintenance and growth of a free-choice society.

Commentary

CARL MARCY
Chief of Staff,
Committee on Foreign Relations, U.S. Senate

THERE IS LITTLE to quarrel with in the able presentation of Mr. Norman Burns. His experience vastly exceeds my own. As a consequence, my comments will be directed not so much at the details of his presentation, but rather at the degrees of emphasis in his essay.

The basic question relating to technical assistance in the

Middle East—or anywhere else, for that matter—is: Does the program further United States foreign-policy objectives?

This point is often overlooked not only by supporters in the United States, but occasionally by practitioners in the field. It is understandably difficult for the humanitarian in the United States and for the veterinarian inseminating cows in Iran to remember that technical assistance supported by the United States is supposed to further United States foreign-policy objectives.

Technical Assistance and the National Interest

In this connection, the last sentence, and particularly the last clause of the last sentence, of the essay deserve emphasizing:

. . . under current conditions in the Middle East and Asia, where unrest and mass poverty fill the people with desires for new solutions to their problems, economic development is a prerequisite to the maintenance and growth of a free-choice society.

Although in its day-to-day operations technical assistance is concerned with raising standards of living, economic development is not the end of technical assistance; it is, rather, the means to the broader end of "the maintenance and growth of a free-choice society."

In an area with the characteristics of the Middle East, economic growth is an indispensable part of the total development process that we believe to be in the national interest of the United States. But we delude ourselves if we think economic growth is the only important part of that process. As Mr. Burns points out, Nazi Germany and Communist Russia provide examples of economic development that has been marked by totalitarianism rather than by freedom. Prewar Japan could be cited as another example. Furthermore, if economic development necessarily leads to the growth of freedom, how are we to explain the Soviet Union's own economic aid program?

Is Response to a "Felt Need" Enough?

Mr. Burns makes the point that if technical assistance is to be successful, it must respond to a felt need and it must lead to the establishment of a local organizational structure to carry on after the foreign technicians are withdrawn. To this should be added that technical assistance must also lead to, or be a part of, a whole complex of socio-cultural-political changes. A part of this, of course, is the establishment of a local organizational structure, or—as Mr. Burns puts it—the institutionalization of the activity within the governmental or private structure of the host country. But the kind of change referred to here goes far beyond simple administrative devices.

A subcommittee of the Senate Foreign Relations Committee, headed first by Senator Hickenlooper and then by Senator Mansfield, spent more than two and a half years in an intensive study of this problem. In one of its reports the subcommittee said:

> The determining factor [as to whether economic growth is or is not in the national interest of the United States] is not economic development itself, but the whole complex of political and social institutions in which economic development takes place and the social and political changes which occur as a consequence of economic development.
>
> Technical assistance is in the national interest of the United States when and only when it not only promotes economic development but also encourages the growth of free institutions within the framework of a free society.
>
> Technical assistance in agriculture may result in sharp increases in crop yields, but it will fail of its purpose (indeed, it may be positively harmful) unless it is accompanied by measures designed to bring about a fair distribution of the increases between landlords and tenants. In many underdeveloped countries, this means land reform. Otherwise social stresses within the

country may be increased, and Communist propaganda may find a greater receptivity as a result of technical assistance than it did before technical assistance was undertaken.

Similarly, technical assistance in education may result in sharp increases in literacy, but again it will be less than fully effective if the school system is not adapted to meeting the country's needs or if the country is flooded with cheap Communist literature and free world books are not generally available. Moreover, it serves the national interests of neither the United States nor the recipient country to increase the number of holders of law and liberal arts degrees in an economy which may already be surfeited with frustrated intellectuals and which needs plumbers and mechanics.

These are matters in which the influence of the United States is necessarily and severely limited. It would be highly improper, as well as self-defeating, for the United States to attempt to dictate a country's policies on such peculiarly domestic sociopolitical questions. But it is entirely appropriate for the United States to take into account a country's own attitude toward these questions when planning a technical assistance program, or when negotiating a technical assistance agreement. And in the subcommittee's judgment, the United States should take such attitudes into account to a greater degree than has been evident in the past.[1]

The Act for International Development speaks of "balanced" development. This is a problem to which Mr. Burns alludes indirectly, but which deserves rather more extended consideration.

Technical assistance can no more be compartmentalized in the recipient state than it can be separated from the foreign-policy objectives of the United States. For example, take the problem of the distribution of emphasis, within the technical-assistance program, between health and agriculture. As Mr. Burns points out, the program frequently meets cultural resistance in both of these fields. People think hypodermic needles are devices of the devil; or they are so attached to traditional methods of farming that they just plain don't want

[1] *Technical Assistance and Related Programs*, Senate Report 1956, May 7, 1956.

to change. Mr. Burns indicates—and the evidence tends to confirm—that this resistance can be overcome more quickly in regard to health than in regard to agriculture. Certainly results are more immediately and spectacularly apparent in the case of health than in the case of agriculture. The wonder drugs can make a very great difference in health almost overnight, but improved agricultural methods take at least one growing cycle, and probably longer, before their results are apparent.

It is sometimes important, in overcoming cultural resistance, to do something that has an immediate impact. To take a specific example, which happens to be in Latin America, but which could no doubt be duplicated in the Middle East, the Plan Chillan area development program in Chile did not really win public acceptance until mass inoculations wiped out hoof-and-mouth disease. It is frequently easier to make an impact in regard to health than in regard to anything else, because it can be done more quickly.

Parenthetically, it might be noted that sometimes the way to overcome cultural resistance in regard to health is through animals. In Chile, the path was found through hoof-and-mouth disease in cattle. In India, some villagers were persuaded to accept antimalarial DDT spraying only after it had been demonstrated that this spraying reduced the insect infestation of their animals.

In any event, for these and perhaps other reasons, technical-assistance programs in health are at least partly responsible for the growing rates at which population is increasing in the Middle East and elsewhere. Medicine has gotten ahead of agronomy. This is not to suggest that medicine should be held back, but that agronomy should be speeded up.

The point I wish to emphasize, however—and one which Mr. Burns touched upon only lightly—is the need for balanced planning of technical assistance, balanced not only among technical-assistance projects themselves, but among other programs and the total social, cultural, and governmental situation. Balanced plans are perhaps more important than big plans.

I have referred to the need of keeping health and agronomy programs in balance. There have been in recent years increasing doubts expressed in the United States about the wisdom, from the American point of view, of encouraging increased food production abroad in the face of increasing food surpluses in the United States. Mr. Burns correctly points out: "Until the caloric availability of food in the Middle East and Asia reaches a more satisfactory level, greater agricultural production in those countries will mean simply more food for the local people to eat." It might also be added that increased production of food—or of anything else, for that matter—abroad is competitive with American production only to the extent that it displaces American markets. Unless foreign production is substituted for American production, in other words, it has no effect on the American economy. Foreign production becomes a threat to American producers only if one assumes that foreign countries will buy from the United States what they do not produce themselves. In view of the purchasing power of the countries of the Middle East, this assumption appears questionable, to say the least.

Indeed, a study of United States foreign trade figures shows that the wealthier—i.e., the more productive—a country is, the more goods it buys from the United States. The following figures, taken from the Senate Foreign Relations Committee report on the Mutual Security Act of 1955, are illuminating. United States exports in 1954, per inhabitant of the country, were $181.97 to Canada, $39.65 to the Netherlands, $13.46 to the United Kingdom, $9.91 to Germany, and $7.67 to Japan. But to Iran, they were only $2.21; to Egypt, $1.77; to Indonesia, 88 cents; to India, 43 cents; and to Pakistan, 42 cents. If this last group of countries could be raised even part way to the level of the first group, American export markets would be enormously expanded.

Mr. Burns has made the point that technical assistance, by itself, is not adequate to cope with the problems of economic development and that capital is also needed. The supply of capital is not, strictly speaking, a problem of technical assistance; yet a technical assistance program cannot be intelligently planned without reference to capital availability. One of the functions of technical assistance is to help capital-short countries use what little they have to the best advantage. And one of the pitfalls of technical assistance is that it may create in the local population desires that there is no immediate hope of fulfilling because of a shortage of capital.

This creates a nice dilemma for the technical-assistance administrator. On the one hand, he cannot succeed unless the people with whom he works have the urge to develop. This necessarily means that they are dissatisfied with things as they are. The line between dissatisfaction and frustration is a fine one.

One of the problems—and also, one of the opportunities— of the technical-assistance program, however, is to keep dissatisfaction from becoming frustration and despair and also to channel into constructive uses the energies released by dissatisfaction.

So we see that it is not merely a combination of technical knowledge and capital that is needed for economic development. A third indispensable ingredient is the state of mind that the Mansfield committee called "the urge to develop."

This urge, the committee said in the report referred to above, "is compounded of many things. It is a great deal more than the desire for more economic goods. It is a recognition that traditional ways of life are incompatible with the fulfillment of such a desire and a willingness to modify traditional habits in order to achieve this goal. People who work only in order to live as their grandfathers did are not susceptible to economic development. If technical assistance shows them how to produce one-fifth more food, they will instead produce the same food and increase their leisure proportionately. This is not economic development, though it may satisfy the social values of the people. In this connection, it is worth recalling the remark of George Bernard Shaw: 'Do not do unto others as you would they should do unto you. Their tastes may not be the same!' "

All of this is involved in the problems of the intercultural transfer of knowledge, and it is gratifying that Mr. Burns put so much emphasis on this phase of technical assistance. Here, the technician in the field is the key man. He must, of course, be technically competent. But he must be much more. He—and, importantly, his family—must combine some of the characteristics of a linguist, a diplomat, a teacher, a sociologist, a cultural anthropologist, a missionary, and a pioneer. And the technician and his family must have the physique and the temperament that permit easy adjustment to difficult environments.

Personnel is a key problem in the technical-assistance program and is perhaps the greatest single limiting factor on the size of the program. The files of the Committee on Foreign Relations contain case after case in which worth-while technical-assistance projects have been delayed for a year, or even two years, after they have been agreed upon with the countries concerned, while suitable technicians were being recruited in the United States.

There is no easy solution to this problem. Arabic and other languages of the Middle East and Asia are not widely spoken in the United States and probably never will be. Even without consideration of the language problem, it is not easy to find a competent technician, temperamentally qualified, who is willing to leave the job he has—usually a pretty good one—and take his family to what seems to many Americans like the end of the earth.

As the technical-assistance program becomes more firmly established, progress is being made in solving the personnel problem. Regional specialization and longer tours of duty are welcome developments.

Technical assistance is frequently referred to as the most popular part of a foreign-aid program, which, in its totality, is none too popular. In recent years, technical assistance has consistently been the only major program that somebody in the Senate has not offered an amendment to cut. Some enterprising student of the social sciences might well devote time to an analysis of why technical assistance—"pure giveaway"—seems popular, while the recent development fund—"pure loan"—seems to have hard sledding.

This state of affairs is even more striking when one recalls that the Act for International Development passed the Senate by a single vote in 1950. Since that time, both the administrators in the Executive Branch and the legislators in Congress have learned a great deal about this "bold, new program." The principal thing learned, I think, is that it is not quite so simple as it appeared then. We still have a great deal to learn. We do not have many of the answers yet, but at least we have identified most of the questions.

One of the questions to which more attention could well be given is the relationship of technical assistance to the overall foreign policy of the United States. This is basically the same question with which this comment opened—namely, does the program further United States foreign policy objectives?

There are some people who think that the objectives—or at least the results—of the technical-assistance program are contradictory to the objectives of foreign policy. On his return from a seven-week trip studying technical assistance in the Far East, South Asia, and the Middle East in 1955, for example, Senator Green reported:

> Unresolved dilemmas in overall American policy show up in a number of countries where the United States is dedicated politically to maintaining the status quo and economically to promoting the kind of development which is impossible within the existing political and social framework.[2]

What we are really concerned with here are the social and political consequences of technological change. These consequences have been inadequately studied, but we do know that they are immense. The prime example, of course, is the United States. Consider the changes in the American society that have come about in a single generation from only three technological developments: the automobile, which took families away from home; the motion picture, which gave

[2] *Technical Assistance in the Far East, South Asia, and Middle East.* A Report by Senator Theodore Francis Green. January 13, 1956. Reprinted in Senate Report 139, March 12, 1957, p. 527.

them a place to go away from home; and television, which brought them back home.

The changes in American politics—except for changes in methods of campaigning—have been less marked, one reason perhaps being that American politics are institutionalized to a high degree. Political institutions, as we know them here and in western Europe, act as a kind of shock absorber, but they are virtually nonexistent in much of the Middle East.

It is in the interests of the United States that such institutions develop in the Middle East—not necessarily in the image of American or European institutions, but indigenously, to provide a kind of home-grown stability that can cope with technological and social change. Unless technical assistance contributes to this process of institutionalization, it is not being fully effective and it may even be counterproductive.

To quote one of the studies prepared at the request of the Senate Special Committee to Study the Foreign Aid Program:

> This internal social transformation is the crucial determinant of the future political development of the countries of Asia and Africa, and such a development appears the best guaranty of their future political independence and noncommitment to the Soviet orbit. If such a middle class imbued by an ideology of economic progress by nonviolent means could have been created in Egypt after the anti-Farouk revolution, the intelligentsia of that country, instead of indulging in pan-Arab "imperialism," might have been so deeply concerned with the solution of the country's internal economic problems that the glamour of enlargement of Egypt's sphere of influence would have paled in comparison.[3]

[3] *The Role of Foreign Aid in the Development of Other Countries.* The Research Center in Economic Development and Cultural Change of the University of Chicago. Senate Committee Print, March, 1957, pp. 76-77.

VII

Structural Changes in Middle East Society

PAUL STIRLING
Lecturer, The London School of Economics,
University of London

THE SOCIETY OF THE OTTOMAN EMPIRE was highly complex and heterogeneous. Recently almost everything in its former territory that can possibly be included in the pantechnicon "culture" has been changing. In the face of so much material, most of it unanalyzed from a sociological point of view, what I can say in one essay is necessarily superficial—an exercise in trying to follow through the consequences of a theoretical approach, rather than an examination of the vast piles of unsorted data. The key to this approach is the notion of "social structure," that is, that all the activities that go on in a given society can be analyzed as the contents of a whole series of more or less defined social relationships which together form the "social system."

What is important to my purpose in this essay is not argument about this approach, but the questions it prompts us to ask. What were the main groups and social positions in the late Ottoman Empire? How were they arranged vis-à-vis each other in terms of power, prestige, and mutual dependence? How have these arrangements altered with the breakup of the empire into smaller political units, the winning of independence, and the accelerating arrival of Western technology and social institutions? Since one cannot speak of change without assuming something that is changing or has changed,

140

I am going to assume, wrongly, a traditional social structure of the Ottoman Empire. This society contained three main types of people—nomadic tribesmen, villagers, and townsmen. The pastoral tribes in their deserts or mountains were largely or completely independent of the central government. The size of the autonomous unit varied greatly and often rapidly. Occasionally, it grew large enough to attack and conquer towns and establish new ruling dynasties. The tribes constantly raided each other, and, insofar as the central government was unable to prevent them, they also raided the settled towns and villages.

The villagers, the most numerous category by far, were the worst off. Those in fertile or accessible country were usually indebted sharecroppers on the estates of absentee landlords; those in more remote areas had no defense against tribal raids but to accept and pay in kind for the protection of other tribesmen. The exceptions, who managed to own their own land, were mainly situated in mountainous areas, or else were settled tribes who retained enough of their tribal organization both to defend themselves against outsiders and to prevent their own leaders from turning into landowning townsmen. So long as they paid their rents and taxes, and refrained from really serious breaches of the peace, they were largely left alone.

Towns are more complex and heterogeneous than tribes and villages. Those of the Ottoman Empire varied from small almost agricultural towns to vast cities like Istanbul and Cairo. They contained landowners, merchants of all types from shopkeepers to owners of important international export houses, a great number of craftsmen, porters, laborers, servants, and so on. Most towns also contained a farming quarter, in which life was much like that of the villages. There were also the administrative and garrison centers, the seats of the centrally appointed governor or the local dynasts, and their armed forces.

The imperial rulers were also city dwellers, but they were a distinct subdivision—the sultan and his ministers and officers. They were drawn mainly from the great hereditary families of Istanbul, supplemented by recruits from a wide range of classes.

The rulers' power rested largely on control of the professional army, and this control in turn rested on the power to pay and feed them, that is, on the ability to collect the taxes, which in turn rested on the control of the army.

Besides these main social divisions, the empire was also divided into thousands of much smaller communities. These groups were organized on three criteria—religion, language, and locality—and formed a multiple structure of semiautonomous groups of many kinds and sizes.

Sunni Moslems were dominant, but they were not, in spite of theological theory, a single community, for they were divided along language, territorial, tribal, and social-class lines into many communities that differed considerably in their application of customary law and of Sunni dogma and ritual. Shii Moslems were divided into a number of sects recognizing different imams, and in practice if not in theory, each sect used its own customary law. The Christians and Jews constituted a number of formally distinct millets, each having its own heads, at once civil and religious, and administering its own personal law. The internal organization of the religious communities was by no means simple. Distinctions into language groups and local groups, and into the three categories of tribe, village, and town, often operated to produce internal cleavages and crosscutting loyalties. Since an individual often belonged to a number of groups based on different criteria and, furthermore, had social relationships that went outside these groups, he could choose the membership or relationship that he felt most advantageous as his guide to action in a given situation.

But if loyalties were complex and conflicting, they were never loyalties to the empire as such. The notion of an Ottoman nation could never have come anywhere near realization. Armenians, Greeks, Catholics, and even Arab and Kurdish communities were mainly interested in preserving as much autonomy as possible. Only members of Sunni communities could in some contexts class themselves in the same group as the rulers and acknowledge direct loyalty to them.

This society was not run by a Western type of bureaucracy. Except for some supervisory officers in the cities, like the inspectors of weights and measures, the official hierarchies were mainly concerned with collecting taxes, preserving order, keeping the military organization in being, and running the religious institutions of the Sunnis. Barth remarks that for southern Kurdistan in 1950 it was a necessary qualification for office that a man already hold de facto enough power and prestige outside his office to be able to exercise his official functions,[1] and we may tentatively assume these to be the normal conditions of the Ottoman Empire. The hierarchy did not consist of channels down which detailed orders could be passed from the center with confidence that the effects at the bottom would resemble the intention of the legislators. Rather the power of government stood outside and between the communities. The official hierarchy was a hierarchy of responsibility for good order and the payment of taxes. Each official was dependent on his superior, whom he supported against his rivals and whom he used as far as possible to defeat opposition among those below him. So long as funds were forthcoming and no serious trouble occurred, he had a free hand.

Each community was left to manage its own affairs—religion, social services, schools, judiciary, internal taxation. They were thus able to see themselves as the center of the social universe, apart from a more-or-less remote overlord. The pomp and permanence of the imperial government and its service in preserving order gave it legitimacy. But loyalty was not to the sultan, but the local community.

This structure was stable, but not rigid. The continual clash of interests constantly brought about slow permanent changes in the structure. Such permanent changes as were taking place internally were never shattering. Indeed, it is hard to see how they could have been, without either drastic changes

[1] Fredrik Barth, *Principles of Social Organization in Southern Kurdistan* (Oslo, 1953).

in technology, or conquest from outside. Both arrived together.

By far the most important thing about the Western nations is their vast power. The people who ruled the Ottoman Empire had been accustomed to assume without question their superiority over the northern infidels. The remarkable technological and administrative advances in Europe in the eighteenth and nineteenth centuries upset this assumption and gave Europe political and economic power, backed by an increasing military advantage. Eventually, the Western nations acquired the prestige of belonging to the one and only civilized and advanced society, the criterion by which all other societies should be judged. Hence the series of imitations of Western techniques and institutions and the adoption of at least some Western assumptions and standards.

Part of this process happened spontaneously. In self-defense, for example, military techniques had to be learned and military equipment purchased. At the same time, the European powers imposed on the Ottoman administration the enacting of a number of "reforms."

These measures entailed a new conception of government. The Ottoman Empire was assumed to be a modern nation-state, and its hierarchy of officials to be a civil service. Measured by these standards both the government and its organs were not unnaturally found wanting by the Ottomans as well as by their European advisers. A series of legislative acts between the late 1820's and 1878—legally and on paper—removed the disabilities of all subject peoples and the feudal rights of fief-holders and of absentee landlords, enforced primary education, introduced proper legal process for all accusations and penalties, and even set up a constitution and a parliament.[2] The officials charged with administering the new laws had been used to a system in which office was a profitable perquisite of their social rank. Naturally, they exercised their talents in the new situation, not because they were immoral, but because they had been formally assigned a role they had

[2] Abdul-Hamid suspended the constitution in 1878 and resisted further liberal innovations until his overthrow in 1908.

never heard of and which they could not in their situation possibly play. Moreover, the new concept of efficient government required the interference of the central government in the innumerable semiautonomous communities.

The prize example of the confusion caused by assuming the hierarchy to be a civil service was the attempt at land registration. Land in the Ottoman Empire was not registered, and in the middle of the nineteenth century the government decided it should be. The power relations in the Ottoman Empire were largely decided by rights over land, since land was by far the most important economic resource. By rights, I mean *de facto* rights as practiced and accepted by the people concerned. These *de facto* rights were always complex, and very often more than one party had a recognized interest in a piece of land. The reformers, however, thought in terms of simple "ownership," and wanted to see the peasant cultivators registered as the outright owners of their own land. They expressly forbade the registration of any kind of joint rights or special rights over a landowner by others. This prevented any legal protection of the rights of tenants, or of the rights of tribesmen to communally owned land, against their sheikhs. In practice, in almost all areas, land passed into the hands of members of the literate class—existing owners, tax collectors, officials, political heads of tribes or sections of tribes. In many cases, of course, the new rights remained for a long time a dead letter because no one had the necessary force to upset the existing arrangements, but where and when the new rights were enforced, the results were very often misappropriation, absentee landlordism, confusion, and protracted litigation.

Technical change is obvious. Aircraft, radio, and such are dramatic marvels. But perhaps even more socially relevant are improved methods of administration. More efficient record-keeping, communicating, and checking up amount to more efficient ways of pushing other people around. Technical and administrative advance go hand in hand. New technical organizations like factories call for new degrees of precision and reliability in the co-operation of large numbers of people. The new devices and new administrative methods give new power to interfere in the daily life of both urban and rural communities.

The positions in the new hierarchy require specialized knowledge and training. Power no longer rests simply on the command of hereditary resources. Important social positions demand indispensable technical knowledge and experience, and those who possess it are able to exercise power through this very fact. This involves the rise of the professional and business class, particularly represented in the Middle East by the army officers, who, while the professions are still small in numbers, are the only professional group that has the means, through its monopoly of armed force, of pressing the government really hard.

In discussing Westernization, people frequently assume that the main factor in change is intellectual conviction. Parliamentary government, a secular independent judiciary, and so forth are intrinsically such excellent ideas that once people know about them they adopt them. We shall be nearer the mark if we look at the social context and ask what in the situation is conducive to the use of these institutions and ideas—if we look for manipulation, not simply conviction.

In 1918, the end of the Ottoman Empire left a politically open situation, with Western powers and various indigenous groups and peoples competing for power and territory. It is not surprising that with western Europe in the ascendant, ideas that had both the prestige of belonging to the victorious allies and the more concrete advantage of being likely to enlist their support should have swept the board. With the establishment of the League of Nations, it was assumed that the nation was the only possible politically autonomous unit, and nationalism was the most obvious political ploy. Egypt, which really lay outside the empire already, had a clearly defined "protected" status and accepted frontiers. Even here the best weapons against the Westerners were the Westerners' own weapons, and Egypt soon achieved nominal independence. Turkey was also by an astonishing feat of arms able to secure national unity and independence. The remaining states were eventually divided into British and French spheres of influence from which, after another world war, emerged six independent Arab states and Israel.

With the mandates and treaties, the direct pressure from the West toward the establishment of Western social institutions intensified. At the same time, the indigenous drive to establish national power and prestige by taking from the West was also gaining ground. Hence technical and administrative change accelerated rapidly.

All the new institutions were based on an entirely new conception of the political entity—the national state—with the government claiming to represent the social unit to which the ultimate loyalty of all its citizens should be given and ready to interfere in the lives of all sections of the population, not merely to maintain order and the status quo, but to produce a permanent state of change along a path of eternal improvement—that is, to pursue "progress" and "civilization." The old divisions into religious, language, and local communities, and into townsmen, villagers, and tribes, which still existed— which, indeed, had in some cases been strengthened by the period of conflict and insecurity—had theoretically no place in the new scheme of things, with which they were plainly inconsistent.

But the new central governments had the benefit of the new techniques and methods of administration. They controlled professional armed forces, which made rebellions unsuccessful, and they were learning how to exert control over the daily lives of their citizens on a scale these semiautonomous peoples had never experienced. The new means of communication—motor car, telephone, and radio—worked in the same direction, bringing parts of the society into contact, forcing them to see themselves as bits of the nation rather than as the center of their own universe. Communities that had been almost self-contained social systems of their own became parts of a single social system with the government and its Westernized servants firmly at the top.

The people who have lost most by the change are the tribes. One-time independent Bedouin communities have

been "pacified," and in many cases settled as *fellahin*. The
new technology has deprived many of them of their main
sources of income—camel-breeding and caravan escort—and
the modern weapons in the hands of regular armies make their
resistance to governments much less effective. The new frontiers cut across the tribes' normal routes of migration and
upset their traditional pasturing practices. Their raids became
either a disturbance of the national peace, or worse still, aggression against another state. They are no longer the cream
of Middle East society, but by the new urban standards bar-
barians, who must first become peasants like their former subjects before they can begin to achieve "civilization." The
working out of the confusion from the Ottoman land reform
has meant that in many cases land held by complex tribal
customary rights has been registered as the personal property
of the sheikh, who is thus converted from a political head into
an absentee landlord. Very large areas of Iraq seem to have
been settled on these terms since 1920.[3] In Syria, the Jezira
area, which was formerly uninhabitable because of tribal activities, is now being cultivated by "merchant tractorists"
who pay rent to the sheikhs.[4]

In Turkey, also, the nomads living in the Taurus Mountains
and in the east have been under pressure to settle. The only
practically important tribally organized people inside Turkey
were the Kurds. The Turkish army has been in action against
them several times, from 1925 to the middle 1930's. Normal
administration is now in force in all Kurdish areas, and assimilation by the teaching of Turkish seems to be proceeding
slowly.

Villagers have also been subject to the civilizing and nationalizing pressure. The degree of political and economic integration of the villages into the national life of Turkey is
striking. The great national effort of the war of independence,
and the symbol it gave the nation in the person of Atatürk,
made the population, which was already fairly homogeneous,

---

[3] Doreen Warriner, *Land Reform and Development in the Middle East*
(Royal Institute of International Affairs [O.U.P.], 1957).
[4] *Ibid.*

nationally loyal from the beginning of the republic, in spite of the government's attacks on religious symbols and institutions. The villagers certainly had a great deal to bear: they were told by legislation how to lay out their villages; they were made to wear hats like infidels; they were subjected to a European code in place of their own sacred law; their religious orders were made illegal; and the training of their imams was prohibited. Finally, they were forbidden to write in the sacred Arabic script, and their children were taught the script of the Franks. What averted the direct impact of this series of attacks on their way of life was the absence of an administration capable of enforcing the reforms in detail. Probably this relative inefficiency saved the regime from reactionary rebellion. As the administration has increased in scope and efficiency, so the reforms slowly have reached the villages piecemeal. Only the hat law was rigidly enforced at the time of its enactment. But now the administration is reaching the villages. The headman receives a stream of official orders—the village houses are to be renumbered, a statement of village accounts is required, an electoral role must be submitted, all dogs not actually required to protect sheep must be put to death, and so on. The office of headman has become unpopular. His official duties, even though frequently evaded, are liable to cause trouble with the authorities, or with the villagers, his neighbors, or with both. They often require him to extract money or information from his fellow villagers. All headmen I have come across are accused of embezzling funds, and all of course have strenuously denied it. Almost all were young men between twenty-five and forty years of age, usually with influential senior kin alive. All with scarcely an exception said they wanted to resign as soon as possible and would never undertake the office again, and in many cases a two- or four-year term of official office [5] was in fact broken by retirement. One result of this is that neither the headman nor anyone else could really exercise any leadership or exert pressure to settle village quarrels. This in turn

[5] The office was reduced from four to two years in 1951.

leads to more recourse to urban institutions and personnel, thus intensifying the process of the decline of rural autonomy.

At the same time, the usefulness of the government has become more obvious locally. Government credit has increased greatly, and one of the main annual administrative contacts for all villages and most villagers is the paying of the old Agricultural Bank loan and the drawing of a new one after the harvest each year. Roads and road overseers have appeared in villages, water conduits and fountains have been built, officials arrive to assess the harvest in bad years for a debt moratorium, medical officers of health make occasional visits, and village health officers and midwives have settled in some villages.

The villager himself goes off to town much more often than he did, hours away in a bus or lorry, instead of days away on foot or donkey. The volume of migrant labor, though it is not, as far as I know, measured by official statistics, has risen very greatly. All these contacts with a self-consciously progressive middle class, which ostentatiously uses a different etiquette (they do not, for example, normally remove shoes when entering a village man's guest room) has made the villager very ready to pour scorn on his own way of life and accomplishments. He sees himself at the bottom of the national scale of social rank.

This process of urban interference to improve village life has gone much less far in Syria and Iraq. With minor exceptions, Syrian governments have been too preoccupied with staying in office to do very much about organizing social services to attack the villages. The peasants on the whole have not been subjected to a stream of officials. On the other hand, as Gullick [6] makes very clear for Lebanon, private enterprise has taken a hand. Buses and trucks, radios, and even some technical agricultural and irrigation change have arrived, though we have as far as I know no recent detailed information on the effect of these on the structure of village society.

[6] John Gullick, *Social Structure and Culture Change in a Lebanese Village,* Viking Fund Publication in Anthropology No. 21 (New York, 1955).

In Iraq, the situation is similar, except that distribution of landholding is even more recent and is even more heavily in favor of the large landowning class. In spite of vast expenditures on dams, and also on roads, bridges, water works, hospitals, and so on, practically nothing has so far been spent on social services for villagers. This is hardly surprising since the government is necessarily dominated by large landlords who do not want middle-class officials wandering about in their villages suggesting reforms. Not only is the first reform suggested likely to be a reduction in the landlord's share of the crop, but middle-class officials are used by the villagers as allies against the landlord's political influence. This is what one would expect a priori, and is clearly brought out in Dr. Salim's study of marsh Arabs.[7] On the other hand, the vast public works that the oil millions have financed have meant plenty of work for sharecroppers who have given up the rural struggle and decamped with their families to town. Whereas at least until very recently the proportion of urban to rural population in Turkey was roughly constant, in Iraq, by all reports, people are moving into the towns. The sheikhs of Amara complain that they are losing workers at a rate that will endanger agricultural production.[8] Village awareness of belonging to the bottom rung of a centrally controlled state cannot fail to grow when many kin and ex-neighbors are living in the cities, being paid wages out of national oil revenues.

The Egyptian situation is still different. A central government has existed for a long time—on and off for a century and a half. The villagers have never had the same autonomy. In recent years both landlord and government have worked to introduce higher output through technical improvement and even social improvements through health clinics and such. The newly liberated estates of the great landlords, now formally owned by the cultivators, have been organized on a basis of officially controlled co-operatives, in which the eco-

[7] S. S. Salim, "Economic and Political Organization of Echchbaysh, a Marsh Village Community in South Iraq" (Unpublished Ph.D. thesis, University of London, 1955).

[8] Economist, June 22, 1957, p. 14.

nomic and administrative functions of the landlords have
been taken over by professional organizers.[9] The crowning
example of government interference with villagers is the program for the settlement of the new villages in the newly re-
claimed Tahrir Province. Peasants picked by psychological
tests are to live in uniform clothes on a strict and thoroughly
uplifting routine.[10] It would be interesting to know what is
actually happening, sociologically speaking, in these new
villages.

It is not only the pressure on villages and their integration
into the national social system that is growing rapidly. The
urban classes are becoming more dependent on the villagers,
both politically and economically.

National power and prestige depend very largely on the
productivity, in an agricultural country, of the peasants. The
politicians may not always see this too clearly, but they all
know that "backwardness" is weakness and at least for this
reason seek reform in the villagers.

The peasants are also becoming a more important political
factor. Any attempt at a secret ballot election in which the
votes are really counted and published is bound in countries
with large peasant populations to make the village vote important. In Turkey, the Democratic party won the 1950 election by appealing to and organizing in the villages, and they
increased their vote in 1954 by the same technique. Officials
are very much more polite to villagers than they used to be;
village taxes have been reduced; the official price of grain, which
is bought by a government organization, has been raised; and
many villages have acquired water works and new roads. In
Syria, the Baath party claims and works for the support of
village sharecroppers, and in Egypt both the Wafd and Nasser
have sought village support. This conscious dependence, however limited, of the townsman on the villager is something
entirely new in the Middle East. It is precarious, because elections are not politically essential. Yet—and this in itself is

[9] Warriner, op. cit.
[10] Ibid.

interesting—the politicians continue to talk about and to hold elections.

Not only has the traditional relationship between town, village, and tribe altered radically. The new nations have also had to deal with the minorities. Here again the most striking changes have been in Turkey. Mustafa Kemal saw the problem very clearly. The bitterness left by the Armenian revolts and massacres and the war of independence against the Greeks was too violent for these minorities ever to accept loyally citizenship in a Turkish republic. By the time the Treaty of Lausanne came to be negotiated, massacres had effectively removed or driven into safer lands most of the Armenian population of Anatolia. The members of the Greek Orthodox millet were a more serious problem, but this was solved by their bodily exchange with Greece, by the Treaty of Lausanne (1923), for Moslems living in what was to be Greek territory.

The various Shii sects in Turkey were officially ignored. Their leadership and organization were indirectly attacked when Mustafa Kemal abolished all the meeting places and organization of the dervish orders, since it is clear that these orders, though ostensibly Sunni, had close relations, at least rurally, with Shiis.[11] Shiis are classed as Moslems for census purposes, so that no accurate figures for their numbers can be given. They do not seem to be numerous among the educated class in Turkey and do not seem to present any political difficulty.

The policy toward Sunni minorities is similar. In the Circassian villages, for example, Turkish is spoken in the schools and by the schoolmasters, and this seems to be accepted as right and proper. Only the Kurds, who include both Sunni and Shii tribes, are numerous enough to form a politically important non-Turkish group. They, too, are taught Turkish, and the policy of Turkification seems to be working so far. It has been said to me that it is the educated Kurds, so far few in number, who object to this policy. But the Kurds are not

[11] J. K. Birge, *The Bektashi Order of Dervishes* (London, 1937).

a united people, and many at least accept cheerfully the status of Turkish citizen.

The official end of the millet problem came in 1926. The Treaty of Lausanne guaranteed the legal equality of the minorities, and this meant that so long as the Sharia or a code based on it was still applied to Moslems, the millets had to have their own personal laws. Partly in order to end this permanent institutional symbol of the non-Turkishness of part of his population, Mustafa Kemal hastened the introduction of a European code of law.[12] With this the last remnant of any formal recognition of minorities in Turkey disappeared. This did not end the social reality of ethnic and religious distinctions, but with a vast homogeneous majority, Turkey was able to claim justifiably to be a modern nation-state.

The Arab states were in a different situation. Their minorities were more numerous, and they were less bitterly hostile to each other. They even had all been united in getting rid of the Turks. Moreover, except for the Arabian peninsula, the major areas were in the hands of mandatory powers. Britain and France could not pursue a revolutionary policy, nor ignore sectarian differences and linguistic minorities, as the Turkish Republican government was able to do. Nor did they start with a single de facto large ethnic majority. Hence, in these countries a different system of personal law continues to apply to the peoples of the minorities. In the political institutions, the existence of these communal loyalties has been clearly recognized, and such institutional differences symbolize and perpetuate the distinctions. Lebanon has a most curious arrangement by which alternate holders of office in ranked order from the president downwards must come from the Christian or Moslem sections of the population, and these in turn divide their allocated offices between themselves according to relative power and importance. In Syria, the arrangements are little less formal. Special arrangements for local government still exist for the areas of the Druses and the

12 See on this subject *International Social Science Bulletin*, Vol. IX, No. 1 (1957).

Alouites, where the French began the experiment of regional administrations for different cultural groups. The Iraqi Christians have a fixed small number of deputies in the Parliament. One of the more important ministers is a Kurd. In the Kurdish areas Kurdish is spoken in the schools and by the administration. Most of the Kurds are not bilingual, so this regime is more or less inevitable. How far are the loyalties in these countries seriously confused? We do not have any definitive evidence. Many early leading Arab nationalists were Christians, and Christian Arabs certainly consider themselves primarily as Arabs. How far the vast Moslem majority of Arab speakers really regards the Christians as part of the Arab nations, I do not know. Many Arabs are still enthusiastically for Arab nationalism as opposed to Syrian, Iraqi, or Jordanian nationalism. Kurds, Armenians, and so on, on the other hand, are more likely, if they are not committed to a struggle for their own independence, to look to the existing national structures—to become Iraqis or Syrians.

The same factors of integration through technological and administrative change that have increased social relations among village, town, and tribe have also operated to reduce the barriers among the communities. Better communications, more officials, more cash crops, more migrant labor, more village social services, enforced national service with the army— all these are bound to build a network of social relations across the communal boundaries, but largely within national boundaries that are more intricate and more numerous than has ever been the case in the past. When the government is so busy governing, no community can retain real autonomy. To bear with the diminution of its autonomy, a group needs to be able to some extent to identify itself with the larger group that the government symbolizes, that is, with the nation. Otherwise, the interference, however well intentioned, is almost certain to be interpreted in a hostile light as an attack on the minority and to lead to increased emphasis on loyalty to the minority as opposed to the nation.

I have been arguing that the structure of Middle Eastern society suffered a complete change between the middle of the nineteenth century and the middle of the twentieth century. The old structure was based upon the preservation of a balance between and the ascendancy over innumerable communities from outside these communities. It aimed at stability, at preventing disorder and rebellion. As such it was highly successful. Its final collapse did not come through the failure of the structure, but through the external accident of European technologically based power. The Ottoman Empire changed quite noticeably, as all societies do. But the changes were not part of the ideology and were in spite of, rather than encouraged by, the political structure. Society was assumed to be the same forever.

Now the same area is divided between territorially distinct and theoretically, but not practically, homogeneous nations, whose governments can preserve order and stability with comparative ease because their police have machine guns and aircraft. This is no longer their preoccupation. Instead they are concerned, on the one hand, with the exclusion of their political rivals from the national government and, on the other hand, with rapid reform and development, in order to preserve, if not to improve, their relative position vis-à-vis other national governments, all equally busy with the same race for technical advance. Society is assumed by the new Westernized rulers to be improving all the time, and government is for all and has the right and duty to interfere with all.

Commentary

AFIF TANNOUS
Chief, Africa and Middle East Analysis Branch,
Foreign Agricultural Service, Department of Agriculture

DR. STIRLING HAS APPLIED HIMSELF successfully to the difficult task of portraying structural changes in a highly complex society. In concentrating upon the broad outlines of the task, he was able to highlight for us major trends and developments over a long period of time, following the break-up of the Ottoman Empire. In the following comments, I shall attempt to supplement his broad analysis by emphasizing certain aspects or by dwelling in more detail upon others. Then I shall permit myself some indulgence in a brief appraisal of the outcome of this intensive, and seemingly overwhelming, process of change in Middle Eastern society.

There is no denying the diversity, numerous autonomies, and conflict of loyalties in the "traditional social structure of the Ottoman Empire" as amply portrayed and emphasized by Dr. Stirling. Differences of identification and cross-identification with family, tribe, village community, urban center, sect, class, and racial extraction have been in operation in this part of the world since the dawn of human history. They are still strong forces to be reckoned with, as each national unit in the region strives to achieve integrated and stable societal organization.

Yet we would be cherishing a distorted and misleading picture of the situation, should we fail to see the underlying forces of unity and cohesion. These, in my view, were mainly responsible for the continuance of a working social order over the centuries and for the persistence of cultural identity against tremendous forces of change. These unifying forces are likely to emerge stronger and more dominant in the future, as Middle East society adjusts to new forms or structures. I

am talking about tribal organization, which has been a con-
tinuous source of contribution to the way of life anywhere in
the region; the farming village community with its basic institutions, firmly established and similarly organized, whether
in North Africa, Lebanon, or Iraq; certain basic values, customs, and mores shared in common by most of these peoples;
and the dominant roles of the Arabic language and the religion of Islam.

Thus when the Ottoman Empire came to an end, these
unifying forces asserted themselves, and the prevailing social
order did not shatter into scores of fragments; it broke into
only two major entities, the new Turkey and the emergent
Arab world. The subsequent division of the latter into mandates, protectorates, and semi-independent units was only
power-politics deep. It could not penetrate to the unifying
societal core, the underlying cohesive web of life.

Another feature, which Dr. Stirling implied or mentioned
briefly in his discussion, should be specially emphasized. This
is the traditional cleavage between the two major segments of
Middle Eastern society, the wide gap that separates the elite
minority at the top from the large masses at the bottom. The
social, economic, and political distances between the two are
great, and the means of communication meager. Yet the two
belong organically to the same social system and are integrated
within the total cultural pattern. From this reality arises a
peculiar conditioning of the process of change and national
development. At the same time it poses a stubborn dilemma
for the elite—how to accelerate the desired change for development as they see it, whereas the social center of gravity lies
among the people, who lag behind on the other side of the
gap.

Indications from various fields of experience have become
increasingly convincing that here is the key feature of Middle
Eastern society, through which past developments can best be
understood and future trends predicted. This is not only significant as a method of approach for students of Middle Eastern culture; it is also of paramount importance for leaders

planning and implementing various technical developments in the region.

Let me touch briefly upon a few supporting illustrations. The "model village" approach to the improvement of living conditions among the peasants, as practiced in some of these countries, may be well designed and sound, but only so far as the elite designers are concerned. Upon actual implementation among the rural people, numerous problems arise because of peculiar social and economic conditions. The result is often unbalanced change and frustrating disorganization.

The agricultural co-operative has proved its worth in many countries (including some in the Middle East) over the past fifty years, as a dynamic agency of progressive change and sound development for the farming village community. But when the elite become impatient, and go so far as to make the co-operative a legal obligation, both the method and the objective of the desired change are unavoidably distorted.

Mechanized farming, now widely sought in the Middle East, serves as another good illustration of the principle we are trying to affirm. It is dynamic and can bring about quick changes in farming and rewarding results, but only when applied at the hands of farmers who are ready for it, under appropriate social, economic, and technical conditions. In many cases the leaders of development in the Middle East have gone ahead with large-scale programs of mechanization without due consideration for these conditions. As a result, the economic returns have not been as rewarding as expected; also undesirable changes in the social and economic organization of rural life have arisen.

We could go on citing many other similar cases from actual experience, but space does not permit. The evidence is convincing, however, that the process of change and development in the Middle East is strongly conditioned by the dominant gap in the social structure; that the elite leadership on the one side and the large majority of the people on the other conceive of change from different assumptions and proceed with it at vastly different rates; that this imbalance in the process is mainly responsible for the various manifestations of disorganization and instability in the region; and that the main answer to the problem lies in a determined effort by the elite to bridge the gap and achieve a more integrated social system that can move ahead progressively as a whole.

To leave the matter at this point would amount to giving a totally negative impression of the situation. We cannot do so, for there is a promising positive aspect, although it is not yet dominant. In each one of the Middle Eastern countries, enlightened elements among the elite have become thoroughly aware of this fundamental problem and have taken some firm steps in the direction of bridging the gap.

Among these steps we may enumerate the following: the Rural Social Centers in Egypt, aimed at the uplift of the village community from within, at the level of the people; the several community development and extension programs now in operation in several countries, in co-operation with United States and United Nations technical assistance agencies; the truly co-operative society of Abadiyeh village in Lebanon, developed entirely by local leadership and initiative; the planned resettlement of rural families and communities in the irrigation scheme of the Ghab in northern Syria, in contrast with the absentee mechanized cotton development of the Jezirah in that country, as discussed by Dr. Stirling; the Dujailah and other land-distribution and resettlement projects of Iraq; the national agrarian reform programs of Turkey and Egypt and by the Shah of Iran on the royal domain; the recent emphasis upon fundamental education under the leadership of UNESCO and the determined trend toward universal elementary schooling.

Dr. Stirling has discussed at length the leading roles played by modern technology and improved methods of administration in the changing Middle Eastern society. I wish to elaborate briefly with two observations. The first is that the process of technical change, so far, has taken place mainly on the basis of borrowing from the outside and imposition from above. It has been, so to speak, set free to take its course, without much consideration for its far-reaching implications and repercussions in the living patterns of the people and the social structure. Concern has been primarily for the immediate result wanted from the borrowed item of technology. Beyond that, the chips have been left to fall as they would and society to adjust belatedly the best it could.

Thus, for example, the modern industrial plant was set up, but there were no plans for the arising labor needs or anticipation of labor problems. The tractor, the irrigation pump, and the automobile substantially increased production and income for the tribal chief, but they helped turn him into an absentee landlord and his kinsmen into landless sharecroppers. Piped water assured an adequate and readily available supply for the village folk, but it did away with the traditional social institution that had developed over the centuries around the village well. Through efficient techniques of communication and transportation, central authorities were better able to prevent raiding, keep peace among the tribes, and push for their settlement, but no provisions were made for adequate substitutes to avoid physical and moral deterioration. The modern system of higher education was set up successfully, but it drew away promising youth from the local communities, thus accentuating the gap in the social structure.

One may argue that all of this, and more, is part of the price any society must pay for its gain from technical advancement. This is true, but only to a certain degree. The difference is great indeed, in the magnitude of arising problems and the degree of disorganization, between a society adjusting to technical change from within its own pattern of culture, and another, like the Middle East, borrowing intensively from abroad. In the former case, it is a matter of healthy, balanced growth, with possible minor crises; whereas in the latter it is intensive, one-sided change, by forces alien to the native culture, beyond the capacity of society to absorb the shock and adjust effectively.

I wish, however, to go one step further and assert that it is not inevitable that the process of technical change in the Middle East should always demand such a high price in disorganization, frustration, and upheaval. Borrowing from culture to culture can take place selectively. Adoption of modern technology can be planned to fit the economy and other aspects of the receiving culture. Social science has advanced sufficiently to enable us to detect tensions arising from new techniques and provide for adequate solutions. The successful adoption of this course, however, rests upon the assumption that there is a thorough understanding of, and respect for, the culture, the way of life of the people. I am talking about the people of the Middle East as they actually live today in their villages, tribal communities, and urban centers.

My observation on public administration in the Middle East is that it has lagged glaringly behind technical change, to the detriment of both and of society as a whole. This is another manifestation of the preoccupation with the tangible material aspects of development and the relative disregard of the human aspect. The underlying erroneous assumption is that technology is sufficient unto itself, that once it is borrowed and established, human relations will take care of themselves and the social system will adjust to the new situation automatically. The process of change does not function this way; stable social organization rests upon the thorough integration of technical change with institutional change.

A few examples will show how this lag in public administration manifests itself. The forms of civil service established in the area are similar to their counterparts in Western countries, from which most of them have been copied. Yet they are vastly different in content and application. There are standards for the selection of civil servants, but actual appointment of personnel to the job submits, to one degree or another, to the practice of nepotism. Full-time service is required from the official, but in many cases he is underpaid and must seek an additional job to meet his needs. The usual hierarchy of personnel is well established, and the pyramid of job classification defines and distributes functions adequately. In practice, however, there is so much centralization of authority that initiative is stifled and efficiency reduced materially. The adopted technology creates new situations in human relations and calls for new forms of organization. These require specially trained and qualified personnel, who are not yet adequately available.

The parliamentary form of government is also adopted from the West, with some adaptation to local conditions, although not enough to achieve thorough integration. The traditional organizations of the tribe, the village, and the urban community, which are essentially democratic, could make fundamental contributions to the developing national systems. The two have not yet joined fronts solidly; hence the lag in governmental organization. Local mutual aid and family solidarity could provide a solid foundation for a national system of co-operatives and credit. Settlement of disputes by mediation and other customary legal procedures could be reconciled positively with national law. The independent character and individuality of tribesmen could be recognized as a potential national asset, rather than the cause for disciplinary measures. The personal touch in human relations, a dominant feature of the traditional culture, could develop into a rewarding method of operation in government and business affairs.

Change is a function of any living culture, a manifestation of growth. It always involves a certain degree of disorganization, calling for some adjustment and reorganization. The problem arises when the rate of change is so rapid, and the resulting disorganization is of such magnitude, that society fails to make effective and timely adjustment. The process is not, so to speak, a blind natural phenomenon; for it results mainly from human behavior. Rational orientation by individuals and groups concerned, therefore, could become an integral and dominant feature of the process. In this reality lies the possibility for society to plan and guide change, to predict its course and adjust accordingly, to soften the shock and benefit most from the results.

The Middle East has been changing at an accelerated rate during the past forty years. The process reached unprecedented intensity and comprehensiveness under the impact of tremendous forces released or generated by World War II. Leading among these have been the spirit of nationalism, the conflict of political ideologies, improved facilities for communication and education, and the revolution of modern technology.

Neither in its organization, nor in its rationalized attitudes and dynamism, was Middle East society well prepared to meet all of these forces and steer a relatively smooth course of development and progress. Differences between countries in this respect are not ignored. The area as a whole, however, has suffered from a continuing state of disorganization and instability, sometimes erupting into critical upheavals. At the heart of the process, or the problem, lies one outstanding reality—the imbalance of a segmented society.

After taking this quick ground view of the various factors and trends in the situation, I wish now to raise my sight and look into the future. I shall do so by asking a few questions. Will the elite succeed in identifying themselves functionally and organically with the masses, not only on the political front, but also fully on other fronts? Will the prevailing spirit of intense nationalism survive its initial role of motivating political awakening and independence, to become a leading force for long-range economic and social development? Will the current impatient and anxious desire for Western technology and forms of organization give way to a more balanced development based upon selection, adaptation, and integration? Will the religious heritage of Islam be revived to play its leading role in the evolving social order?

The trend of change and the future of Middle Eastern society are inevitably tied up with these basic questions. In my observation, the indications are strong that all of these eventually will be answered in the affirmative.

VIII

Recent Developments in Islam

P. J. VATIKIOTIS
Department of Government, Indiana University

IT WOULD BE PRESUMPTUOUS to attempt a total assessment of recent developments in Islam, for it is not possible to encompass all that pertains to the millions of Moslems living in Asia and Africa. One's knowledge is, at best, limited and could, if used to pronounce broad generalizations on Islam today, be dangerously misleading. Islam, to borrow Professor Franz Rosenthal's phrase, "is an eminently historical religion." It is still making history, and to analyze history in the making is difficult. One may construct theories about the past, but the present impinges on the future, and the theorist, unaware, turns prophet. One may venture merely the formulation of hypotheses regarding current trends in Islam on the basis of recent developments.

Such hypotheses as I shall offer will be limited to the Arab countries, Turkey, and Pakistan, with only passing comment on Iran and North, West, and East Africa. I will focus attention on those recent developments in Islam that tend to increase or lessen tension in the Middle East.

Scientific technology and its pragmatic outlook have seriously challenged the traditional unity of Islam, resulting in a pervasive uncertainty, extending to law, literature, politics, and education. One has only to recall the encroachment on the sacred law of positive legislation adopted by almost all the Moslem countries to meet pressing social and economic

165

problems.[1] The sacred law, as the perfect embodiment of the social-religious-political ethic and ideal, is thus being compromised. What does this signify? Is the Moslem actually convinced that earthly existence can be improved by man-made laws?

Furthermore, in the recent past we have witnessed in Syria and Egypt the abolition of confessional jurisdiction and the discontinuance of religious bequests (waqfs) for private use, both measures being designed to expand the jurisdiction of civil authority.[2] There is novel experimentation in literature, expressed in the battle between classicists and innovators.[3] One observes a radical deviation from traditional Islamic forms. The metrical but unrhyming verse is gaining legitimacy. The short story—in its Western form—is increasing in popularity. The art of representation—painting, sculpture, freehand, woodprint—is steadily developing.

All this would seem to indicate that Islamic society having defined its aims has deliberately chosen to move along a certain path. Why, then, the gnawing uncertainty? I submit as my first hypothesis that, the changes mentioned notwithstanding, the Islamic societies of today, even though reluctant to admit it, are caught on the horns of a great dilemma: on the one hand a steadily growing desire to adopt the techniques of modern civilization for their advantages in terms of welfare and national strength, and on the other hand a marked reluctance to abandon traditional ways of life and values. Deep attachment to traditional Islam manifests itself in varying degrees of intensity among the different Moslem countries. Though anxious to fit Western technology into an Islamic

---

[1] In Saudi Arabia one still finds strong opposition to modern legislation. A 1950 royal decree providing for the payment of income tax (daribat ad-dakhl) instead of the religious zakat (alms) was strongly opposed and quickly suppressed.

[2] May, 1949, in Syria, and December, 1952, in Egypt. See G. Busson de Janssen "Les Waqfs dans l'Islam Contemporain," Revue des Etudes Islamiques (Paris, 1953), pp. 43-76.

[3] See the "language debate" between Ta Ha Husayn and Abbas M. al-'Aqqad in al-Ahram, LXXXII, and al-Gumhuriyya, III, passim, of June-August, 1956. See also discussions on literary trends in al-risala'l-gadida (Cairo, 1956–1957), passim.

context, these countries have only partially succeeded, inasmuch as their desire to borrow from the West is mixed with resentment towards it.[4] Moslems, from North Africa to Pakistan, are calling for economic and social reform, insisting, however, that such reform should be undertaken in harmony with the principles of Islam. How this harmonious adjustment is to be achieved is not clear.[5] Does modern legislation derive from the principles of the Sharia as such or from the general spirit of Islam? The most recent constitutions of Syria and Pakistan require, ambiguously, legislation derived from the principles of the Sharia. Similar ambiguity is reflected in the new Egyptian constitution, which declares Egypt a "democratic socialist Republic" with Islam as the religion of the state. Thus, in the most recent rationalizations of social-political organization, Islam still asserts itself.

Let us take the still older case of Turkey. It is commonplace to refer to Turkey today as a modern state in the midst of the patriarchal, dictatorial, and fake parliamentary regimes of the Middle East. Such a characterization, I am afraid, is rather hasty, reflecting not the fact but the seeming success of Atatürk's ruthlessness. Prudence would withhold the final word on Turkey.

Under the Ottoman regime, Turkey achieved a highly elaborate Moslem judicial system and religious hierarchy. The Islamic institutional structure was indeed a feat of Ottoman statecraft. Yet so serious were the maladjustments in the twentieth century, and so violent the resentment against it, that Atatürk undertook to legislate it out of existence. Then, suddenly, at the end of World War II, a counterreaction appeared, which, since 1950, has constituted a veritable "revival of Islam."[6] So far, repercussions of this revival have not been

---

[4] On this problem, see the excellent discussion in G. von Grunebaum, ed., *Unity and Variety in Muslim Civilization* (Chicago, 1955), especially pp. 357 ff.

[5] See especially the *Islamic Review* (Woking, Surrey), XLI (August, 1955), 6-13, and the *Islamic Literature* (Lahore, Pakistan), special issue, "Islamic Civilization versus Western Civilization," VIII (May-June, 1956), Nos. 5, 6.

[6] B. Lewis, "Recent Developments in Turkey," *International Affairs*, XXVII (July, 1951), 320-31. Also, his "Islamic Revival in Turkey," *International Affairs*, XXVIII (1952), 38-48.

such as to challenge seriously Kemalist principles—especially that of laicism. Yet the revival is genuine enough for us to question the durability of the revolutionary ideology underlying the Kemalist order—especially as the basis for a national myth totally acceptable to the masses.

Agitation for religious education has been the foremost manifestation of the recrudescence of Islam in Turkey. The issue was first discussed in the Grand National Assembly in December, 1946. The timing of the issue raises many interesting questions. Was it a spontaneous reaction to the monolithic regime of the Peoples Republican Party, with its thought-control aimed at the generation of a secular-republican climate of opinion? Or, again, was it a sincere Islamic antagonism to an imported philosophy and way of life?

These questions cannot be fully answered here, but it appears that the authorities were unable to continue ignoring the basically Islamic ethic of the people. Positivist doctrine, apparently, was unable to displace the Islamic value-system, strengthened as it is in Turkey by other cultural and folk elements. The government established the Faculty of Theology at Ankara in October, 1949. Working closely with the Government Religious Agency (Diyanet Isleri Resligi), it serves as a center for Islamic studies and trains religious teachers for state schools. It has been editing and translating Islamic classics while a committee of the Faculty of Literature at Istanbul is preparing a Turkish edition of the Encyclopedia of Islam. By the end of 1955, the government announced that religious instruction would be available in middle (orta) schools for those who wished it.[7]

The textbooks adopted for purposes of religious instruction are interesting. One by A. Hamdi Akseki, entitled Islam Dini, gives a modern ethical content to Islam and tries to reconcile Islamic tenets with a republican-humanistic philosophy. Another, Ilkokul Kitaplari-Dini Dersleri II, prepared by the government in 1954 for use as a primary school text, goes further by imparting a utilitarian aspect to faith, emphasizing the

[7] See Howard A. Reed, "Revival of Islam in Secular Turkey," Middle East Journal, XIII (Summer, 1954), 267-82.

ability, worth, and active life of the individual Moslem. "My faith in God," one passage asserts, "brings me security and makes easy for me even the most difficult tasks. I never fall into hopelessness." Could this be a precautionary antidote to a possible relapse into traditional lethargy? Furthermore, it asserts the brotherhood of man rather than that of Moslems alone: "All people are brothers whatever religion they have." [8]

Here is a calculated policy by which the government seeks to guard the Kemalist gains in the social, economic, and political spheres. The government is loath to permit the reappearance of religious groups with political—even social—influence. Having recognized the necessity of minimum concessions to religious sentiment, it is anxious to direct that sentiment to ends acceptable to it.

The Turkish public has been showing great interest in Islam, as indicated by the proliferation of periodicals, magazines, pamphlets, and books devoted to Islamic subjects. Some of these publications reflect a reformist view—an attempt to give to Islam an orientation consonant with scientific thought. This is not a novel attempt by Moslems, as we shall see presently in the case of Pakistan. More novel is the attempt paradoxically to utilize the revived interest in Islam as a means for bolstering the brief secular-republican tradition begun by Atatürk. Ismail Hakki Baltacioglou, editor of Din Yalu (Religious Road), is probably the most active exponent of this object.

It would appear, at least on the surface, that the religious challenge is being adequately met by the Turkish government. One might further assume that the revivalist movement in Turkey is, under official guidance, taking on the character of a spiritual, personalized religion, compatible with the secular requirements of the state. Indeed, the Turkish ruling elite has rationalized its support for religious education by viewing it as the basis of character-building and national solidarity. In a speech delivered at Konya in December, 1955, Prime Minister Adnan Menderes, though reiterating the basic principles

[8] See the translation by Helen L. Morgan, "A Turkish Textbook in Islam," The Muslim World, XLVI, No. 1 (January, 1956), 13-23.

of Kemalist secularism, emphasized the fact that "Turkey was and would always remain Moslem." It is also quite probable that the Democratic party of Celal Bayar was able to command wider popular support in both the 1950 and 1954 elections through its religious concessions.

We have seen how the Sharia with its intricate institutional structure in Turkey was abolished overnight. Its formal absence, however, does not seem to have minimized the traditional attachment to Islam by the Turkish people. Then is formal reinstatement of the Sharia necessary for Islamic revival and reform? If not, can Islam be a religion of the "spirit"? Can it be an ethical outlook? These are some of the questions that Moslem Turks must answer if they propose the integration of Islam as a religion into the social and political philosophy of the Kemalist Revolution.

It is unlikely that the Turkish rulers will countenance any new formula short of separation between religion and state. Their sober realization that continued support from the masses meant partial identification with the popular myth, Islam, is bolstered by realism. The government's realistic attitude is reflected in its quick action against the fanatic Nation or Millet party of Fevzi Cakmak, when that group was using Islam for political agitation. At the same time, as a result of its religious compromise, the government lost some of its adherents. The Freedom party, for example, is a splinter group consisting of those members in the Democratic party who felt republicanism was being compromised. Semiofficial organizations, like the Divic Ocagi (Society for Preservation of Ideals of Revolution), also sprang up to lobby against the government's religious policy.

Whether the Turkish authorities will succeed in reintroducing into Turkey an Islam influenced by the borrowed ideas of Western liberal-humanist tradition remains to be seen. Realizing that Islam as an emotional force is still a determinant of political life, the elite has used it to broaden the base of its popular support. What is more curious, however, is its fanatic use by the mob. It would not be an exaggeration to say that even the Turkish government itself was shocked and surprised by the September, 1955, Black Friday in Istanbul.

Some have gone so far as to interpret Turkey's partnership with Iran, Pakistan, and Iraq as a Moslem alliance, through which Turkey is vying for Islamic leadership. Admittedly Nasser of Egypt is not very popular with the Turkish press and government. Yet it would be a mistake to interpret the alliance as related to anything but the political, military, and strategic interests of Turkey.

In its recent development Turkey has been the most consistent among the Islamic countries. Now she has officially agreed to reconsider Islam as the religious force strengthening her national existence. It remains to be seen how this reconsideration will be accomplished and how it will affect the future development of Turkey. That task alone carries the uncertainty of reconciling two opposite social ideals—a positivist one and a religious one.

The emergence of Pakistan is possibly the most significant event in contemporary Islam. Its establishment as an independent nation-state is the fulfillment of the aspirations of the pre-1947 Moslem League of India. The fact that Pakistan is predominantly Moslem is not of particular significance, for so are Egypt, Syria, and Iraq. What is singularly interesting, however, is that Pakistan has declared itself an Islamic state, an Islamic republic, and claims to have adopted an Islamic constitution, which has succeeded in reconciling the parliamentary concept of limited government with the universal sovereignty of God. Constitutional debates lasted some seven years, from March, 1949, well into 1956, the basic issue being the formulation of a concept of an Islamic state. A corollary consideration, depending on the successful resolution of the basic issue, was the accommodation of this Islamic state to a twentieth-century environment.

By an Islamic state the Pakistanis mean a political community governed by the precepts of Islam as revealed in the Koran and recorded in the Tradition. God, to whom universal sovereignty belongs, rules by delegating authority to the state of Pakistan, exercised through its people according to His limits. Because it is an Islamic state, the Pakistanis argue that it embraces the principles of democracy, freedom, equality, tolerance, and social justice.

The first problem that arises is how to distinguish between the sovereignty of God and that of the people. A related problem is how to establish a legal framework for the distribution of sovereign power, a problem especially complicated in the case of a federal state like Pakistan. In Pakistan that is done by a written constitution. Is this constitution supreme law in Pakistan? If it is, what happens to the higher law of God? If that law is reflected in the constitution by a strict observance of the Koran and Tradition in legislation, who determines discrepancies between the two? Indeed, what interpretation of Tradition and which school of law is to be followed?

Legislation in accordance with the sacred law presents serious problems of jurisdiction. It cannot have uniform applicability because non-Moslems cannot be subjected to the Sharia. Indeed, within the Sharia itself the diversity of sects precludes uniformity.[9] At the one extreme, secular opinions point to the basic incompatibility between an Islamic state and a democratic parliamentary system. At the other, fanatic supporters of the idea of the Islamic state have claimed that Islam is not one among many religions, but the one final, universal religion. It is very difficult to conceive of an open free system that permits such dry finality. One of the basic conditions of a free parliamentary system is the entertainment of alternative solutions, a flexibility that permits change with circumstance. A system based on doctrine preconceived by nature cannot tolerate radical deviation.

Because of these and other problems, there is today in Pakistan great confusion over what constitutes an Islamic state. To meet this problem some are taking a new look at the Tradition with a view to giving it a modern and uniform interpre-

[9] It should be noted that the recommendation for a nominated Board of Mullahs (doctors of religious law) to review and pass on the constitutionality of legislation has met with great opposition. See Grace J. Calder, "Constitutional Debates of Pakistan," I, II, III, The Muslim World, XLVI (January, April, July, 1956), 40-60, 114-56, 253-71.

tation. In February, 1955, a special issue of *Islamic Literature*, published in Lahore, was devoted to the question of the "Islamic State." In 1956 the same journal concentrated on "Islamic versus Western Civilization." The latter inquiry reflects the desire on the part of Pakistanis, who suffer from dangerous romanticism, to show perfect harmony between Islam and scientific philosophy. But it is an apology at best; it does not tackle the real problem of Moslem doctrine. It is one thing to liberalize a religious message; it is another matter to make it work. In spite of these efforts there is still no clear definition of what an Islamic state is. Those subscribing to the idea do so because of emotional attachment to an ideal, not because they are reasonably convinced of its practicability.

Apart from the romantic modernists just cited, there are also in Pakistan those who call for a pure theocracy, arguing that Islam is nothing less than God's direct rule on earth. Self-government is to them heretic, because it implies man's ability to regulate his social-political existence. Abu'l-Ala-al-Maududi, the foremost exponent of the theocratic doctrine, has formed an Islamic Society (Jama'at-i-Islami) of Pakistan, representing this conservative ideal. Fortunately or unfortunately, it also acts as a political party of the opposition.

The question of an Islamic state of Pakistan is actually unresolved, marked still by uncertainty and contradiction. Emotional attachment to the traditional view of man ruled by the sacred law is complicated by the desire, through modern legislation, to provide for the economic and social well-being of Pakistan. Thus tension is inevitable when, as in Pakistan, there is an attempt to use a Western-conceived and -organized state structure for the implementation of traditional Islamic values. What is more, the tension will increase as the rulers of Pakistan try to foster and identify a homogeneous national object of loyalty, namely, the Republic of Pakistan. That cannot be achieved by retaining a dual framework of government, one for Moslems, the other for non-Moslem minorities. It looks more to us as if the Pakistanis have established a republic inspired by "Islamic nationalism" (really nationalism idealized through Islam) rather than an Islamic state that is a republic.

In the Arab countries developments have been more complicated. All we can hope to do here is mention a few of these developments on the basis of which we may hypothesize on the general trend. The past five years have seen the steady revival of the concept of an Islamic community (umma), especially in Egypt. Influenced by the ideas of modern nationalism, this is not merely a community of faith, but a political community as well. Writing in a special issue of al-Hilal (January, 1957), on "Our Arab Nation," Nasser asserts that Arabs are the only people with a qibla (direction for prayer), a potential source of national strength and international leadership. In the same issue, Ahmad Zaki emphasizes the sharpened cultural-religious antagonism between the Arabs and the West. Ahmad Hasan al-Baquri, Minister of Waqfs, writing in 1956, underlines the religious basis of the Arab social and political renascence.[10] Besides these specific instances, there is the usual but accelerated idealization of Islamic historic personalities in popular magazines.

Recent measures by the Egyptian government in the field of education are significant. A law that became effective in December, 1956, makes obligatory the teaching of Islam to Moslem pupils in Christian schools operated by foreigners. Noncompliance with this law renders a school liable to seizure by the state. The Republic of Egypt was proclaimed in May, 1953, in the name of Allah and the Koran, while Naguib, in accepting the oath of allegiance (bay'a) from the ulema first and the people later repeated the words of the first caliph, Abu Bakr.[11] Could this be a reiteration of Islam as the foundation of all legitimate political power? The results of the June, 1956, plebiscite for the adoption of the new constitution were publicly expressed in the form of the bay'a. In both

[10] See al-Hilal, LXV (January, 1957), special issue, "Our Arab Nation," 6-7, 41-44, and al-Ithnein, No. 1170 (November 12, 1956), 17.

[11] "O people, I have been designated to be your chief even though I may not be the best among you. If you judge my conduct as satisfactory retain me. If you find me in error correct me."

Jordan and Saudi Arabia one reads about the frequent denunciation of Western culture as a degenerating influence upon
Moslem society.[12] In 1955, the Egyptian Ministry of Waqfs
established an office to supervise and encourage the role of
the mosque and the imam in community life, to promote the
kind of preaching that would extend Islamic education. (A
royal decree in Arabia [1955] prohibits students from attend-
ing primary and secondary schools abroad.)

Here we might venture a hypothesis: For the Arab countries, during the interwar period, nationalism was a formula of
national salvation derived from and based on Western ideas.
The tendency today is to reject the Western origin of nationalism and to base it on Islam. Western nationalism embodied
in the imported concepts of liberal constitutionalism and representative institutions failed to work in the Arab countries.
This failure was due partly to the resistance of a traditional
society unacquainted with Western concepts. Consequently,
even revolutionary regimes in the Middle East today must
integrate this traditional element in their political program.
Islam seems to offer the common ground for this accommodation. They also feel that Islam can ultimately free them from
intellectual dependence on the West.

If this is a fair estimate of the present trend, we must look
closely at any recent attempts by Arab Moslems to establish
an Islamic basis for their national existence. Interwar experience showed that the Moslem intellectual and political leaders
were unable to undergird any change with a social philosophy
acceptable to the masses. Educated Moslems had roman-
tically embraced the idea that adoption of certain forms would
of itself produce change. They failed to realize that mere
form, however ideal, can produce only what the social context
permits. It was this confusion of the Western-educated Moslem that deprived him of influence. His thought, though liberal, failed to provide the conditions necessary for the healthy

[12] This trend may be especially noted in the Saudi Arabian daily, al-bilad
as-su'udiyya (August, 1956). A new Jordan monthly, hadi 'l'islam, contends
that the danger of "imperialism" to Moslem society is to be found lurking
even in the Western-run schools and hospitals, as well as Western literature.

development of Arab Moslem society. Those, on the other hand, who rejected religion found themselves lacking any contact with the masses. And those clinging to conservative religious orthodoxy refused to re-examine their position in the light of a changing world, thus gradually alienating all those inclined to creative thought.

The debate that raged in 1949–1951 between Khalid Muhammad Khalid (calling for a complete separation between state and Islam and the socialization of national programs) and Muhammad al-Ghazzali (purporting that ideal social justice was found in Islam) is almost a thing of the past. Neither did this debate seem to have greatly affected the traditional observation of ritual by the masses.[13] Indeed, a more serious attempt to restate the position of Islam began in 1955 in India through a fresh examination of Tradition.[14] In the Arab countries, mass Islamic movements, which purport action on all fronts—social, economic, educational, and political—thus avoiding the creation of an intellectual gap between them and the public, have had greater success in the recent past. The Moslem Brotherhood is a good example. Although officially suppressed in January, 1954, at its Egyptian home base, the brotherhood is still a formidable religious-political force in the Arab world. Its suppression in Egypt required the establishment of an Islamic congress to promote the Islamic quality of Arab nationalism in the face of alien challenges and penetration—a recognition of the brotherhood's success.

A pressing problem facing Arab Islam is the construction of a formula for unity. The political fragmentation of the Arab countries, themselves a product of nationalism, would indicate that the nation-state as an object of loyalty must be fostered. But, individually, these countries do not show the

[13] See the well-known work From Here We Start by Khalid M. Khalid (Cairo, 1949), and its refutation by Muhammad al-Ghazzali in The Beginning of Wisdom (Cairo, 1951). (Translations by American Council of Learned Societies, Near East Translation Program, Washington, D. C., 1953.)

[14] See excerpts of the call in 1955 by Hyderabad Academy of Islamic Studies for the re-examination of Tradition in The Muslim World, XLV (July, 1955), 299-300.

homogeneity necessary for a uniform national myth. We may, therefore, assume that a nationalist Islam may prove an alternative. It can have greater appeal because it is a traditional concept—it is indigenous (native). We saw how previous adoption of a liberal ideology by the intellectuals deepened the chasm between them and the masses. It produced a two-level society without contact, sympathy, or understanding between them. The social-political consciousness of the few was unable to produce a new order, because it was counteracted by the traditional conservatism and inertia of the many. The masses, with their devotion to the past, were beyond the reach of the intellectuals. It is not strange, therefore, that Islamic nationalism can have a greater appeal; it asserts the sentiment of religious-communal solidarity—a vague, yet emotionally acceptable, concept.

Parallel to the emergence of this new brand of Islamic nationalism, there is a general decline in liberal thought, a general discrediting of the intellectual. This is reflected in the decay and collapse of parliamentary government in many of the Arab countries and the growth of strong monolithic regimes. These are characterized by vociferous reaction to and rejection of Western ideas and principles, accompanied by a conscious utilization of state power for the identification of national aspirations with the principles of Islam.

Before we can inquire whether resuscitated Islam can serve as the basis for renewed spiritual strength and a means to achieving homogeneity and solidarity among the Moslem Arab countries, we should note any forces that militate against it. First, there is no consensus among Arab Moslems regarding the validity or desirability of this trend. Political considerations at this time preclude general agreement. The Islamic orientation of Saudi Arabia, for example, does not prevent political estrangement from Egypt or Syria. The same divergence of opinion is found among intellectuals.[15] In North Africa,

---

[15] Cf. Abd ar-Rahman al-Bazzāz, "Islam and Arab Nationalism," *Die Welt des Islams* (1954), Parts 3-4, pp. 210-18, where he asserts that "Arab nationalism devoid of the spirit of Islam is like a body without a soul," and Sati al-Husri, *al-'uruba awwalan* (Beirut, 1955).

Habib Bourguiba of Tunisia contends that "constructive nationalism" is preferable to the Islamic variety.[16] Consequently,
there is today a division of the Arab Moslem world marked
by a struggle for power. This struggle for power is aggravated
by the vacuum that the retreat and disappearance of foreign
control has produced.

The problems of Islamic Arabic society are also complicated
by external shocks. The psychological trauma resulting from
the establishment of Israel has yet to be assessed. More irri-
tating has been the Anglo-French invasion of Egypt in the
fall of 1956. Have these two encroachments upon the Arab
Moslem world sharpened Islamic antagonism to the extent of
rejecting Western norms, while, at the same time, causing
greater political fragmentation in the area?

Other developments in the Arab countries tend to under-
mine the identification of national aspirations with a revived
and active Islam. Everywhere, in Iraq, Egypt, Arabia, Syria,
and North Africa, governments are concerned with the economic and social development of their respective countries.
As their programs for reform acquire shape and meaning there
is a gradual emergence of a proletariat and a middle class. As
education becomes widespread, as services are extended to a
larger portion of the population, these and other classes will
demand greater participation and representation in the social-
political process. As the gap between the few who have tradi-
tionally held power and the masses is narrowed down, new
centers of power will arise, demanding a role in political life.
The possible transformation of the social structure from its
traditional form may totally change the role played by the
various groups in Arab society and politics. At present, these
emerging groups are not finally committed in their allegiance.
They are rather uprooted and confused. Will Islam be able to
command their allegiance in the future?

On the basis of recent developments, it is improbable that
resuscitated Islam will serve as a basis for Arab solidarity
and integration. Political considerations causing differences

[16] See his article "Nationalism: Antidote to Communism," *Foreign Affairs*,
XXXV (July, 1957), 646-53.

among the Arab countries still predominate. Although appealing, Islamic nationalism has not, so far, broken through individual national barriers. Neither has it seriously accommodated the techniques required for the administration of a modern state in its total interpretation of existence. The question of the compatibility between Islam and modern nationalism is unresolved. Instead, the dualism consisting of a desire among a few for modernization, on the one hand, and a mass attachment to a traditional view of society, on the other, paralyzes national development and minimizes the chances for greater unity.

Reformulating our hypothesis, we may conclude that there is today an attempt at a Moslem renascence throughout the Islamic countries. This revival, however, is marked by struggle, tension, and uncertainty regarding the future. External forces such as the political-economic-strategic interests of the West and communism are actual factors in this struggle. In seeking national strength some of these countries are rejecting Western-inspired principles of national existence in favor of a new Islamic base. Unfortunately, this new Islamic base is still vague and not formulated in clear terms. It is more of an emotional stimulant than a formula of positive action. The dualism of values between sections of the Moslem public— one set of values primarily learned from the West, the other native—is still an obstacle to the creation of a homogeneous society. This dichotomy is widened by the increased use of non-Islamic techniques for the promotion of national welfare. Political and economic considerations continue to direct policy in a Moslem world quite divided in its loyalties.

The recent Islamic revival is still negative in character. The attempt among Moslems to gain intellectual as well as political freedom from the West has not been accompanied by a parallel introduction of a native value system, one that is not only rationalized by the intellectuals, but is also emotionally accepted and followed by the mass. Thus, the positive aspects of this revival are still vague and confused. Whether Islam, in rejecting influence from abroad, will succeed in generating its own formula for social and political salvation is the

most exciting unknown factor of the future. Now that Islam
has revived its political aspirations, this task becomes critical.
Similarly, it is always dangerous to telescope changes that require centuries into a short span of years. It is doubly dangerous when there is no agreement on what changes, and in
which direction.

Commentary

GEORGE MAKDISI
Associate Professor of Near Eastern Studies,
University of Michigan

SINCE THE END OF WORLD WAR II, there has been a growing
literature in the West in interpretation of Islam. There are
several reasons for the growing interest indicated by this literature. Except for a small number of specialists, Islam is little
known in the West. It is important strategically. It has oil.
It is an important factor today in world equilibrium. Whatever the reasons, Islam is receiving an increasing amount of
attention by an increasing number of interpreters.

Americans, by virtue of the preponderant role in world
politics that has become theirs, are in need of understanding
more about the peoples of the world and especially about the
peoples of the East. Not long ago, Americans felt no special
need to learn foreign languages. Today experiments are under
way, not in colleges, not in high schools, but in grade schools,
with a view to teaching foreign languages at an early age. Instead of expecting others to speak their language, Americans
are beginning to make the effort to speak the language of
others. It is with this attitude that the interpreter must approach his subject. He must make the effort, a sympathetic

effort, to understand it, to deal with it on its own level, in its own climate, in its own terms.

For this reason, essays such as Mr. Vatikiotis' should be welcomed for the light they might throw on a little-understood part of the world. If I disagree with Mr. Vatikiotis on certain points, some of which are fundamental, I do so in good faith (as I believe he stated them in good faith), in the interests of both the people interpreted and the people to whom the interpretation is addressed. The preceding essay is, I believe, meant for a local audience, and some of its terms or generalizations need, in my opinion, to be examined more closely, and some distinctions concerning them should be made.

The Umma

I would like to comment first on what Mr. Vatikiotis sees as the influence of modern nationalism on one of the most fundamental concepts in Islam. He describes the Islamic community, the term for which is umma, as follows: "Influenced by the ideas of modern nationalism, this is not merely a community of faith, but a political community as well." He is right, of course, in describing the umma as a community that is both religious and political, for this has been its characteristic since its very beginnings, thirteen centuries ago—it is, therefore, hardly due to the influence of modern nationalism. Indeed, it is this very characteristic which has made for the most important tensions Islam has experienced, not merely recently, but throughout its history. I shall come back to these tensions later on.

The Islamic System Is Flexible

In reference to Pakistan, the following observation is made by Mr. Vatikiotis: "One of the basic conditions of a free parliamentary system is the entertainment of alternative solutions, a *flexibility* that permits *change with circumstance.* A system based on doctrine preconceived by nature cannot tolerate radical deviation." Lest it be thought that the Islamic system is unqualifiedly inflexible, I would like to make the following distinction.

Legislative power, in the ideal Islamic state, belongs to the Koran, which contains God's revelations to His *umma,* or community. These revelations are not only of a religious order; they envisage a definite civil organization. Now the *umma* is based on the Koran; hence its essentially *religious,* but also *political,* nature. The revelations of God to His community stopped with the death of the prophet Mohammed. In its history since that time, Islam undoubtedly has encountered many particular situations not explicitly referred to in the Koran. Yet it has survived the difficulties it encountered. The story of how it survived these difficulties, a story that may also be regarded as that of its tensions, has been told in several works. What matters here is that this survival could not have been effected without the attribute of flexibility.

On this subject of flexibility, I would like to quote some passages by Moslem jurists as quoted by the Italian scholar David Santillana in the book entitled *Legacy of Islam.* Santillana makes the following statement (italics mine):

> Having as its scope social utility, Muslim law is essentially *progressive,* in much the same way as our own. . . . It is not *unchangeable* and depending on mere tradition. The great schools of law agree on this point.

He then quotes the Hanafites as saying:

> The legal rule is not unchangeable, it is not the same as the rules of grammar and logic. It expresses what generally happens and *changes with the circumstances* which have produced it.

He also quotes the following passage, which shows how the law is conceived as admitting custom and following it in its evolution:

It is a general rule that every law is based on use or custom itself. . . . It might be said on one side: we must follow what is established, for we cannot make law, having neither the knowledge nor the authority required: we must solve questions which are submitted to us according to what is to be found in the books. But on the other hand, to apply laws which are founded on ancient usage, once that usage is changed, is to set oneself against general opinion, and to prove one's ignorance of religion. The truth is that whenever a law is based upon the custom of a particular time, *that law must change when the conditions which called it into being have changed.*[1]

It is, of course, perfectly admissible to speak of rigidity or inflexibility in Islam, but this must not be attributed to its whole system of theology: dogmatic, juridical, and mystical. One may speak of inflexibility in matters of dogma, in much the same way as one would speak of it in other religions. But one must be careful not to apply the same inflexibility in the field of juridical theology, unless it be to say that some schools of law are less flexible than others. But of the fact that they must be flexible, there can be no doubt. This application of inflexibility was in fact attempted in the eleventh century in Spain, by the well-known jurist and theologian Ibn Hazm, with disastrous results to the school of which he became the foremost exponent, the Zahirite School. In a work that remains to this day one of the fundamental studies of Islamic legal theory, the Hungarian scholar Ignaz Goldziher traced the development of this school and the role that Ibn Hazm played in it.[2] Ibn Hazm transferred the rigid rules of interpretation in matters of dogma from the field of dogmatic theology to the field of juridical theology, or Moslem law. The school that he so developed paid a heavy price for its rigidity, by becoming extinct. There are no Zahirites today in the Moslem community.

[1] David Santillana, "Law and Society," in *Legacy of Islam*, Sir Thomas Arnold and Alfred Guillaume (London, 1931, reprinted 1949), pp. 305, 306-17.
[2] Ignaz Goldziher, *Die Zahiriten: Ihr Lehrsystem und ihre Geschichte. Beitrag zur Geschichte der Muhammedanischen Theologie* (Leipzig, 1884), esp. pp. 115 ff.

Vagueness in Political Concepts

Mr. Vatikiotis is right in attributing vagueness to definitions of political concepts in Islam, such as the term *state*, or what constitutes an Islamic state. It is true that such terms as *state, nation, fatherland*, or *motherland*, as used in the Middle East, are still in need of having their contents studied. But it should be pointed out that the West, in its own sphere, and in spite of its long experience in the field of political philosophy, shares with the East this attribute of vagueness. In his recent book on *Man and the State*, Jacques Maritain has the following to say about the difficulty of defining these terms and of the confusion surrounding them:

> There is no more thankless task [Maritain begins his first chapter] than trying rationally to distinguish and to circumscribe—in other words, trying to raise to a scientific or philosophical level—common notions that have arisen from the contingent practical needs of human history and are laden with social, cultural, and historical connotations as ambiguous as they are fertile, and which nevertheless envelop a core of intelligible meaning. Such concepts are nomadic, not fixed; they are shifting and fluid. Now they are used synonymously, now in opposition to one another. Everybody is the more at ease in using them as he does not know exactly what they mean. But as soon as one tries to define them and separate them from one another, hosts of problems and difficulties arise. . . .
>
> . . . . .
>
> . . . The confusion between, or the systematic identification of, *Nation* and *Political Society*—or *Political Society* and *State*— or *Nation* and *State*, has been a woe to modern history. A correct restatement of the three concepts in question is badly needed.[3]

Easy, or Hasty, Criticism

The Orientals look at the West, and especially at the United States today, as being materialistic. Some go so far as

[3] Jacques Maritain, *Man and the State* (Charles R. Walgreen Foundation Lectures; Chicago, 1951), pp. 1, 2.

to say that there is no difference between the United States and Communist Russia in this regard.[4] In other words, the West denies the spiritual in its deification of the material. This unqualified view is, of course, wrong. Some of us, who are Christians, may attribute it to a condition of near-sightedness on the part of the critic; others of us, who are still practicing Christians, may well wonder whether it may not be more accurately attributed to the West's own failure to make plain the spiritual values upon which it was nurtured. In any case, this same type of criticism is in turn indulged in by Western observers, who may not be excused even if they do so by mere force of habit. Orientals are then seen as "xeno-phobic," "emotional," "steeped in lethargy," and the like. Westerners themselves have their good share of these human qualities. A conscious effort needs to be made to avoid such easy criticism, which is of no value and which needs to be scrapped in order to clear the way for serious dialogue. For instance, if Orientals have only partial success in "fitting Western technology," rather than explaining it as due to re-sentment of the West, the explanation might conceivably lie in the thing itself and its relationship to their way of life. People of a long tradition are not easily brought to change their tried ways, ways from which they know what to expect. Progress, in any part of the world, against the strong current of tradition, is slow, even in a Western country such as ours.

The Ideal Islamic State

The ideal Islamic state is a theocracy; in the words of Pro-fessor Louis Massignon,[5] a lay and equalitarian theocracy. A theocracy, because it is a system of government that is founded on precepts revealed by God; a lay theocracy, because Islam has no sacerdotal system, no priests nor ministers as represen-tatives of God; equalitarian, because all Moslems are equal

[4] See, for instance, Sayed Kotb (tr. J. B. Hardie), Social Justice in Islam (Washington, D.C.: American Council of Learned Societies, 1953).
[5] La Passion d'Al-Hallāj (Paris, 1914–1922), p. 719.

in the eyes of God. Under this theocratic system, the Koran is the sole legislative power; the judicial power belongs to every believer who is qualified to apply its precepts because of his knowledge of the Koran; the executive power, both civil and canonical, belongs to God alone, and can be exercised by only one intermediary, one single leader, the caliph. The community of believers takes the oath of obedience to God (bay'a) in front of this delegate, who has neither legislative initiative nor judicial authority.

The Historical Reality

This is the *ideal* Moslem state. In actual practice, things happened differently. The history of Islam shows an incongruity between the ideal and actual fact. The very first challenge was that of the customs of the people encountered by Islam once it broke out from its confines in Arabia. These customs were incorporated in due course into the Islamic system. True, voices were continually calling for reform and the return to primitive Islam; but the orthodox, who remain to this day the overwhelming majority of Islam, always sought for a "middle road" acceptable to the majority, a middle road that shifted according to the needs of the times.

Islam Today

Today, the impact of the West presents Islam with new problems, new challenges. No one can deny the difficulties with which Islam is confronted. The problems are all the more difficult to deal with for having occurred with a speed that was breath-taking and for having taken hold of Islam at a moment when it had just come out of a long period of isolation. Islam was caught, as it were, out of practice in dealing with them. It is perhaps significant that the Wahhabites as well as the Salafiya, the modernists of Egypt, had to reach back across the centuries to the doctrines of a thirteenth-century jurist in order to find a solution for their problems.[6]

Even if Islam had no external troubles whatever, it would have the internal difficulty of reconciling its ideal system, which identifies the spiritual and the temporal with the day-by-day concrete realities of its existence on earth.

Louis Gardet[7] has, I believe, grasped the true elements of the problem facing Islam today. In describing the Moslem community as a universalism, he lists the particularisms with which it has had to deal; namely, the tribe, the race, and now, the nation and the economic groups.

In dealing with the tribe, he shows how the Moslem community was able to maintain a unity of command by calling upon the tribes to obey a higher principle of submission to God's will. Side by side with this unity, however, there remained the tribal *esprit de corps*, the *'asabiya*, founded on blood ties. This explains how the traditional hostilities of the tribes more than once triumphed over the unity and solidarity of the *umma*.

In dealing with the races, the Moslem community could tolerate only one racial particularism, the Arab one—and this on the historico-religious level, not on the politico-social level where only Islam counts, the rights of all believers being the same. This legitimate superiority, legitimate from a religious point of view, comes from the fact that the Koran is in the Arabic language, revealed to an Arab prophet; it is, in other words, because of the special religious mission of the Arab race. When the superiority was of an exclusive type, on the politico-social level, the other races of Islam demanded equality within the Moslem community. We have concrete examples of this in history, such as the Mawali and the Shu'-

---

[6] See Henri Laoust, *Essai sur les Doctrines Sociales et Politiques de Taki-D-Din Ahmad b. Taimiya* (Le Caire: Institut Français d'Archéologie Orientale, 1939), esp. pp. 506 ff.

[7] Louis Gardet, *La Cité Musulmane: Vie Sociale et Politique* (Etudes Musulmanes, No. 1; Paris, 1954). See the technical term "umma" in index, esp. pp. 208-221.

ubiya movements of the Umayyad and Abbasid periods respectively.

In the modern period, the Moslem community has come up against the particularism of the nation. The personal status of the Moslem had developed outside of the idea of nation in the modern sense. The political evolution from tribe to nation is an evolution of people from *jus sanguinis* to *jus soli,* or a fusion of both. This evolution has nothing to do with Islamic societies. The *umma* recognizes neither law. It will tolerate them, but on the condition of fusing them both into *jus religionis.*

Gardet sees two ways open to Islam on the question of nationalism. First, Islam may continue in the path of its present evolution, which will end in a total secularization of the state. Turkey is the example. The other way is for Islam to restore traditional values, making them more flexible and adaptable to the needs of the times, englobing the nations already constituted, not by transcending them—for the Moslem community is not supranational—but rather by grouping them under the obedience of a specifically Moslem principle, therefore political and religious.

The first way would bring about the triumph of secularism, and therefore of the pro-Western intellectuals, at the expense of the unity of the *umma.* The second way has difficulties familiar to Islam. The unifying propensity of its values on the temporal level would always run the risk of creating conflicts between the *umma* of the Prophet and the autonomy of each Moslem *umma,* or nation. But once the Moslem community is regiven a full politico-religious authority, it would naturally tend, if not to dissolve the intermediary unities, at least to group them in its own way.

Gardet then comes to the economic question, which is related to the political one. He asks if the Moslem world will be condemned to division into absolutely sovereign states, at a time when the age of nationalisms, enclosed within themselves, seems to be on the way out.

European nations, in order not to die out, are in search of a larger principle that could regroup their legitimate differences without destroying these differences. Will not Islam, constituted into independent nations conceived according to the modern Western type, run the risk of being definitively dissociated at the mercy of the great politico-economic groups? Since the unity proper to the Moslem world is politico-religious, will it be able, in face of the "great powers" of the world at present, powers with strong economic structures, to find a coherence sufficient really to constitute a temporal whole? Will it be capable, in order to bring this about, of assuming the heavy economic problems regarding which its own traditions still remain unarmed?

Division into national utilities has emphasized the economic weakness of each Moslem state. National independence has been bought at the price of economic subjection with regard to some power or other. And economic subjection is the worst of all, because it is not felt as much as the political kind.

The Moslem world has the roots of its religious unity in values that are properly political, terrestrial. If it intends to maintain its religious unity, therefore, it appears required, at the present time, to assure itself of a sufficiently strong economic basis.

The sentiment of solidarity of the Moslems is perhaps stronger now than it was in the Middle Ages. The Moslem world reverberates from one corner to the other, when troubled. This shows the universalism of Islam. Its divisions are not of the same fratricidal character as those that are found in the West. They should be understood against the background of the analysis just made.

The greatest hope of Islam is a unitary recasting that would respect legitimate local differences. It is too early to say whether the unifying elements of the umma could or could not change from being politico-religious, to becoming politico-economico-religious, thus constituting a sufficient factor of power and equilibrium. Perhaps the 1952 Egyptian agrarian reform is an indication for us that the problem has now been stated in its fullness.

This is, very briefly, the analysis given by Louis Gardet, an analysis that should be read in its entire text in the original. He points out the elements of the problem and the direction the solutions may take. His book, La Cité Musulmane (The Muslim State), deserves to be made available to the English-reading public; just as some years before it, another enlightening book by Professor H. A. R. Gibb was made available in French.[8] It is, incidentally, surprising to me that a work by Professor Wilfred Cantwell Smith,[9] just off the printing press, carries no mention whatever of Louis Gardet's work.

. Mr. Vatikiotis rightly points out what he refers to as a "dualism of values," Western-inspired and native—that the few are for modernization, while the masses are for the traditional view of society. But then he says that this paralyzes national development and minimizes chances for greater unity. I should think that in a democracy that yields to majority opinion, the voice of the masses would be heeded. It would then appear that what the Moslem people want is not a form of society that is Western-inspired, but one that is Moslem-Oriental-inspired. In concluding these brief comments, and with this in mind, I would like to pose the question with Gardet whether Islam would not do well to by-pass the "nation" in the modern sense of the word and find its unity in the Moslem community (umma), rethought according to its fundamental political and human values.

[8] H. A. R. Gibb, Modern Trends in Islam (Haskell Lectures in Comparative Religion, 1945; Chicago, 1947; French translation by Bernard Vernier, Paris, 1949).
[9] Islam in Modern History (Princeton, 1957).

Problem Studies

IX

The Cyprus Problem

CHRISTOPHER MONTAGUE WOODHOUSE

Director-General,
Royal Institute of International Affairs

THERE ARE SOME PROBLEMS in international relations that are, in the strict sense, insoluble, and I believe the Cyprus dispute to be one of them. For by a solution I mean a settlement that all parties to a dispute can be induced by mere reason to accept as giving them adequate satisfaction of their claims. And in the case of Cyprus I can see no settlement satisfactory to the Greeks that the Turks could be persuaded to accept by mere reason, and vice versa. This follows from the positions of principle that they both have taken up and from which neither will voluntarily depart: the Greeks, that they will accept no settlement that does not include the possibility of the eventual union of Cyprus with Greece (*enosis*); and the Turks, that they will accept none that does not exclude that possibility. What is true of the Greeks and Turks on the island is also true of the Greek and Turkish governments on their respective mainlands. Either government would almost certainly fall if it openly gave way on these points of principle in the foreseeable future. The existence of a British interest in the island also complicates and aggravates the problem, but the British interest did not create it, and the problem would still exist even if the British interest did not.

Why does this problem exist, and how did it come into existence? These are, respectively, questions in the field of international politics and of history. It will be convenient to

193

take the second question first, since in the Mediterranean area world history contains much of the answer to most problems. I shall not, however, as do some enthusiasts in this dispute, go back to the Mycenaean age or the Byzantine Empire to establish whether the Cypriotes are Greeks or whether Cyprus ever has been Greek. It all depends on how you define a Greek; and personally I define a Greek as someone who thinks he is a Greek and wishes to be one. By this definition, there are certainly over 400 thousand Greeks in Cyprus. But there are also nearly 100 thousand Turks, by a similar definition.

To establish the beginning of the problem, it is necessary to go back only to 1571, when the island was captured by the Ottoman Turks from the Venetian Republic (whose forces were commanded in the siege, according to Shakespeare, by Othello, the Moor of Venice). During the next two or three generations, the Turkish conquerors created the Cyprus problem in its modern form by pursuing the same policy that was being simultaneously pursued by the British in Ireland, where it was called "Plantation"—that is, the introduction of a large nonnative population with a different language and religion to establish and maintain an ascendancy over the conquered inhabitants. Thus for the first time, just over three and a half centuries ago, a Turkish-speaking, Moslem minority originating from Anatolia was planted in Cyprus alongside a Greek-speaking, Orthodox majority who considered themselves the kin of the equally subjugated inhabitants of the Greek mainland.

This situation continued substantially unaltered for three hundred years, though there was a momentary flurry of expectation during the Napoleonic wars that either the French or the British would occupy the island. (Rather ironically, in view of later events, the British decided not to do so in 1814, chiefly because Cyprus proved to have no deep-water harbors and was therefore judged unsuitable for naval operations.) The first change in status came in 1878, when the British government entered into a secret bilateral arrangement with the Ottoman Sultan, immediately before the Congress of Berlin, by which the island was to be occupied and administered (but not annexed) by Great Britain, in exchange (among other conditions) for guarantees of the Ottoman Empire's security against Russia. Cyprus remained under titular Ottoman sovereignty for another thirty-six years, and the notorious "tribute" continued to be collected by the British government on the Sultan's behalf (though it went in fact not to the Sultan, but to the bondholders of the Ottoman debt in western Europe, on which the Sultan had defaulted). This "tribute" even continued to be collected up to 1927, long after the next change of the island's status, which came in November, 1914, when Great Britain annexed the island by Order in Council after Turkey had entered World War I on the side of Germany; this annexation was recognized by Turkey in the Treaty of Lausanne in 1923, a treaty to which Greece was also a party. The last change up to date came in 1925, when the island was constituted a crown colony, which is still its juridical status. It was governed under a limited constitution up to 1931, when serious violence broke out and the constitution was suspended. The constitution has not yet been restored, though not for want of trying on the part of the British government since World War II.

Meanwhile, however, the Greeks of the European mainland had achieved independence as a result of the national revolt that began in 1821 and culminated in the great naval battle of Navarino in 1827. Ever since that date, and especially since the recognition of the independent kingdom of Greece in May, 1832, the Greeks have consistently pursued a policy of expansion designed to bring all the territories inhabited mainly by Greeks into their national boundaries. The extreme form of this policy was known as the Great Idea (Megáli Idéa) and aimed at re-establishing the Greek capital at Constantinople. It is noteworthy that when a new dynasty came to the Greek throne in 1864, the King was called not King of Greece, but King of the Hellenes, implying that all the Greeks everywhere were destined to become his subjects; and when his first son was born, he was christened Constantine by popular demand, with the implication that he would one day rule in the capital of Constantinople. This Great Idea at one time

nearly came about; and although no reasonable Greek clings
to it today, there are still quite a lot of unreasonable Greeks.
For them at least the island of Cyprus represents on many
grounds the minimum territorial claim to which they have a
natural right.

What are the grounds of this claim? Many of them have
been suggested already, but it will be convenient here to
draw them together. First, there is the claim of population.
No census has been held in Cyprus since 1946, but an official
estimate at the end of 1955 gave a total population of about
524 thousand, in the following proportions: Greeks, about
80 per cent; Turks, nearly 18 per cent; others, 2 per cent. It
is fair to point out that the Greek population has greatly increased, both proportionately and absolutely, under British
rule since 1878, as a result of good administration and unrestricted immigration from Greece; it is fair, but it is also, from
the Greek point of view, irrelevant. The large predominance
of the Greek population is, of course, the basis for the Greek
claim to self-determination for the island. Self-determination
is different from enosis, since union with Greece is only one
of the forms that self-determination might theoretically take;
enosis should be compared to Anschluss rather than to independence. But there can be little doubt (as was shown by an
unofficial plebiscite in 1950) that if self-determination were
to be settled by a simple popular referendum, enosis would
in fact be the outcome.

Second, there is language, and third, there is religion. The
Greeks of Cyprus speak a language that is recognizably distinct from mainland Greek, but no more so than the Cretan
or the Corfiote dialect. And they all belong, virtually without
exception, to the Greek Orthodox Church, which has always
played a powerful role in the political leadership of the
Greeks and was largely responsible for the fact that Greece
ever became an independent country at all. It is worth noting
that the title of ethnárkhis, or leader of the nation, which is
now applied to the Cypriote Archbishop Makarios, was in-
vented by the Ottoman Turks as a device for establishing control over their Greek subjects. The first ethnárkhis was the

Patriarch of Constantinople in 1453, and he was designated as such by the Sultan immediately after the Ottoman conquest of the city.

Fourth, there is tradition. This is a difficult thing to define, but quite easy to illustrate. When the Greek national rising began in 1821, many Cypriotes also rose in revolt against the Turks, and some escaped from the island to fight on the mainland. Hundreds, if not thousands, were executed as rebels, and among them were a number of priests, including the then Archbishop of the island. In 1828 a Cypriote delegation demanded the island's inclusion in the Greek state that was about to be formed. When the British arrived in 1878, they were greeted with appeals for enosis, or union with Greece, from the first day. The claim was admitted to be understandable, if not more, by no less authorities than Gladstone in 1897, Churchill in 1907, and Lloyd George in 1919. Moreover, the island was actually offered to the Greeks in October, 1915, on the condition of Greece's entry into World War I on the British side; but, unfortunately for the Greeks, their government hesitated and the offer was withdrawn.

Fifth, and connected with the argument from tradition, there is the argument from history. I have mentioned the Greek policy of expansion to incorporate Greek-inhabited territories since 1832. It is important to appreciate that this urge to expand has been not only consistent, but generally successful; and there has not yet passed a single full generation since 1832 during which the boundaries of Greece have remained unaltered. The principal advances have been the acquisition of the Ionian Islands from Great Britain in 1863; Thessaly from Turkey in 1881; Macedonia, Epirus, and Crete, with other islands, from Turkey again in 1913; western Thrace from Bulgaria in 1920; and the Dodecanese Islands from Italy in 1947.

The process has only broken down and failed in one or the other of two circumstances. The first has been when Greece has gone to war in support of her claims, and lost the war, as she did over Thessaly in 1854, over Epirus and Crete in 1897, and over eastern Thrace and Smyrna in 1919–1923. The

second case has been when the power already in occupation
of the territory claimed by Greece has set about systematically
annihilating or de-Hellenizing the Greek population, as
Turkey, Bulgaria, and Albania have done at various dates.
Presumably neither of these circumstances is likely to occur
under British rule in Cyprus. The result is that most Greeks
believe that their further claims, of which Cyprus is the only
active one, but not the only possible one, are not merely just
but are also, in the long run, bound to succeed if they per-
severe. History supports this view, provided the Greeks avoid
catastrophic mistakes; but this has not always prevented them
from making catastrophic mistakes.

Finally, and almost parenthetically, there are certain special
factors about the particular urgency and violence of the claim
to enosis today. The claim has been more or less active since
1878 and seldom dormant; but seldom, too, has it been so
vigorous as in the last five years. There are several contributory
reasons why this is so. It is due partly to the fact that, since
the Truman Doctrine in 1947, Greece is no longer so dependent on British good will for her survival; partly to the general
decline of the British position in the Middle East, coupled
especially with the decision to transfer general headquarters
from the Suez Canal zone to Cyprus in 1954; partly to the
grave economic situation in Greece, from which the agitation
for enosis has served to distract public attention; partly to the
personal antipathy between Sir Anthony Eden and Field-
Marshal Papagos, the British and Greek protagonists at a
crucial period; partly to Communist agitation; and partly to
the conjunction in the same generation of two dynamic
Cypriote leaders, Archbishop Makarios and Colonel Grivas.
But all these factors, of course, constitute no part of the
Greek case over Cyprus. They merely happen to exacerbate
it at the present time.

It will be seen that the Greek case over Cyprus is predominantly emotional rather than rational. In the Turkish
case the balance of reason and emotion is reversed. For a long
time nothing was heard of the Turkish case, for the simple
reason that the Turks had the strongest of all cases—that

there was no case to answer. They argued, when they argued at all, that the sovereignty of Cyprus had been settled by the Treaty of Lausanne, which Turkey would never have signed if there had been the least hint that Great Britain might ever surrender that sovereignty, and all that was necessary, therefore, was to respect the treaty. But purely as a question of international law, this case proved inadequate, once the British government showed the first sign of willingness to consider a change of sovereignty. For, in fact, the Treaty of Lausanne by no means precludes Great Britain from ceding Cyprus to Greece or to anyone else. On the contrary, that treaty is the sole and sufficient basis of Great Britain's right to dispose of the island in any way she wishes. In recent years the Turks therefore have found themselves obliged to defend the status quo on other grounds or to demand the partition of Cyprus or its retrocession to themselves.

Many grounds have been adduced by the Turks. Some of their grounds need not seriously detain us, and of these I will just mention three. First, there is the argument from history, that Cyprus was Turkish for three hundred years and has never been Greek. This is a contention that merely rests on definitions of words, and these would not be generally accepted. Second, there is the political argument that the Greek Cypriotes are predominantly Communist-inclined, and therefore the cession of the island to Greece would help to promote the cause of international communism. But I think myself that the charge is absurd, and the inference is a *non sequitur*. Third, there is the argument that Cyprus is geographically an extension of the Turkish mainland, being about forty miles from Turkey and over six hundred from Greece. This argument could have been (but was not) even more forcibly used to oppose the cession of the Dodecanese Islands to Greece in 1947 and could indeed be very widely extended —for instance, to support a French claim to the Channel Islands or an American claim to the Bahamas from Great Britain. None of the above arguments is, I think, likely to be taken very seriously today.

It is better to concentrate on the serious and substantial

elements in the Turkish case. First, there is the real Turkish
fear on behalf of its national minority in Cyprus, despite all
the Greek offers of guarantees and claims of fair treatment
to minorities elsewhere. The fear is a fact and has helped to
promote strong Turkish support for the seemingly desperate
expedient of partitioning the island if the British withdraw.
Second, there is the fear of the force of precedent. Cyprus is
not the last possible Greek territorial claim at Turkey's expense, and a similar case could be made out on nationalist
grounds for the cession to Greece of the islands of Imbros
and Tenedos, which occupy a strategically vital position
covering the Dardanelles. And this leads to the third, and
even more vital, strategic argument, that Cyprus in unfriendly
hands would be a threat to the security of Turkey's southern
coast. The fact that Turkey already has close neighbors to
the north, east, and west whom she looks upon as at least
potentially hostile is not in Turkish eyes a very good reason
for putting up with another one to the south as well.

All these Turkish arguments are also British arguments
against enosis. This is so not only because Great Britain feels
a moral obligation to safeguard Turkish interests, but also
because Great Britain has an interest of her own in Cyprus.
The British case has been conducted and presented in the
last few years in a way that has done much to obscure the
fact that there really is a British case; but there is, and it is
a case that also vitally concerns the free world as a whole.
Many irrelevancies have been officially put forward as if they
formed part of the British case when in fact they do not, and
these I shall mention only briefly in order to identify and dis-
miss them. They may be true, but they are not the reasons
why the British have sought to retain Cyprus.

First, there is the economic argument that the Cypriotes are
much better off under the British flag than they would be
under the Greek flag. This is no doubt true, but perfectly
irrelevant to the Greeks, who would reply that what they
want is not good government, but Greek government. (Also,
of course, they would not admit that these are two different
things.) Second, there is the argument that the British must

stay in Cyprus to prevent communal trouble between Greeks and Turks. To this the Greeks would reply that communal trouble arises solely from the British policy, which they believe to be deliberate, of playing off the one community against the other. Third, there is the danger of political instability being exploited by the Communists, either in Cyprus or in Greece. Here the reply would be that if the danger of communism seriously existed, Greeks are the only people who could effectively combat it and the only real danger to the stability of political democracy in Greece arises directly from British failure to solve the Cyprus problem. The point in all these cases is that they are not the real reasons why the British have sought to hold on to Cyprus; they are simply excuses, in which few responsible people seriously believe.

The real reasons, like those of the Turks, are almost wholly bound up with defense. Like those of the Turks again, they are not limited to the context of NATO, since both Great Britain and Turkey have commitments in the Middle East (for instance, under the Baghdad Pact) that they do not share with either NATO or Greece. And there are other British interests that are also international interests common to all the free world, but in which Greece shares only to a relatively small degree—for instance, oil on the Persian Gulf and free traffic through the Suez Canal. These are the reasons why, for instance, a base on Cyprus under Greek sovereignty would be inadequate for British purposes. The operation against Egypt in November, 1956, is a case in point, where the presence of a large Greek minority in Egypt might have made it exceedingly difficult for the Greek government to facilitate a British operation from a Greek base.

This question of strategic interest is extremely intricate and cannot be discussed briefly. But it is worth summarizing the three phases of British interest in Cyprus under this aspect: first, the period from 1878 to 1954, when Cyprus played virtually no strategic role at all, despite the circumstances of its original occupation and despite two world wars fought in the Mediterranean; second, the period from 1954 to 1956, after the British decision to withdraw from the Suez Canal

zone, when the island was deemed essential for the maintenance of British interests, not so much in the event of a
major war with the Soviet Union as in the event of local upheaval within the Middle East; and third, the period beginning early this year, after the Anglo-French attack on Egypt,
since which time the British interest in the island has come to
be regarded as having widened into the concept of a NATO
interest. On these developments of strategic opinion, I will
comment only by reminding you that in the rather similar
case of the Ionian Islands in the last century, the British government argued as late as May, 1861, that British control
over them was indispensable to the peace of the Mediterranean, exactly eighteen months before deciding to cede them
to Greece.

At present, however, in the case of Cyprus, considerations
of defense are still paramount. And there is another consideration related to defense, which may be designated, I hope
without prejudice, as old-fashioned imperialism. Without
going into the ethics of the question, it is still important to
bear in mind that Great Britain remains the center of an
empire and depends both for her security and for her prosperity on the continuation of her imperial connections. The
British Empire was created partly for trade, to enable us to
survive, and partly for defense, to protect our trade. Cyprus
belongs to the category of possessions that were acquired in
order to protect our trade routes, which means that it has
no economic value in itself. It is therefore important as a
link in a chain rather than for its own sake. The British have
seen many such links broken since World War II, and they
are beginning to get fed up with the process.

Where, the British ask themselves, is it going to end? If
Cyprus goes the way of the rest, next it will be Gibraltar or
Aden or Hong Kong; and finally the British Empire will be
reduced to nothing but Malta, with its paradoxical demand
for *enosis* with Great Britain. This consideration may seem
absurd and obsolete to the Greeks, as also to most Americans;
but it is nevertheless a real factor in the formation of British
public opinion and therefore should not be ignored. And it

should not be forgotten that, although American public opinion is basically anticolonial and although the pro-Greek lobby is relatively very strong in the U.S.A., both the Department of State and the Pentagon at present—I repeat, at present—regard Turkey as a more reliable ally than Greece and are therefore inclined to prefer that Great Britain should retain Cyprus rather than cede the island to Greece. Moreover, the Pentagon, with the case of Okinawa in mind, is likely to endorse the British military view, as long as that view is sustained by the British defense authorities, that on a small island the maintenance of an effective base requires complete control of the whole island.

Parenthetically, it is possible, though not yet certain, that a good deal of the above argument should be put in the past rather than the present tense—in other words, that the strategic and imperial bases of the British case are already becoming, or have become, obsolete and that this is already recognized by the British authorities. This seems to me inevitable in the long run, and there have been recent hints that it is already so. In that case there would remain only two reasons for not giving effect to this recognition by withdrawing from Cyprus at once. One is the possibility that the island may still be useful to NATO; the other is the danger of communal violence between Greeks and Turks, and even of war between Greece and Turkey. There is a bitter irony for the Greeks in these two reasons. For if Cyprus had been ceded to Greece ten years ago, NATO could certainly have had whatever use it wanted of the island today; and ten years ago the danger of Greco-Turkish conflict over it did not exist, as witness the peaceful facility with which Rhodes, another Greek island with a Turkish minority and one much nearer to the Turkish coast than Cyprus, was ceded to Greece by Italy in 1947. But be all this as it may—and none of it, like other hypothetical propositions about the past, is indisputable —the essential point I am trying to make remains unaffected. For the arguments that I have been elaborating were the bases of the British case for retaining Cyprus, whether or not they remain valid today. And whatever judgment may be passed upon them, these are, as a matter of history, the reasons why the Cyprus problem has developed into the deeply painful and tragic form in which we face it now.

I have now outlined as best I can the thinking of those principally concerned on the subject of Cyprus. It is time to summarize and conclude. I do not think much is to be gained by recapitulating recent history in detail: the three successive attempts by the British government, in 1948, 1954, and 1956, to re-establish constitutional government; the outbreak of violence in 1955; the three Greek appeals to the United Nations between 1954 and 1957; the British attempt to negotiate first with the Greek and Turkish governments and then with the politico-religious leader of the Greek Cypriotes, Archbishop Makarios; the deportation of the Archbishop to the Seychelles in 1956 and his liberation in 1957; the innumerable attempts to find a form for words defining the future of Cyprus in a way satisfactory to all parties. All this points to only one conclusion: the British government cannot solve the problem because, in the normal sense of the word *solution*, the problem is insoluble; and this will remain so as long as the Greeks and the Turks stand fast on logically irreconcilable principles. But clearly this deadlock cannot last forever. What, then, is likely to be the eventual outcome?

Failing a total transformation of the situation in the Near and Middle East by war or revolution, I myself can see no eventual outcome that does not lead, in one way or another, to the achievement of the Greek claim to *enosis*. But I must emphasize that this is not something I recommend. I recommend nothing, since it is not, in my view, the function of non-responsible students of international affairs to recommend, but only to observe and to record. However, you have a right to expect at least a forecast. I draw my conclusion from the fact that the British government, which three years ago denied that there was any Cyprus problem, has since early 1956 explicitly conceded the principle of self-determination for the island, reserving only the questions of method and timing. This means that Great Britain is willing at some unspecified future date to surrender sovereignty over the island. So the question arises, to whom?

At present there are in view six distinct possibilities, of unequal probability: to the United Nations; to NATO; to Greece; to Turkey; to the Cypriotes as an independent people; or by separate self-determination, which means partition of Cyprus into a Greek and a Turkish unit. Without elaborating reasons, I regard retrocession to Turkey as inconceivable, and partition, more hesitantly, as improbable, although the latter course has recently been officially favored both in Great Britain and in Turkey. An independent Cyprus is hardly practicable: outside the British Commonwealth it would not be viable, and the events of the last two years have made independence within the Commonwealth virtually unimaginable, especially since there is, unfortunately, no such thing as the Cypriote people—there are only Greek Cypriotes and Turkish Cypriotes. Independence in some form could, of course, be conceded on paper, but I doubt whether it would be real, and if real, I doubt whether it could last. (It should be emphasized, too, that independence is the one thing that no one at all in Cyprus has ever asked for.) Some form of NATO solution would be welcome to Great Britain, but that is resolutely opposed by Greece and is therefore unlikely to be acceptable to NATO. A surrender of sovereignty to United Nations trusteeship would, I think, only be an intermediate step towards cession to Greece. In the long run— which may be a very long run indeed—I consider that cession to Greece is the only possible outcome, though it will perhaps only be achieved by a very determined and very expensive American intervention.

It could, however, be quite easily achieved in the fairly short run, if the Greeks were to show a little wisdom. If the Greeks were to accept the constitution devised by Lord Radcliffe in 1956 (or any other constitution whatever, however limited and restrictive) without any explicit reference to self-determination, then I believe that nothing could prevent them from achieving *enosis* within a decade. Even this would not be a solution in the normal sense, because it would be much resented by the Turks, but it would be possible for the Greeks to achieve it, if they were clever, in a way that the Turks would find very hard indeed to resist. The ground for this contention lies in the history of previous cases (such as the Ionian Islands and Crete) in which *enosis* was achieved despite the imposition of constitutions designed to make it impossible.

I greatly fear, however, that things have now gone past the possibility of wisdom on the part of either the Greeks or the Turks. In the short run, therefore, only an imposed settlement is possible. And since, if the British alone sought to impose a settlement, the dissatisfied party would certainly appeal to the U.S.A. against it, I can see no authority ultimately capable of imposing it except the United States government. What form it might take I will not presume to predict, but I still do not see any form that it could take in the short run that would not lead in the long run to the achievement of *enosis*. Whether the Greeks or the Cypriotes will be happy when they have it is another question, the answer to which I will not try to anticipate.

Commentary

A. J. MEYER
Associate Director, Center for
Middle Eastern Studies, Harvard University

AS MR. WOODHOUSE has made admirably clear, Cyprus today is a microcosm of the incredible snarl of recent events in the Middle East and of the deteriorating position of the Western powers. He has likewise enunciated the basic irony of it all—the descendents of Aristotle and Aphrodite caught in an arrangement starkly devoid of both reason and love.

Few could quarrel with Mr. Woodhouse's analysis of the political and strategic problems or with his forecast. For better or worse, Cyprus seems destined ultimately for some form of Greek stewardship. With equal assurance, one may forecast an interlude of temporary rule quite different from today's military government. Hopefully the interlude will bring more normal life to the island, and Cypriotes will select their destiny in reasonable tranquillity.

That the West has a political stake in Cyprus—link in the chain of the British Empire, listening post in the eastern Mediterranean, police station for mainland uprisings, guard post for the jugular vein of Europe's Far East trade and oil supplies—goes without saying. Even though the Suez landings (which had, after all, to be launched from Malta due to the lack of port facilities in Cyprus) reportedly recast British military thinking, this little island is still highly important to the countries of the Western alliance. This importance will certainly increase, during the next decade at least, with the rise of what Charles Issawi has recently termed "the emerging Arab monopoly" of eastern Mediterranean trade routes.[1]

Important, in turn, to politics on Cyprus is its economy. In what follows, I shall treat the island's productive plant and discuss the economic implications of various settlements under consideration. While Cypriotes today, in the heat of *enosis*, would undeniably choose rule by Greece rather than an adequate currency system run by what they deem a benevolent old British nanny, times may change. Urban unemployment and poverty have a way of shaping political decisions, and once political settlement is reached, more pernicious difficulties could arise.

Disregarding J. M. Keynes' warning to economists that "in the long run we are all dead anyhow," I shall begin by predicting a long-run decline for the Cyprus economy, with the downward toboggan reaching top speed five to seven years from now. International disaster, military-base construction, soldier pay, and soaring world copper prices have for two

[1] Charles Issawi, "Crusades and Current Crises in the Near East: A Historical Parallel," *International Affairs*, XXXIII (1957), 279.

decades pulled the Cypriotes' living standards to unnaturally high levels. Major slashes in income seem virtually inevitable.

The island's fundamental economic problem is that of a healthy, rapidly expanding population (which at present rates will exceed one million by the year 2000) within a limited land area and with all available agricultural land already under cultivation. The island's other resources—seasonal rainfall that varies widely, a porous rock formation that deposits most of the rainfall in the sea, dwindling copper reserves, and strategic location—ameliorate, but do not eliminate, the demographic pressure.

Half the population lives from agriculture and is slave to Cypriote inheritance and farming practices. Disinterested in primogeniture, Moslem and Christian farmers alike divide land in varying degree among surviving heirs. Resultant over-fragmentation has reduced holdings to an average of 15 acres per farm family, half of which lies fallow each year. The culti-vated 7½ acres join with a pegged price and customary fruit- and vegetable-growing to provide a cash income to rural Cypriotes of $60 to $70 yearly. (He realizes another $30 to $40 from sources described below.) The average farmer, meanwhile, spends half his workday traveling between his fragmented plots, which average 12½ per acre holding. The "lot viable" on Cyprus is estimated by crown colony agricul-tural experts to be 23 acres, and the point of no return has long since passed. Large concentrated holdings are virtually unknown in Cyprus.

The average Cypriote farmer spends an estimated quarter of his waking hours in productive work, another quarter in the village coffee house, and half his time traveling from plot to plot. His earned income of slightly over $100 per capita yearly permits no surplus for investment in improving his land. As an agricultural producer he generates neither the raw materials for industrialization nor the demand for manufactured products.

Population pressure did not, thanks to impure water and the malaria mosquito, reach intolerable proportions until about 1938. Then, thanks to the influx of British troops, base expansion, wartime shortages of goods, and, in the postwar years, soaring world copper prices, the island's economy improved immeasurably despite the basic imbalance.

For the past two decades, rural Cyprus has exported its surplus population to the island's six district towns, which in turn have burgeoned under the stimulus of war-induced prosperity. British-trained technicians eliminated the malaria mosquito, dug clean wells, and installed an excellent highway grid. Tourism gained momentum until it became a major foreign-exchange earner. Small-scale industrial development began.

Industry has increased phenomenally on Cyprus since 1938. From a virtual handful of establishments applying machinery to the productive process—mostly mines, and a few small bottling works and wineries—industry has grown until last year's census listed thirteen thousand establishments employing fifty thousand people, almost 20 per cent of the island's labor force. The district towns are dotted with small factories, making hard and soft drinks, clothing, housewares, and the like. Statistically the record is impressive.

Yet the new industrial census likewise reveals definite soft spots. It shows, for example, that really efficient, high-productivity output is confined to the copper mines; that of the 50,000 workers, 13,500 are working proprietors; and that only half of the "industrial" labor force works in plants employing more than ten workers. In view of low productivity, levels of investment, and purchasing power in rural Cyprus, the local market probably cannot expand much further. Since 1953, there has been a steady decline in investment in industry.

The island's copper mines are the one industry that is really productive on modern standards. Owned by American, British, and Greek interests, these export yearly to Europe more than $25 million worth of copper concentrates and pyrites and iron pyrites. The mines are models of safety, cleanliness, and efficiency, and the six thousand workers enjoy high wages and advanced programs for social security. The almost $10 million paid in tax-royalty each year by the mining industry pays more than a third of the crown-colony operating budget. Unfortunately, the copper mines are an island within an island as far as the Cyprus economy is concerned. Highly specialized and capital-intensive, the mining operations require tools and machinery that with few exceptions can come only from abroad. Integration of the industry into the local economy is virtually impossible, except via the medium of crown-colony expenditures (using tax money paid by the mining companies) and employee wage bills, which have undoubtedly stimulated some local small-scale industry. Local importers and entrepreneurs likewise do well, serving as middlemen for a large part of the mines' external purchasing.

Entrepreneurship is often said to be short in Cyprus. The island's bankers maintain that their problem is not shortage of funds to loan, but rather a shortage of businessmen with bankable projects. American and British visitors never tire of pointing to the lack of capital-intensive whirring factories as symbolizing an incompetent entrepreneurial class.

The Cyprus businessman, on the other hand, faces real obstacles when he tries to turn Nicosia and Larnaca into Middle Eastern versions of Manchester and Liverpool. Consumer preference is against him; British goods are still preferred to Cyprus-made items of similar price and quality. Most manufacturers are traders only vaguely accustomed to advanced production techniques. Family loyalties load payrolls with brothers and cousins rather than with competent, paid managers. The mass of Cypriotes possess meager purchasing power. A share of the east-west banking and entrepot trade, which makes nearby Lebanon what it is today, is denied the Cypriote by inadequate and expensive port facilities and sterling-area currency restrictions.

The island has done well from tourism during the postwar decade and before the recent troubles earned about $6 million yearly from visitors who came to summer on Mount Troodos, visit the setting for Othello in Famagusta, or savor life on the beaches of an island famous for having given the world such unlike products as the goddess of love and copper ore.

Cyprus has also done extremely well from two decades of transfusions of United Kingdom military funds. Increasing steadily since 1940, these topped $18 million in 1954 and $27 million in 1955, for example. Devoted 50 per cent to local works expenditure, 25 per cent to soldier pay, and the remainder to buying direct services and employing Cypriote workers, these funds account indirectly for much of the island's employment and prosperity.

The Cyprus economy takes shape, therefore, as one absorbing each year about $50 million annually from abroad in the shape of United Kingdom expenditures, tax-royalty from copper exports, tourism, and mining wage bills. Under this stimulus—$100 per year per Cypriote—an impressive set of national income figures emerge. Secretariat economists estimate the per capita income at about $300 per year—higher than Turkey's, about equal to that of Greece and Lebanon, and just under Israel's.

Why, then, the gloomy prediction made earlier in this essay? By Mediterranean standards the Cypriote is well off, unemployment is not yet *really* a problem, and, for reasons already stated, the West has a real stake to maintain on the island. On the surface, the complacency on the subject often attributed to the Colonial Office would seem understandable.

But complacency vanishes as one contemplates future economic change on the island. Proved copper reserves are dwindling (as are prices, from 50¢ to 30¢ a pound in less than eighteen months), and within a decade the island could face drastically lowered tax-royalty income. The airbase construction program has about run its course, and military outlays will, according to present plan, be halved in the very near future. As Britain reshapes her post-Suez occupation military thinking about Cyprus, the funds for Cyprus could drop even lower. Tourism has long since dropped to nothing as a foreign-exchange earner. Conceivably, in five years the island's $50 million yearly from the West could become $25 million, or even less. The resultant impact on employment and poverty and hence on political action could be startling.

It seems doubtful indeed, even to this optimistic American,

that the Cyprus economy has sufficient vigor to generate self-sustaining growth without the stimulus of capital transfers from military sources and copper exports. Hope lies in the maintenance of the island's outside income and in the linking of this financial support to a political settlement. The interim governing arrangement, therefore, becomes the crucial launching platform for Cyprus' ultimate political destiny.

A look at the economic implications of the various settlements under discussion is illustrative. I shall begin with the least attractive proposals and move on to those offering more hope.

The most hopeless arrangement of all is that involving partition of the island, with Greece and Turkey assuming stewardship of the two dominant national groups. As with partition schemes elsewhere in the world, problems of displacement and resettlement, trade, currency, use of ports, and policing of partition boundaries would pose difficulties that could easily make Cyprus a permanent trouble spot, another link in the dreary chain of strife induced by partition. Separation conceivably could keep Greco-Turkish relations elsewhere in a state of constant tension, and the island could rival the Israeli-Arab state boundaries as a focal point for trouble. From an economic point of view, partition would represent the essence of fatuity.

Slightly, but only slightly, better would be establishment now of Greek or Turkish rule over the island. Both nations are beset with severe economic difficulties that make them sorely dependent upon outside economic assistance. For either to succor Cyprus economically seems unreasonable indeed. Neither nation, moreover, has demonstrated particular skill as an administrator of island possessions. Should Greece acquire Cyprus, Turkish Cypriotes would be restive, perhaps mutinous. Should Turkey get the island, Greek and Armenian Cypriotes would feel the same.

Next on the list of undesirable alternatives would be United Nations trusteeship, an arrangement with relatively little to recommend it. Ill-equipped to serve as sovereign authority, maker of laws, collector of taxes, and administrator of currency, the United Nations could only be useful for the briefest of interim periods—and then only as a last resort. One discernible benefit to be gained from United Nations stewardship would be a focusing of United Nations technical assistance resources on the island's economic and social problems.

Better than any of the foregoing, but nevertheless highly imperfect, would be continuation of British rule during an interim period leading to self-determination. As Mr. Woodhouse has made clear, British public opinion may well dictate such a stand by Her Majesty's government. In such an instance, Cypriote resistance would probably intensify. The wounded *amour propre* of a Mediterranean people can no more be discounted than can the renowned stubbornness of the British. And economic conditions could well deteriorate with Britain's changing strategic outlook toward Cyprus, 30¢-a-pound copper, and the United Kingdom's incapacity to finance an American-type aid program.

To my mind the best guarantee of stability for Cyprus—and the only one that would mollify Cypriotes sufficiently to promote a calm decision at the time of self-determination—would be some form of NATO trusteeship. Admittedly a difficult bargain to make, such an arrangement could afford Greece a face-saving say in Cyprus matters, should placate Turkey (which would view British withdrawal with real misgivings), and should make possible furtherance of Anglo-American strategic aims in the eastern Mediterranean. Cyprus, thereby, while acquiring Greek and Turkish participation in its rule, could likewise maintain the pipeline to the dollar and sterling areas upon which its survival depends.

A NATO trusteeship, with accompanying dollar and sterling credits, could make possible a comprehensive economic development scheme—via stimulated economic measures such as those in Puerto Rico and Ghana, for example—which might check the incipient disaster not far off. A development commission with a broad investment program could not guarantee economic solvency for the island, but it at least could make a good try. And the try is clearly in the West's interests.

In summary, I agree with Mr. Woodhouse that chances seem

good for Cyprus ultimately to end as a Greek island. Even
then, and in the interim, the Atlantic alliance needs the base
as a listening post and springboard for police action in the
Middle East, and it is of crucial importance that an interim
arrangement be made that will afford domestic tranquillity in
Cyprus and promote union among NATO partners. To me,
nothing short of NATO rule could do this, and a comprehensive economic development scheme must provide mortar
for the structure. Without that amalgam, given current trends,
any political settlement is foreordained to failure.

X

Israel

LINCOLN B. HALE
Foreign Policy Association

WHAT A COMPLEX TASK is an evaluation of Israel. Here is
a modern nation being built on a tradition two thousand to
three thousand years old, the seed bed from which democracy
came. The bearded exponent of the old with flowing fore-
lock worships, works, and creates alongside his clean-shaven
modern colleague. At the same time, fourth- and fifth-genera-
tion Sabras, Jews born in Palestine, seek to integrate Western
and Oriental immigrants as Israelis. It is a little country, the
size of New Jersey, yet, in variation of climate and geography,
Galilee of the north is suggestive of New England, and the
Beersheba region of the south, of Arizona. It is a nation challenged and unwanted by its neighbors, yet it has a host of
non-Jewish and Jewish friends from the United States to
Burma. Here merchants and professional men have become
farmers and fighters. Its economy is precarious, yet, year by
year, the money has been found to balance a budget and permit development to proceed at a rapid pace. Western in
outlook, it sits like an island in a curious contradiction to the
prevalent social patterns of its geographical setting. It is a
nation beset with controversy as it seeks its place among the
nations of the world and strives to develop its national life.
What are its aspirations? What are its achievements? What
can be its future?

To understand the emotional drive that has propelled Jews
toward Palestine in the last seventy years, one must appreciate
the uplifted glass at the conclusion of the annual Passover

services as through the centuries the words have been spoken: "Next year in Jerusalem." In another strand, the pogroms and the persecutions of the late nineteenth century led Theodor Herzl and other Jewish leaders to the conclusion that the only solution for this problem would be the establishment of a homeland, a place where Jews from around the world would be welcomed. Herzl, although predisposed toward Palestine, had also advocated another location. However, as the several early Zionist congresses resolved the issue, the centuries-long identification with Jerusalem asserted itself, and the movement was under way to re-establish Jews in the Holy Land.

There is no need to trace the history of this movement whereby doctors, teachers, lawyers, and others purchased land as part of the Zionist movement and established co-operative and collectivist villages, seeking to create the agricultural society they considered basic to the creation of a homeland. The movement developed slowly in the first quarter of the twentieth century. The intrusion of Western ideas into the Arab Eastern Oriental scheme of life quickly drew opposition. This was strengthened by the Arab nations' judgment that the political decisions following World War I were to give them preferential treatment. Great Britain, with responsibility for the mandate in Palestine, was faced with increasing tension and strife. The economic improvement resulting from mandate activity and the developing Jewish community contributed to an improvement in the standard of living and set in motion a limited Arab immigration as workers were attracted from the neighboring areas.

Pressure for immigration to Palestine steadily mounted as the implication of Hitler's Aryan policy became clear. Great Britain, caught in the middle of a most difficult conflict, and herself an object of attack by some Jewish groups, was unable to cope with the situation. Finally she turned back the mandate to the United Nations. As a solution, the United Nations proposed separate Arab and Jewish states joined in an economic union. This proved unsuccessful, even though approved by a formal United Nations resolution.

As this process of development and settlement proceeded,

Arab resistance mounted. The new society being created in their midst was a threat to their traditions and culture. Their previous contacts with the West had made them wary. They were becoming increasingly resentful of colonialism. The stirring of nationalism added to the emotional, psychological reaction to this Western, indeed foreign, organism coming into existence at the heart of their world. On the day Great Britain left Palestine in May, 1948, the state of Israel was born amid chaos, terrorism, and war. The events of 1948 are still unclear. Claims and counterclaims are made by the Jews and Arabs. The Jewish position emphasized both the failure of the Arabs to implement immediately the United Nations partition plan and the combined attack by the armies of the neighboring states. The Jews also contend that the refugees left their homes at the instigation of Arab leaders who promised them a return to their lands once their successful military action had been completed. The Arabs, on the other hand, contend that the Jews invaded the land allotted the Arabs by the United Nations plan and instituted a reign of terror involving the massacre of civilians, with the result that the population was driven out of the country and dispossessed of its property and land. They insist it was the Jews and not they who had failed to accept the United Nations decision.

There is undoubtedly some truth in each of these positions. Each party shares some degree of responsibility for what has transpired. There is some justice on each side. The definitive book or statement clarifying and evaluating events, particularly those of 1948, has still to be written. It presents the difficult task of sorting out the objective documentary evidence from material emotionally highly colored by the force of events and the reactions of peoples involved.

The result at present seems to be a confused, complex mixture of right and wrong. The predominant coloring is gray, rather than either black or white. Moreover, the passing of time makes a return to these original causes and conditions more and more difficult. The present situation should be dealt with realistically. Any attempt to enforce a solution now based upon 1948 conditions might well bring as unjust a result as it is claimed the armistice growing out of the United Nations recommendation and the resultant strife produced. The need is for temperate discussion and negotiation that recognize both the past and present and seek a solution that is as just and fair to all concerned as is possible.

It is important to recognize that the element of persecution and the determination of world Jewry, as expressed in Zionism, to succor its own were prime forces in this historical development. It is doubtful that Israel would have been born as she was had there not been fifteen years of Hitlerism. Could the development have been slower? Could there have been more moderation?

One can suggest that to understand the nation of Israel one must have the historical perspective of the centuries, be it one thousand, two thousand, or four thousand years, as well as that of the decades, be it twenty, fifty, or seventy years.

As one analyzes the elements that provide the driving force of Israel, one recognizes: first, a historic religious identification, although 80 to 85 per cent of her citizens are secular in outlook; second, nationalistic aspirations, historic in part, but also similar to the current aspirations of all peoples in the Middle East; and third, a fellowship of clan or family that gives a unity and purpose to these people who have resisted assimilation in large measure for two thousand years. These three factors, separately or in combination, provide individuals with a positive drive that adds up to the "spiritual" force that lies behind the amazing progress and development of Israel.

Out of and against this background, Israel's aspirations, as I see them, become clear:

1. To become a nation within the family of nations, discharging her full responsibility politically, economically, culturally, and socially in the creation of a world at peace. From her traditions she feels she has a contribution to make to a world society.

2. To come to terms with her neighbors so as to help create regional stability and permit economic development of all countries of the area. She recognizes the difficulty in achieving

this goal, but knows that her future lies in becoming an integral part of the Middle East.

3. To permit the absorption into Israel of all Jews who desire to come, thus providing a home for the persecuted and homeless Jews of the world. She is aware of the serious economic difficulties of resettlement, development, and eventual absorption of these people in productive enterprises. She feels that she can handle the problem of overpopulation by more intensive agricultural and industrial development without territorial expansion.

4. To re-create and develop further a distinctive Israeli culture based on the older Hebraic tradition. She is convinced in the face of the covert and overt anti-Semitism that is part of modern society that such a cultural-spiritual creation will bring dignity and security to many Jews around the world who will never identify themselves politically with Israel.

Out of this complex of aspirations, fears, historical antecedents, political influence, human emotions, and the instinct for self-preservation, there has developed a crucial Arab-Israeli conflict fraught with danger for the world. The intensity of feelings, the emotional involvement of many people around the world on one side or the other, and the hardening of positions and judgments make temperate discussion looking to solution of the impasse extremely difficult.

Questions suggest themselves. Could the League of Nations, the United Nations, Great Britain, and other nations have played their roles to have prevented this impasse? Was the movement to establish a Jewish homeland in Palestine a mistake? Could this movement have been prevented? Can Israel hope to achieve her aspirations? To what extent are the Arab objections justified? Could the Jewish leadership have followed a more moderate course of action? Have the Arab nations served their best interests by adopting an intransigent position where discussion and negotiation are extremely difficult? Has Israel undertaken too ambitious a program for her potential resources? Is a definitive moral, ethical evaluation for action possible? What is a reasonable solution to the impasse that now appears to exist? These are some of the imponderables that are a part of this complex situation.

In the brief span of her existence Israel has provided an excellent demonstration of development. The dynamic drive of her people toward the achievement of her ideal, coupled with a conviction that the Holy Land could bloom again, has worked wonders. Her eager and intelligent utilization of the know-how and economic assistance of the United States mutual security program has resulted in the Israeli program being among the best of these country programs. Similar use has been made of the United Nations technical assistance program. The initiative of Israeli scientists and leaders has made its contribution. All these efforts have been integrated and co-ordinated by the Israeli government.

Techniques of land reclamation, water spreading, development of water resources, irrigation, agricultural research, and cultivation methods have made large areas literally bloom again. Studies made in 1955 and 1956 by the agricultural section of the United States Operations Mission and the Ministry of Agriculture indicated that Israel might approach self-containment in food and fiber with a population of two million people. This assumed maximum water usage and the export and import of produce. Groves have been planted that should increase the exportable orange crop of eight million cases to some fourteen million by 1962. Approximately nine million trees are being planted each year as reforestation continues apace. The harvesting of forest products has started. As water becomes available large areas under irrigation are producing industrial crops of cotton, peanuts, and sugar beets. Behind this development is a continuing program of research that considers cost factors, seeks to improve plants or to discover new species, and concentrates on more efficient agricultural production per unit. This experience and these achievements have led to the utilization of the services of technicians from Israel in other countries where the climate and the geographical conditions are similar.

Israel has explored carefully her natural resources. Potash, bromine, phosphate, copper, iron, oil, marble, glass sands, and clays are being exploited. Potash from the Dead Sea has the best potential. The quality of the mineral deposits is relatively poor. This gives concern as Israel, forced to develop her maximum potential, proceeds with their exploitation even though the economics of a given development are open to question. Current oil production provides about 5 per cent of Israel's yearly needs. Hopes for additional wells are still strong. A recent strike some three miles from Heletz has not yet been identified either as part of the original field or as a new structure.

Israel has rehabilitated her railroad system. United States aid and German reparations have provided Diesel engines, cars, and self-propelled Diesel trains that carry an increasing share of the traffic load, relieving road transport. There is being developed a merchant marine, which at present is composed of twenty ships, but is being expanded to thirty. The road system has been placed in good condition through rehabilitation and new construction. The system provides hard-surfaced roads to all villages. Electric power development is three years ahead of the anticipated needs. Oil is the fuel. There is no coal and only a limited hydroelectric possibility in the Jordan River Development Plan. This explains the intense interest in nuclear development for power and as a possible energy source for desalting sea water to provide "life-giving" water.

Israel has demonstrated through her health and sanitation program that the disease problems of this part of the world can be conquered. Her healthy, sturdy, clear-eyed children are the symbols. An extensive system of modern hospitals and clinics assures medical service for the population and remedial medicine for the immigrants as they arrive from Eastern countries. Her professional and research leadership is excellent. As an example, during the current year Israel will produce sufficient Salk vaccine to meet her needs for polio protection of her children.

The elementary educational system unified in 1953 provides good quality instruction for all children, Arab and Israeli, and keeps pace with the immigrant population increase. The curriculum has taken an increasingly prevocational trend, recognizing that youth must be prepared for the agricultural and industrial economy crucial to Israel's survival. At the higher educational level the Hebrew University, the Technion, and the Weizmann Institute are providing for skilled leadership. Each has rapidly been developing its physical plant. Secondary education is available mostly in private schools and hence is limited. This poses a serious problem, as a larger proportion of able youth must achieve a higher degree of education to meet the leadership needs of the country. The inherent financial problem has prevented temporarily the creation of additional public secondary schools.

Cultural development has been a part of the total growth of the country. Three major theaters operate in Tel Aviv, producing the best of the classic and modern repertoire in Hebrew translation as well as indigenous plays dealing with the current Israeli scene. Each theater provides traveling troupes that take their productions to communities throughout the country. A rich musical life is spearheaded by the Israel Philharmonic Orchestra, founded in 1936. It presents world-renowned soloists and conductors from Europe and the United States. A three-million-dollar concert hall will be opened in Tel Aviv this October. Orchestral concerts are presented in selected cities and villages. Chamber music and solo concerts are numerous. Several art colonies and writers' groups with quality leadership make their contribution. A rich program of archaeological exploration is being carried on at selected sites in a land where the hills and plains speak of the past. Great care is being taken to preserve the dance forms that have come with the immigrants. These cultural activities permeate the whole community, including the villages, and stimulate activity and participation. The response of all groups in the population to these avenues of cultural experience is spontaneous and enthusiastic. One can only speculate as to its contribution to Israel's inner strength. In my judgment, it is a most significant factor. Man does not live by bread alone.

One of Israel's major problems is economic. Can she hope in a reasonable time to approach economic viability? In 1956 her exports were covering only some 25 to 30 per cent of a foreign-exchange budget that was approaching $400 million. The balance was provided by German reparations, United States economic aid and world Jewry. A goodly share of these funds is being applied to the capital cost of settlement and development projects, including agriculture and industry. As the plant is built, capital savings may be possible in the future.

Only in the last five years has Israel recognized that the industrial potential comparable to the exploitation of agriculture must be developed. This is difficult due to limited natural resources and the absence of an adequate internal fuel supply. A drastic increase in industrial export will be required because of the need to import raw materials to be fabricated for export. Israel is now engaged in a vigorous program to meet this challenge. Behind her insistence on freedom of navigation from Elath is the hard economic fact that her industrial development must have a trade route to the east coast of Africa and to Asia. The United States Operations Mission is giving major emphasis to industrial management to help develop the technical and management skills required if a country with a high standard of living is to compete in the export markets. Israel must export or face dire consequences.

Israel's immigration policy greatly complicates the economic problem. Since 1948, Israel has settled some 750,000 immigrants. During 1957 she anticipates that 100,000 newcomers will reach her shores. This indicates that by January, 1958, the total population will be 2,000,000, including 1,800,000 Jews and 200,000 Arabs. A large proportion of these immigrants have had no financial means, and those from the Middle East and North Africa have had little familiarity with modern agricultural techniques or industrial skills. Thus the cost of their transportation to and settlement in Israel has been provided, followed by training programs either formal or on the job, to prepare them to support themselves. Recent immigrants who have come from eastern Europe are skilled artisans who are urgently needed to assist in industrial development.

This situation has called for a constantly increasing number

of full-time jobs in agriculture and industry. The development
in industry and to a lesser degree in agriculture has not been
able to keep pace with the need. At the present time there
are not sufficient income-providing jobs in these fields for
the population, so that heavy immigration is a real economic
hazard. Far too large a percentage of people is employed in
government, in services, and in public works. The Jerusalem
Post of August 1, 1957, recognizes the implication of the
problem when it says editorially in discussing a new housing
project to be backed by American private capital:

> The ultimate success of the endeavor as far as the local econ-
> omy is concerned will depend on the ability of the new immi-
> grants to repay the loans advanced for their housing. With this
> in view, far reaching changes ought to be introduced in the
> industrialization and rationalization of national productivity
> for it is clear that the employment of so many immigrants on
> publicly provided emergency works is no contribution to the
> problem of absorption, however important temporary employ-
> ment of this nature may be from the sociological point of view.

This problem is further complicated by certain internal
conditions. Israel's standard of living is relatively high, ex-
ceeding that of Greece and Italy. It reflects the Western
orientation of her leaders. Her people enjoy a daily diet in
excess of 2,800 calories. At the same time her productivity
rate is low, with some improvement recently. These two factors present a critical condition, which must be dealt with if
she is to compete successfully in the export market. Favorably,
Israel has become increasingly productivity- and management-
minded in recent months as her leaders have faced the need
for industrial export.

However, she has a labor government closely related to the
Histadrut, which controls 80 per cent of labor and as owner
is the private manager of some 30 per cent of industry. The
inherent urge to protect labor, which is in excess supply, to
continue welfare benefits, and to maintain a standard of living that has been established on a low productivity rate indicates the difficulty of raising production to meet interna-

tional competition. Moreover, there is the urge for labor to maintain its privileged position in relation to private enterprise, whose capital is so necessary for essential development.

This situation, although currently a serious problem, may well be a passing phase, which time will correct. Jewish behavior patterns are basically individualist rather than collectivist. Liberal economic policies favorable to foreign investors are being proposed now to attract private capital. These must be scrupulously implemented. Indeed the integration of the Histadrut as well as the Jewish Agency into the state of Israel to create a functional whole is a matter of time and part of the process whereby prestate factors that helped to make the state possible should be absorbed.

Israel's agricultural potential is limited first by water and second by land. At the moment she is approaching the limit of agricultural expansion permitted by her water resources. This situation, with additional but limited land area, creates a powerful incentive to obtain early use of the Jordan River water and to carry on research in the technique of desalting sea water. A break-through in the latter, which would provide reasonably cheap water, would be a boon to all arid countries. The development of her industrial potential is just getting under way. Success is imperative. Determination, skill, and sacrifice could bring results. Indeed her industrial potential is limited by her development of know-how and skill in producing competitively for and creating an export market—a Herculean task.

A second major problem is Israel's international political status. Can she integrate herself into the political framework of the Middle East? She has established good relations with the majority of the 200 thousand Arabs within her borders. They are sharing in the advantages of development and the improved standard of living. Educational, health, and other benefits are being utilized. However, Israel, faced with the area's political problem and the possibility of fifth-column activity, has felt compelled to maintain minimum security restrictions on the movement of Arabs in Israel. This is a regrettable necessity. This fact creates misunderstanding and is disturbing to her neighbors. As Israel's population increases, her Arab neighbors have some basis for fear of territorial expansion, especially when a minority group in Israel contends for it. There is also indication that her neighbors, because of Israel's dynamic quality, may be as fearful of a peaceful penetration as of military aggression, should relationships be reestablished.

The failure to implement the armistice, coupled with continued Arab hostility and Israel's reprisal technique, created a most difficult situation. Both Israeli and Arab leaders, along with the United Nations representatives, must bear responsibility for failure to work out agreements and techniques that would have prevented loss of life and eliminated tension. This continued failure may well have added to the tension and hostility. The move to give the United Nations police powers, if extended, may be effective. The observer-team technique was essentially reporting and evaluating events after they had occurred and did not permit preventative action. The emotional tension made negotiation by the United Nations leaders under these conditions difficult or impossible.

Israel's relations with the United Nations have been difficult. She undoubtedly acted in accordance with her best interests and under deep provocation. But disagreement with the United Nations observers and condemnations by the Security Council and General Assembly are regrettable episodes. As Israel looks to her future, it is apparent that her peace and security are vitally dependent upon her relationships with her Arab neighbors and the United Nations. One wonders if there are still avenues of negotiation that her initiative might discover.

At the present time it is apparent that outside leadership, from the United Nations and/or other countries, should take the initiative to open lines of communication between Israel and her neighbors. Strong moral suasion might well be used. A first prerequisite to an easing of tension is a settlement of the Arab refugee problem. Time has hardened attitudes and filled Israel's land area with an immigrant population. It is my judgment that Israel should, and will, accept the return of a limited number of refugees, possibly a hundred thousand, and will assume the financial burden of resettlement of bona fide Palestine refugees. This settlement should bring with it a determination of permanent boundaries. It is my judgment that consideration should be given to returning or relating the Gaza area to Israel in order to permit its fullest exploitation for the indigenous population and some small segment of Palestine refugees. International agreements involving the United Nations and other world powers should guarantee the border settlement. This would reassure the Arab fears of Israel expansion. Should a full settlement not be possible immediately, every effort should be exerted to find segments that might be handled to open the communication lines among the leaders. These might include the Gaza strip, Jordan River water, Haifa as a free port, refugee settlement, a clarification of the Suez status, and other regional activity that diplomatic skill might discern.

An interesting adjunct to the political problem is internal. People from sixty-five nations constitute the population of Israel. There is a basic distinction between families from Western and Eastern countries. Israel is seeking within her own population to solve the problem of integrating people with an Occidental and Oriental tradition bound together only by a common Jewish heritage. The present leadership is Western. What will the passing years bring as Eastern elements exert their influence? Can Israel, from her internal experience, make a contribution to the area and to the world problem of reconciling the Oriental traditions with twentieth-century Westernism?

In conclusion, what of Israel's future? It is clear that her present situation is precarious, both economically and politically. These ideas and questions can be suggested. Israel is a bastion of democracy because of her philosophical and idealogical unity with the West. The skill, knowledge, and capacity for development that she has demonstrated should be used to assist other nations. At some point she is certain to face a critical economic crisis. Can she maintain her present standard of living? When the period of crisis is over and the

pioneering drive gone, will she sink into the traditional social-
economic pattern of the Middle East? Can she exhibit the
flexibility necessary to adapt to the area and to gain the confidence of her neighbors? Can she be the crucible and/or a
catalytic agent that can help the culture and tradition of the
Moslem world find its accommodation with the twentieth
century or vice versa? Can she win through to economic viability with a minimum dependence upon world Jewry?

Any objective appraisal raises serious questions about Israel's
economic future. Her difficulty would be partially eased if the
political problems could be solved and normal trade relations
with her neighbors could be resumed. However, she appears
to be attempting an impossible feat. Yet one who has come
to understand the dynamic spirit that is Israel will hesitate
to sell her short. This spirit could be the critical determining
factor. She has made tremendous strides against great odds in
the past nine years. She might just succeed in winning
through. She will be watched with keen interest. We must
await the events to know the answer.

Commentary

HARLAN CLEVELAND
*Dean, Maxwell Graduate School of Citizenship
and Public Affairs, Syracuse University*

A TOLERANCE FOR FAMILIAR THEMES is standard equipment
for anyone who would study any aspect of American foreign
policy. But he who tries to probe the future of the state of
Israel must cultivate this highest form of patience to an un-
usual degree.

There is, inevitably, that paradox about Israel as an efficient
democracy in the Middle East, a Western island in a sea of

Oriental feudalism. There is the vivid memory of Hitler, and the statistical shocker—six million human beings liquidated. There is the now-tiresome argument about whether, in 1948, the Arab refugees were pushed out by the Israelis or pulled out by the Arabs—and the solemn conclusion that there is truth in both contentions. There are the brooding questions about the need for a Jewish homeland, about the intransigence of the Arabs, about the roles of Herzl and Ben Gurion, Balfour, Peel, and Harry S. Truman—rhetorical questions, unanswerable and little relevant today.

Mr. Hale has mercifully spared us most of these familiar strains. But even he has not failed to suggest, as someone nearly always does, that "to understand the nation of Israel one must have the historical perspective of the centuries, be it one thousand, two thousand, or four thousand years."

Perhaps it *would* be helpful to take such a long view. But, in my observation, those who take the most vigorously historical view of Middle Eastern affairs are the least prone to make practical suggestions as to how we—Israel, the Arab nations, the European democracies, and the United States—are going to untangle ourselves from the mess in which that long and bitter history has now left us. Statesmen acting for reasons of past history rather than future weal have brought us to the calamitous condition in which we now find ourselves.

More than to understand the perspective of the past, it seems to me, our problem in the Middle East is to escape it.

Israel's very location is historic. Palestine was originally only one of the places where a Jewish national home could have been established; in the end, historical symbolism won out over other factors in the decision, and the experiment was launched in one of the most unpromising tracts of real estate available, surrounded by peoples unlikely to be overjoyed by the ingathering of new and ambitious neighbors. What the Israelis have done, and plan to do, with their economically godforsaken Promised Land is nothing short of heroic; but equally heroic efforts in a more fertile and less controversial area would have paid off in richer coin.

This decision, too, is past. Tied by history to its ancient
dream, the state of Israel is there to stay. But that dream, of
a Jewish homeland, is Israel's weakness as well as its strength.
The future is wrapped in this enigma: can the dream be
blurred and compromised enough to permit the state of Israel
to survive?

I approach this question frankly as an advocate of the national survival, the economic growth, and the political democracy of the new Israeli state. I do not consider this advocacy
inconsistent with the wish that the Arab states will likewise
find their own way to responsible leadership and economic
growth. Indeed, as will presently appear, I believe that, unless
both objectives are sought, neither will be achieved. The
Arabs are there to stay, too.

It is precisely because it is in our national interest to wish
Israel well that we Americans must on occasion separate ourselves from the torrent of encomium and invective about
Israel and look hard at the conditions of her survival. Her
peculiar history has left at least four roadblocks in the path
of progress; it can do no harm to look at them realistically.

The Sharing of Sovereignty

One legacy of the past is the arrangement whereby some
of the attributes of sovereignty are shared by the Israeli government with nongovernmental organizations, the Histadrut
within its borders and the agencies of world Zionism outside.
Histadrut, the massive labor organization that is also Israel's
largest industrial combine, was a kind of shadow government
in Palestine long before Israel was a state. It controls much
of the welfare and social-security apparatus and many of the
central investment decisions, which the government might be
expected to administer.

Mr. Hale assures us that the exercise of a kind of sovereignty
by the Histadrut, while a serious problem, "may well be a
passing phase, which time will correct." Let us hope he is
right. But one sees very little evidence piling up to indicate

that the Histadrut has abandoned its extraordinary function as social-security agency, housing agency, pioneer movement, and business trust. It still envelops its membership in a life-long bureaucratic benevolence that starts with feeding pregnant mothers and ends only with the provision of tombstones. Its leaders are still prone to refer to the government as a "child," to wax scornful about the unwillingness of Jewish capitalists to invest in Israel, to regard manual labor as the most virtuous form of contribution.

There is, of course, a good deal of pressure on the Histadrut these days to turn over governmental functions to the government, and this pressure will probably continue as long as the government coalition remains under the control of labor leaders, some of whom, like David Ben Gurion himself, grew up in the Histadrut movement. But as the dominant Mapai party loses the electoral base of its domination—it lost ground in Israel's last national election—will there not be a tendency for the Histadrut's leaders to hold fast to their power, for fear of having it transferred to political elements less in sympathy with the welfare-state philosophy that the Histadrut imported from Central Europe?

There is already some indication that the Mapai party leaders are hedging their bets in this respect. According to one observer, the General Zionists have favored the nationalization of industry while the Mapai leaders to their left opposed it. The General Zionists wanted housing projects and labor exchanges nationalized while Mapai favored their control by the Histadrut. In this unique nationalization fight, the argument turns on which of two more-or-less sovereign public institutions will get control, rather than on the more orthodox issue of public vs. private ownership. If, as Mr. Hale says, "Jewish behavior patterns are basically individualist rather than collectivist," these patterns seem to have been effectively submerged in the building of economic institutions in Israel so far.

Outside of Israel, the state is heavily dependent on the organized sentiment and nongovernmental resources of world Jewry to forward the dream in practical ways, through economic development and the maintenance of adequate military strength. It is true that decisions about defense and foreign policy seem to have been made increasingly by the central government of Israel itself, leaving the contributors to Israel's financial revival with less current authority over the use to which these contributions are put. But as long as Israel leans so heavily on contributed funds, the influence of the contributors will be great enough to constitute something like a suspensive veto over major moves by the Israeli nation. And with Israel forcing the pace of its development program to the limit, and necessarily maintaining sizable military forces as well, the prospect of a diminishing flow of funds from abroad (and consequently a veto power of diminished authority) has at best been pushed many years into the future.

Zionists and Jews

In the world as a whole, of course, the Zionists of Israel are still a minority within a larger Jewish community. The evidence is growing that the Zionists in Israel resent the standoffishness of many Jews who are willing to help Israel with annual gifts, but prefer to live "dispersed" in New York or California rather than "ingathered" in Jerusalem or Beersheba.

A nation that depends so heavily on good will and contributions can ill afford to let its petulant nationalism get out of hand. The latest explosion on this subject, as reported by *Time* magazine, has Ben Gurion exploding at Nahum Goldmann, President of the World Zionist Organization. Back in 1951 the Prime Minister had laid down the principle that "a Zionist must come to Israel himself as an immigrant." Now he has carried the doctrine one step further. "There seems to be general agreement," he says, "that a Jew can live in America, speak and read English and bring up his children in American culture and still call himself a Zionist. If that is Zionism, I want no part of it." [1]

[1] *Time*, August 26, 1957, p. 55, col. 1.

Many Israelis born in Palestine, who are nicknamed for the prickly cactus plant called sabra, already show a fanatical self-assurance that is a great strength within Israel, but a danger to Israel's nationhood in the family of nations. The contempt of some Israelis for American Jews who incomprehensibly want to remain Americans is already showing around the edges; the pride of some Israelis in their nation's accomplishments sometimes shades over into a feeling that Israel has become a kind of secular Jewish Vatican. Two years ago a prominent citizen of Tel Aviv, who visits New York every year, was speaking to me of his pride in his Israeli citizenship. "These days when I go to Brooklyn or the Bronx," he said half seriously, "I feel as an Englishman must feel when visiting in the dominions, in Australia or New Zealand."

It is to be expected that Israel's national interest will come increasingly into conflict with the interests of Jews who are not, by the Ben Gurion definition, Zionists. As this happens, Israel will dissociate itself from the influence that necessarily accompanies the private contributions—and eventually from the contributions as well. The important thing is for this process not to develop too fast for Israel's own good.

Meanwhile, it is surely quite unnecessary for Ben Gurion or any other Israeli leader to patronize their overseas supporters as second-class Jews who do not have the courage of their Hebrew convictions. The indispensable support from American Jews depends heavily on not forcing Americans to choose between their Jewishness and their Americanism, but on the contrary leaving plenty of room for a cultural and financial loyalty that does not trespass on that special brand of loyalty called patriotism.

Aid vs. Viability

The sharing of sovereignty with private agencies, at home and abroad, has noticeable effects on the allocation of economic resources. Israel is the only country of the world (unless postwar Nationalist China be counted as another) where the amount of aid from all sources has been so great as to bring into question the capacity of the recipient to absorb it efficiently. Part of this aid is never really subject to the Israeli government's control—it is earmarked for a special welfare purpose or memorial building projects. (The Weizmann Institute is a lovely monument to the dedication of those who helped finance it. But would Chaim Weizmann himself have insisted that scientific research in a pioneer society must be done in a marble building?)

In circles interested in Israel's economic development, one hears a good deal of talk about "viability." There is no doubt that a viable and competitive economy is one of the long-term goals established by the Israeli government. But there is also no doubt that this goal appears rather far down on the list of priorities that have practical meaning in the Israel of today; on the list of significant goals, unlimited immigration and rapid industrial development certainly rate much higher than the achievement of balance in Israel's international trade. And Israel's socialistic capitalist, the Histadrut, is already on record with the strong opinion that social, rather than economic, reasons should dominate the pattern of Israeli domestic investment.

As Israel gets ready to celebrate the tenth anniversary of its statehood, it is still importing more than three times as much as it is exporting and covering the resulting payments deficit with massive contributions, bond sales, reparation payments, and government grants and loans. Israel's spokesmen alternate between pride and defensiveness in commenting on this situation.

Prime Minister Ben Gurion, of course, is not at all defensive about Israel's rapid economic growth and the resulting dollar gap. On one recent occasion he challenged a group of economists to re-examine economic laws in the light of Israeli experience. His view, said to be widely shared in Israel, was thus described in the London Economist: "The cold rules on a balance sheet do not apply when people are working in a state of high development-fever." [2]

[2] "Israel's New Immigration Problems," Economist (London), August 10, 1957, p. 471, par. 1.

Whether the pace of development outranks in importance the need to have enterprises pay depends on the purpose of the exercise. Mr. Ben Gurion would say that the purpose is to build a Jewish national state, not to make sure that every component of this experiment balances its budget. And he would be right, at least in the relatively short run. But now, after eight or nine years, the question of the long run is bound to assert itself. Israel's very success in the agricultural sector now requires special attention to the development of industry, for the new workers immigrating from abroad will mostly have to be absorbed as workers in new industrial enterprise. As the *Economist* remarks, under these conditions "the principle of profitability will have to be heeded if the burden of subsidies to be paid by the government is not to become intolerable."

When it comes to the external balance of payments, a note of defensiveness is liable to creep into the discussion. The useful little pamphlet called *Facts about Israel*, published by the Israeli government, summarizes the foreign trade situation in these words: "Israel's foreign trade shows a marked adverse balance, caused by large scale immigration and heavy capital investment. This is usual in underdeveloped and rapidly developing countries. However, exports have been steadily expanding."

Exports have indeed been expanding rapidly, so that even with imports also expanding, exports have jumped from less than 12 per cent to nearly 30 per cent of the value of imports in the years from 1949 to 1956. But even this brightened outlook would be regarded as appallingly dim in any other "underdeveloped and rapidly developing country." "Large scale immigration" is not at all usual in underdeveloped and rapidly developing countries; the only significant example that comes to mind is Australia, and Australia's passion for industrialization is rapidly removing it from the "underdeveloped" category.

Mr. Ben Gurion is frequently quoted as saying that Israel's economic destiny is to become the "Switzerland of the Middle East." But if peace were to break out tomorrow, would Israel's cost structure be such that it could compete with the industrial nations of Europe in providing producer and consumer goods to the even less developed countries of the Arab world? When, eventually, a free exchange of goods does prevail in the Levant, is there any guarantee that the "Switzerland of the Middle East" won't be Switzerland—or perhaps a resurgent, cost-conscious, sales-minded Germany?

An independent analysis of the past few years of Israel's industrial development might reveal a record of unusually high costs, relatively low productivity, and an extraordinarily high proportion of the labor force working in nonproductive pursuits. It might also reveal a disturbing number of cases in which American and British Jews are perfectly willing to contribute their personal funds to Israel's future, but cannot justify to their boards of directors the investment of company funds in the kinds of private enterprises on which Israel's future may crucially depend. The dream is a powerful, indispensable incentive to economic development; but Israel's whole future will be in danger if, in pursuing the dream, a hothouse economy is improvised out of external grants and domestic subsidies.

The danger is not, essentially, that outside contributions may dry up. They show no sign of drying up; aid to Israel, especially from private groups and persons, has been very generous, and funds from Germany and the United States are currently on the rise. The danger is the opposite one: that in the continued presence of free-and-easy aid from abroad, the pressure to build industries regardless of cost, competitiveness, and profitability will be irresistible.

The Aims of Statehood

History has left Israel with some cruel political dilemmas, too. The politics of older nations consist of arguments about the means of government; but in this new nation, born in such a hurry from so long a history of struggle and privation,

the key political issues are likely for some time to revolve
around the fundamental objectives of statehood.

Israel's aims or "aspirations," as Mr. Hale sees them, are
four: to become a nation within the family of nations; to
come to terms with her neighbors; to permit the absorption
into Israel of all Jews who desire to come; and to re-create and
develop further a distinctive Israeli culture based on the
older Hebraic tradition. The inherent contradiction in Israel's
aims is laid bare by this summary of them; it is the third and
fourth objectives that make the first and second so difficult
to pursue. How much should Israel compromise about unlimited immigration and the recapture of the Hebraic tradition, in order to become a nation and live at peace with Arab
neighbors?

The attempt to recapture the essence of Jewishness may or
may not remain a serious objective. The Hebraic tradition
will no doubt generate much useful and vigorous emotion,
translatable with some effort into practical physical progress
for the building of Israel. And yet the Israeli mood seems
curiously nonreligious. As Max Ascoli has recently noted, Ben
Gurion's preoccupation with the Old Testament is perhaps
the one respect in which he is not truly representative of the
people he leads. If the spiritual vigor of Judaism is lost in
Israel, how much incentive will there be for a "return to a
distinctive Israeli culture"? To an outsider, it seems likely that
the most distinctive thing about Israeli culture during the
next couple of decades will not be the Hebraic revival, but
the building of those Western-type social institutions necessary to control a process of phenomenally rapid economic
growth.

The key issue, in the politics of ends, seems more likely to
be that of unlimited immigration. Not long ago, it seemed
that the flow of Jews to Haifa and Tel Aviv was drying up;
indeed, for a short time there was actually a net outflow of
population from Israel. But now the faucet of immigrants
has been turned on again, hard. Something like a hundred
thousand exiles are expected to be "ingathered" this year—
three times as many as in 1955, nearly twice as many as in

1956. Most have been coming from North Africa and the
Arab portions of Asia Minor; but eastern Europe is once
again opening up a channel for Jewish emigration. According
to one recent visitor:

> . . . the Israelis made a secret agreement with the Gomulka
> government of Poland last winter which is resulting in the emi-
> gration of more than 45,000 relatively skilled if somewhat com-
> munistic Polish Jews to Israel, and the Hungarian government
> has recently been permitting relatively free Jewish emigration
> also.

The visitor remarked to the Prime Minister that he must
be satisfied with the progress of the Polish immigration. "I
wish I could have made that agreement with Bulganin!"
said Ben Gurion.[3]

Unlimited immigration is a cornerstone of Israeli policy;
the long and troubled history of the Jews made it so, and the
1948 Proclamation of Independence so proclaimed it: "The
State of Israel will be open to the immigration of Jews from
all countries of their dispersion." Yet the independent observer may legitimately wonder whether Israel must or can
maintain this policy in practice. The economic burden is
extraordinarily heavy, even if much of it can, for some little
time yet, be transferred to Israel's supporters abroad. The implications of this immigration for Israel's internal politics
are also disturbing: the moderation and democratic understanding represented by the western and Central Europeans
are becoming a smaller and smaller leaven in a larger and
larger loaf. But most important of all, unlimited immigration
is one of several factors that retard the making of a regional
peace.

Below and behind the immigration issue is that touchiest
subject of all—the moral basis for a nation based on race or
religion. Can the centuries of anti-Semitic discrimination
elsewhere be atoned by maintaining a state whose ends are

---

[3] E. A. Bayne, in a letter to the American Universities Field Staff, Inc.,
"Israel and the Doctrine" (American Universities Field Staff, Inc., July, 1957),
p. 7, pars. 1, 2.

expressed in the discriminatory terms of race or religion? How will the perennial minority, now in Israel the majority for once, handle the Christian and Moslem minorities in its midst? It is a tribute to the breadth of Israel's leaders that they are painfully aware of their own dilemma. Most critics have found the treatment of the Arab minority surprisingly good, in spite of the maintenance of military control in the areas of greatest Arab concentration. But the discrimination is there, nevertheless; Arabs are tolerated and treated fairly only when and because they are not a threat to Jewish control of the state. Against any move to let Arabs immigrate into Israel in large numbers, the Israelis would fight with the same stubborn righteousness with which some United States Southerners fight the use of his vote by the Southern Negro, or some New Yorkers resist the influx of Puerto Ricans into New York City.

Road to Reconciliation

The future of Israel is bound up with that of the forty million Arabs around her. Somehow Israel's presence in the Middle East must eventually be rationalized in Arab politics. To this process, the Israelis can make more of a contribution than they presently admit in public. So can we Americans.

With our American enthusiasm for spectator sports, it is natural for us to approach the Arab-Israeli rivalry by choosing sides. There are, of course, the xenophiles who identify themselves completely with Israel—as other elements in our society have at times identified themselves with England or Formosa or the Soviet Union. They start every foreign policy discussion with the assumption that the Israelis must always be right because they have long been "oppressed so hard they could not stand." On the other side there is a smaller number of violent partisans who favor the Arabs, plagued by the chronic difficulty of deciding which of several potentates is in truth the Arab side. The rest of us are less violent because we are less involved. But we, too, are often guilty of cheering or booing rather than analyzing. It's time to remind ourselves that there is a third side to any overseas rivalry—the American side.

It is fortunately not up to us to decide who is right and who is wrong in the Middle East. Maybe there is no true answer to that kind of question: both sides are right according to their own reading of history and loudly righteous about it as well. The fanatical Israel-firsters of the Herut party, always a threat to peace with their trigger-happy resort to terrorism, sometimes push the more moderate parties farther than they would otherwise go in sponsoring anti-Arab reprisal raids. And the autointoxicated leaders of Egypt and Syria, excited by Soviet encouragement and Czech arms, also make it hard for more moderate Arabs to sit down with the Israelis to rationalize an irreversible *fait accompli*.

In this complex network of tensions, our problem is not to decide whether Ben Gurion is being too stubborn or Nasser is overplaying a weak hand. Ours is the more difficult task of dealing with the world as we find it.

American resources, American prestige, and American military force have been sucked into the Middle East by sympathy for the persecuted, by the British exit, by the Russian competition, and by the turbulent rivalries among states too small to act as responsible nations and too strong to be left to settle their own affairs. We will be immersed, for decades, in the flux of Levantine politics. A set of flexible American aims, understood in outline by the public at large, might be the first step in getting ourselves organized to handle this real, if unwanted, responsibility.

Our primary aim, in the short run, is clearly to build a security system that smothers any and all aggression in the area and freezes the borders so hard that they are no longer changeable by action of small nations in the area. The United Nations police force may be a useful precedent here; but let us decide now that United States military power will have to be used—and that, consequently, Americans will occasionally get hurt.

Our second aim must surely be to encourage every development in the area that promises some improvement in the responsibility of Arab leadership. At present there is literally nobody on the Arab side with whom the Israelis could negotiate a regional peace settlement, even if the Arabs showed a will to negotiate. It is therefore in Israel's interest, too, that the forty million Arabs around her be effectively governed, by leaders who can make substantial concessions without more than a normal fear of assassination. Pursuing this aim may lead to the building of regional institutions, such as an Arab Development Bank;[4] it may involve helping the more stable elements in some countries to gain strength by other forms of direct or indirect co-operation with the United States and other free nations. Altogether it will be a very difficult operation, with rewards long delayed.

Our third aim should be to help the Israelis achieve an economic independence that is real and encourage them to deal generously with the key issues in controversy between them and the Arab states. Every massive raid or intransigent statement from the Israeli side strengthens the position of Arab extremists and weakens the elements that will have to achieve power if there is ever going to be a negotiation about peace or about anything. Israel's experience with her neighbors has been (from her point of view) bitter indeed; but if Israel is truly a Western democratic enclave in the Middle East, her leaders have some responsibility for not reverting to Old Testament reciprocity even when provoked. Until Israel handles her own affairs with more of an eye to moderating Arab extremism, the development of responsible Arab leadership will be periodically set back by renewed fears of Israeli attack.

A fourth aim might well be to encourage a rethinking of Israel's unlimited immigration policy. If Zionist policy seems to be deliberately creating an uncontainably explosive population problem for tiny Israel, even moderate Arabs will never believe that Israel isn't going to spill over into Syria, down into the Jordan Valley toward Jericho, or into the Sinai Des-

[4] This scheme is discussed in my article "A New Aid Plan for the Middle East," *The Reporter,* XVI, No. 7 (April 4, 1957), 9-12.

ert of Egypt. On this subject the American Jewish community perhaps has a special opportunity to serve the interests of peace and therefore of American foreign policy. In a new generation of Jews less touched by personal misfortune, there may be more room for the view that world Jewry is big enough for both a Zionist homeland and the national assimilation of Jews elsewhere. If Israel can escape from a history that teaches that Jews are, everywhere and always, the persecuted ones, the principle of unlimited immigration may begin to be modified. Only when it is modified will a major danger to Israel's internal health and external relations be removed.

If we can find the ways of encouraging events to move along these lines, the time may come when practical talks can be held about the resettling and compensating of Arab refugees, dividing the waters of the Jordan, drawing some definitive national boundary lines, freeing intraregional trade, and settling the future of Jerusalem. The Soviet Union, assisted by several breeds of local extremists in the area, will try to prevent that day from coming. But vigorous American leadership, combined with the impatience of awakening Arab peoples and heroic restraint on the part of the Israelis, might just turn the trick. Since there seems to be no easier alternative, it is worth a good long try.

XI

Some Legal Aspects
of the Suez Situation

A. L. GOODHART

Master, University College, Oxford University

THE NUMBER OF LOCAL QUESTIONS concerning the various aspects of what may compendiously be called the Suez situation are threatening to become legion. It is therefore possible to comment only briefly on three issues that, although inter-related, give rise to separate and distinct considerations. These three issues are the action taken by Israel in the Sinai Peninsula, the subsequent action taken by Great Britain and France, and, earliest of all in point of time, the nationalizing of the Suez Canal Company by Egypt.

Before discussing them, however, it is of primary importance to refer to the basic problem concerning the use of force in the settlement of international disputes, because in each of the three cases this was the dominant issue. The question has not been finally answered, and it remains today the most difficult one in the field of international relations, from both the legal and the moral standpoint.

The Provisions of the United Nations Charter

Article 2 (4) provides that:

All Members shall refrain in their international relations from the threat or use of force against the territorial integrity or

243

political independence of any state, or in any other manner inconsistent with the Purposes of the United Nations.

Article 24 confers "on the Security Council primary responsibility for the maintenance of international peace and security."

Article 36 (3) provides that:

the Security Council should also take into consideration that legal disputes should as a general rule be referred by the parties to the International Court of Justice in accordance with the provisions of the Statute of the Court.

The only occasion on which a member of the United Nations is entitled to use force independently is in self-defense. Article 51 provides that:

Nothing in the present Charter shall impair the inherent right of individual or collective self-defense if an armed attack occurs against a Member of the United Nations, until the Security Council has taken the measures necessary to maintain international peace and security.

These articles, if taken by themselves, would seem to provide that it is only when an armed attack occurs that a state may use force to protect itself. The use of force for the redress of grievances, however serious, or for the elimination of future dangers, however great and immediate, must be regarded as illegal, unless it is possible to read certain implied terms into the Charter.

It is obvious that this rule must give rise to the gravest abuses if the United Nations is not able and ready to redress the grievances or to meet the threat of danger. Article 1 (1) therefore places on the United Nations the duty:

to take effective collective measures for the prevention and removal of threats to the peace, and for the suppression of acts of aggression or other breaches of the peace, . . .

This provision gives the United Nations full power to see that justice is done, because illegal acts that are of any importance must necessarily constitute a threat to the peace. If the Charter had not given to the United Nations Organization both the right and the duty to act whenever one state violates the rights of another, then it would have been fatally defective, for it would have encouraged and protected all wrongful acts short of aggression. A state that was careful not to stage an armed attack would then be able to violate all its established international duties with impunity.

The interpretation of the Charter therefore gives rise to two questions. The first is whether the duty placed on the United Nations to maintain peace by the prevention of illegal threats and other wrongful acts by one state against another and the duty placed on the individual states not to use force except in defense when there is an armed attack on it are correlative. The second question, which arises only if the United Nations is unable or refuses to act owing to the exercise of the veto or some other cause, is whether the aggrieved state may take adequate independent steps to protect its rights by the use of force.

It is in the answer to these questions that the basic conflict of opinion seems to lie. The strict view, so ably set forth by Professor Quincy Wright in his article "Intervention 1956," [1] is that there is no immediate correlation between the duties of the states and the duties of the United Nations. As the Charter provides that the states may use force only in self-defense, this provision must be regarded as absolutely binding even though there is no other means by which the redress of grievances can be secured or future dangers met.[2] The use of armed force by a state is only justified when there is "the instant and overwhelming necessity for defense." This seems to have been the principle accepted by the State Department in Washington in relation to the various facets of the Suez situation, although it is not entirely clear that it is regarded to be of universal application. Thus in his message to Congress on January 24, 1955, when there was the danger of an attack on the island of Quemoy, President Eisenhower stated that

[1] Quincy Wright, "Intervention, 1956," Amer. Jour. of International Law, LI (1957), 257-76.
[2] Ibid., p. 269.

preventive action might be taken against a concentration of Chinese troops on the mainland if this constituted an immediate threat.

But in considering the strict interpretation of the Charter, it is important to note that Article 51 permits acts of self-defense only "if an armed attack occurs." It says nothing about threats, however dangerous or imminent. Professor Wright's definition [3] of an act of aggression as "the use of, or threat to use, armed force," cannot be read into the Charter because "a threat" is obviously not "an armed attack." Therefore, in suggesting that a state may use force against an immediate threat, [4] both President Eisenhower and Professor Wright are departing from the strict construction of the Charter. However reasonable this view concerning threats may be, it can find no support in the actual words of Article 51. It can only be read into the Charter as an implied term dictated by reason.

In contrast to the narrow, literal interpretation of the Charter, there is what may be termed the liberal interpretation, which emphasizes that the Charter should be read as a document purporting to create a practical system of international government. To adapt Chief Justice Marshall's famous dictum, we must never forget that it is a constitution that we are construing. The instrument must be read as a whole and not merely as a collection of separate independent articles. Although a provision may be phrased in absolute terms, this does not mean that it is necessarily applicable whatever the circumstances may be. Thus, to take an analogous illustration, there are absolute phrases in the United States Constitution that have been construed to be subject to the war and the police powers of the government.

If this method of construction is applicable to the Charter, then it would seem to be reasonable to hold that the renunciation of the use of force in Article 2 (4) is not of an absolute character, but is dependent on the proper enforcement of international order by the United Nations. If, owing to the

[3] *Ibid.*, p. 270.
[4] *Ibid.*

exercise of the veto or for some other reason, that body proves to be impotent in certain particular circumstances, then an aggrieved state cannot be left without the possibility of redress.

This interpretation of the Charter does not mean that there will be a return to the anarchical conditions that existed before the creation of the United Nations. In spite of the attempts made by the founders of the League of Nations and by the signatories of the Kellogg-Briand Pact to outlaw war, international law at that time failed to draw an adequate distinction between just and unjust wars. The Charter of the United Nations has attempted to remedy this by drawing a distinction between aggression and defensive action. In the case of an armed attack on the territory of a peaceful non-aggressive state, it recognizes the defender's inevitable right of self-defense, just as all state laws recognize the individual's right of self-defense against a personal attack.

There are, however, other forms of aggression that may give rise to greater differences of opinion. If State A encourages its mobs to murder the nationals of State B who are living within its borders, is State B prevented from taking any action to protect them until it has been authorized to do so by the Security Council? If State A forcibly seizes the merchant ships of State B that are in its harbors, must State B acquiesce on the ground that this is an exercise of state sovereignty? If State A accumulates a large number of containers of poison gas along the frontier of State B and announces that it will use these when a favorable opportunity arises, can State B do nothing by itself to abate this threat, even though it is clear that the exercise of the veto by Country Z will prevent the United Nations from taking adequate action? It is noteworthy that ordinary state law gives its citizens powers of self-protection in similar circumstances, although the administration of state law is far more efficient than that of international law.

On the question concerning the use of force, Mr. Dean Acheson, the former United States Secretary of State, has said in his article "Foreign Policy and Presidential Moralism":

> But we must never forget that between an opponent who is
> prepared to use force to gain his end and one who is not pre-
> pared to use force to defend his interests—the former is usually
> the winner.

He continued:

> But, as has been said, under the President's moral philosophy
> force is immoral. Except when employed by others against one-
> self force must be opposed only by moral and political pressure.
> This means that it can only be effectively opposed when it is
> employed outside the Communist empire and by our own Allies.
> Soviet force used in Hungary, Indian force used in Kashmir,
> or Egyptian force used to conduct raids into Israel and to deny
> it use of the Canal or the Gulf of Aqaba cannot, within the
> President's limitations, be effectively opposed because the users
> are immune to our moral and political pressure.[5]

Mr. Acheson suggests that such an extraordinary result can
only be reached "by a combination of phony law and fuzzy
morals." The "phony law" is due to a misinterpretation of
the Charter, which is too readily assumed to be "both simple
and clear."

It has been argued, however, that the "armed attack" must
be the sole criterion of guilt, because it is only in this way
that it is possible to determine who is the real aggressor.
This is an argument of despair, because it must be remem-
bered that in the cases of both Czechoslovakia and Poland,
Hitler alleged that they had initiated attacks on Germany. It
ought not to be impossible for the Security Council to determine whether the "armed attack" has been caused entirely
or in part by the wrongful acts of the other state and for it
to take the action that is appropriate to these circumstances.
Such an interpretation of the Charter would seem to be more
in accord with reason and justice than the one that places the
entire emphasis on the "armed attack."

[5] Dean Acheson, "Foreign Policy and Presidential Moralism," The Reporter, XVI, No. 9 (1957), 10-13.

Was Israel entitled to take action in the Sinai Peninsula?

The answer to this question is obvious for those who hold that Article 2 (4) and Article 51 of the Charter prohibit the use of force except in defense against an armed attack. As the Egyptians did not launch an armed attack, it follows that the Israelis must have been at fault in taking the action they did. If this view is the correct one, then the further question of whether the Israeli action was a reasonable measure of self-protection against a threatened future attack is irrelevant because that would not fall within the purview of Article 51.

But for those who agree with Mr. Acheson, the law is not so simple and clear. They will take the following facts into consideration in determining whether Israel was justified in her action. Although Israel was elected a member of the United Nations in 1949, the Arab countries have refused to recognize her existence and have maintained an active boycott against her. Although this boycott seems to be clearly "inconsistent with the Purposes of the United Nations" [Article 2 (4)], which all the members have agreed to fulfill in good faith, the United Nations has taken no active steps to bring it to an end. The Arab countries have also declared the destruction of Israel to be a major tenet of their policy, a destruction that is to be accomplished by an unprecedented massacre. As long as these threats were merely verbal, it might be argued that they did not constitute an immediate danger, but a more ominous situation arose when Egypt and her allies were supplied with armaments and airplanes by Czechoslovakia and the U.S.S.R. in 1955. It became increasingly serious when Egypt seized control of the Suez Canal on July 26, 1956, because this use of force was declared to be a triumph of Arab nationalism, which "marches forward; it knows its road and it knows its strength" (Colonel Nasser's speech on July 26, 1956). It became imminent when on October 23 a joint Egyptian-Jordanian-Syrian command was announced, to be headed by the Egyptian commander-in-chief in the event of major hostilities with Israel. During this period (October 20 and 24) there was a resumption of *fedayeen* raids across the Israeli-Egyptian frontier in which Israeli civilians were murdered. It did not come as a surprise, therefore, that on October 26 Israel began mobilizing and that on October 29 her forces crossed the armistice lines and invaded the Sinai Peninsula. The United Nations, which had remained impotent during all this period, although it was its duty to remove threats to the peace, then took action against Israel.

It is also important to note that the United Nations had failed to take any positive action in the disputes between Israel and Egypt concerning the Suez Canal and the Gulf of Aqaba. The Egyptian government had justified its refusal to allow Israeli ships passage through the canal on the ground that a state of war still existed between the two countries in spite of the fact that on September 1, 1951, the Security Council had adopted a resolution that found that the Egyptian action was "inconsistent with the objectives of a peaceful settlement between the parties and the establishment of a permanent peace in Palestine set forth in the Armistice Agreement." For more than five years thereafter Israel appealed unsuccessfully to the United Nations for aid in this matter, but no adequate steps were taken. There is some difficulty in seeing why, if Egypt was allowed to use force to keep Israeli ships from using the canal and the Gulf of Aqaba, Israel was not equally entitled to use force to secure a right of passage that had been recognized by the United Nations.

When all these circumstances are taken into consideration, it is not clear why the United Nations took unilateral action against Israel when her forces entered the Sinai Peninsula and refused to pay any regard to the preceding hostile threats and acts on the part of Egypt. It would have been more in consonance with justice and with the purposes stated in Article 1 (1) of the Charter if effective collective measures had been taken to restore order and to prevent future threats in an area in which peace has been continually endangered for more than a decade. On this point Mr. Acheson has said:

"Two wrongs," the President admonishes us, "do not make a right." Now it is quite true that the provision against the use or threat of force is in the treaty—for that is what the Charter is—but it clearly applies both ways, to Egypt as well as to Israel. Furthermore, equally basic in the Charter is the recognition, in Article 51, of the inherent right of self-defense, a right recognized in all law.

Assuredly in our own courts if a plaintiff should ask for an injunction against a continuing trespass, which he had provoked by his own preceding trespasses, he would find that he as well as the defendant would be enjoined. For among the famous maxims of equity are these: He who seeks equity must do equity; he who comes into equity must come with clean hands; equality is equity.

Depth of feeling may be useful in the field of morals, but it is an untrustworthy substitute for clarity of thought in that of law—and even, I suggest, in that hybrid product referred to as the moral law. If we are going to talk law, let us talk good law.[6]

Was the action taken by Great Britain and France in violation of the Charter?

Here again the answer will seem clear and simple to those who hold that the provisions of Article 2 (4) and Article 51 are absolute in character, whatever the surrounding circumstances may be. The war (because such it clearly was) between Israel and Egypt was obviously not an "armed attack" against Great Britain and France, and therefore they were not entitled to intervene, however vital might be their interest in maintaining the safety of the canal. It was their duty, it was held, to do nothing until the Security Council had determined on a course of action and then only if the Council called on them to apply the necessary measures (Article 41).

But would the Security Council have agreed on a course of action if Great Britain and France had not intervened? It is clear that the U.S.S.R. would have exercised its veto against

[6] *Ibid.*, p. 13.

any action that did not entail the unconditional withdrawal
of the Israeli forces from the Sinai Peninsula. On the other
hand Great Britain and France were entitled to hold that
this withdrawal should be coupled with adequate guarantees
that the rights, and the very existence, of Israel should be
protected in the future. Unanimity on the Security Council
could only have been secured if Great Britain and France had
been prepared to surrender a position that they regarded as the
only proper basis for a just solution in the Suez area. They
were later forced to surrender this position, but it is doubtful
whether this has contributed to a stable peace or strengthened
the status of the United Nations. There is therefore no reason
to think that the Security Council would have been able to
agree on a course of action at the time when Great Britain
and France intervened at Suez.

What steps then ought they to have taken to protect their
vital interest in the canal? They could have done nothing,
trusting to an immediate and overwhelming victory for Israel.
As experience has shown, this would have been the wisest
step, but it entailed the danger that the other Middle Eastern
countries would join in the conflict. It was not possible on
October 30, the date of the ultimatum, to foretell that the
Israeli action, which began on October 29, would prove so
successful. On the other hand, they could have joined with
the United States and the U.S.S.R. in forcing Israel to withdraw unconditionally, thus giving a complete victory to Colonel
Nasser, which he could have exploited in the future. Faced
with this choice, the British and the French took the view that
they were entitled to intervene to protect what they regarded
as a vital interest of their own by bringing to an end a conflict
that was due for the most part to the threats directed against
Israel by Egypt and by the preparations for her destruction.
In that way a situation could have been established that
would have made possible a just and stable settlement.

Professor Quincy Wright agrees that "the vital interest of
Great Britain in the flow of traffic through the canal cannot
be questioned," but, on the other hand, he holds that "under
the Charter the Members cannot constitute themselves police-

men to stop fights between others, without United Nations authorization." [7] He seems to regard this principle as absolute, even when it is clear that such authorization cannot be obtained.

In this connection it is interesting to note that under the common law it is not only the right, but a matter of legal duty, for a civilian to intervene in putting down breaches of the peace if the police have failed to do so. This provision, which has not weakened the authority of the state, is regarded as an essential adjunct to the ordinary administration of the law when an emergency arises. The intervention of the civilian is not limited to circumstances in which he is called on by the police to come to their aid; it is his independent duty to take action for the preservation of the peace.

It has been suggested, however, that the intervention by Great Britain and France was not made in good faith, but was a disguised attempt to regain control of the canal. It is difficult to reconcile this view with the fact that less than two years previously, on July 27, 1954, the British government had agreed with Egypt to move her troops out of the Suez Canal zone and had immediately implemented this promise. To occupy hostile territory is always an expensive and painful process, so that it is not clear why the British government, without any apparent reason, should have suddenly adopted an entirely different policy. It is more reasonable to believe that the intervention was made for the purpose of establishing peace in a zone where such peace was a vital British interest.

If we hold that the Charter prevents such intervention in a matter that is of vital interest to the country concerned, we are placing a burden on the United Nations that that novel organization may not be able to bear, because any failure on its part to take the necessary action will have disastrous results. In such circumstances membership in the United Nations would be a source of danger and of weakness to the law-abiding nations.

[7] Wright, op. cit., p. 273.

Was Egypt entitled to nationalize the
Universal Suez Canal Company?

On the night of July 26, 1956, Colonel Nasser seized the
property of the Suez Canal Company by force and expelled
its officials. The pilots, employed by the company, were compelled to continue to work under threat of imprisonment.
There had been no previous negotiations, and no warning
had been given either to the company or to the users of the
canal that such a step was contemplated. On August 4 the
governments of France, the United Kingdom, and the United
States issued a statement protesting against this "arbitrary
and unilateral seizure."

It is unnecessary to consider here the various conferences
and negotiations that followed during the next three months,
except to note that they proved unsuccessful. On September
23 the British and French governments requested a meeting
of the Security Council to consider the situation. On October
13 the Security Council adopted a resolution, submitted by
Great Britain and France, setting forth the requirements that
any settlement of the Suez question should meet, and inviting
the Egyptian government to make known promptly its proposals. The second part of the resolution, which recommended that, pending the conclusion of an agreement, the
Suez Canal Users' Association and the Egyptian authorities
should co-operate, was vetoed by the Soviet Union, thus leaving Egypt in complete control of the canal. The Egyptian
government made no proposals, but private talks were held
between the Secretary-General of the United Nations and the
Egyptian Minister of Foreign Affairs. Professor Wright is
correct in stating that Egypt finally accepted the principles
set out in the resolution,[8] but it is important to note that this
acceptance was dated November 2, 1956, three days after the
Franco-British intervention at Suez. The acceptance has since

[8] Wright, op. cit., p. 263.

been repudiated, so that it will be necessary to reconsider the whole question.[9]

It is also important to remember that the Suez Canal Company holds very large assets in countries outside Egypt. The question is therefore certain to arise as to whether Egypt, by having purported to nationalize the company, has acquired title to these assets.

It cannot be disputed that from the standpoint of interna-

[9] Although the question whether Colonel Nasser finally accepted all the six principles on October 13 is now of minor importance, nevertheless it is of interest to present the facts.

The third principle provided that "the operation of the Canal shall be insulated from the politics of any country." Concerning that principle Mr. Selwyn Lloyd said:

"I would draw the Council's attention, in particular, to the third requirement, providing for the insulation of the operation of the Canal from the politics of any country. The representative of the United States rightly described that requirement—I think I quote his actual words—as being the essence of the matter."

Similarly Mr. Dulles said:

"In my opening statement I spoke of the principles which govern a just solution of this problem. I emphasized one in particular, namely, that the operation of the Canal should be insulated from the politics of any country. I said that if that just principle were accepted, I believed the remaining problems could be resolved. That principle has been accepted, and I adhere to my belief that the remaining problems can be resolved."

But Dr. Fawzi's speech shows that the Egyptian acceptance was so qualified as to be meaningless. He said:

"Sub-paragraph (c) of paragraph 1 is aimed at providing for what it calls the insulation of the operation of the Canal from the politics of any country. It is my delegation's view that, to begin with, this expression is rather unfortunate as well as misleading, and allows scope for various and contradictory interpretations."

The subsequent negotiations between the Secretary-General and Dr. Fawzi show that Egypt never intended principle 3 to have any practical content. The creation of any sort of international body to control the operation of the canal was firmly rejected. In the final letter which M. Loutfi, the Permanent Representative of Egypt to the United Nations wrote on November 2, transmitting a communication from Dr. Fawzi, this rejection was repeated. It is therefore clear that the Egyptian interpretation of principle 3 was at no time in accord with the obvious meaning attached to it by the draftsmen of the resolution.

tional law every nation has the right to nationalize the companies it has created unless there is some special reason that may negative such a right. Thus, to take an illustration that has been frequently cited, Great Britain has nationalized its coal mines, its railways, and its electricity companies, but it has never been suggested that this was contrary to international law, although foreigners undoubtedly owned shares in these companies.

Why then did France, the United Kingdom, and the United States protest against the Egyptian action? They based their protest on this ground:

> But the present action involves far more than a simple act of nationalisation. It involves the arbitrary and unilateral seizure by one nation of an international agency which has the responsibility to maintain and to operate the Suez Canal so that all the signatories to, and beneficiaries of, the Treaty of 1888 can effectively enjoy the use of an international waterway upon which the economy, commerce, and security of much of the world depends.[10]

It is unfortunate that so much of the argument concerning Egypt's right to nationalize has been concerned with the technical question of whether the Suez Canal Company is an Egyptian company or not, because the problem to be considered is of far greater importance and of wider import. The point at issue is whether, even if we assume that the Suez Canal Company is an Egyptian company, Egypt has expressly or by necessary implication agreed not to nationalize the company during the duration of the concession.

The statutes of the Universal Suez Canal Company were approved by the Viceroy of Egypt in 1856. They provided (Article 3 and Article 73) that although the company had its seat at Alexandria, its administrative and legal domicile should be in Paris. The company was to be administered by a council of thirty-two members, representing the principal countries concerned in the enterprise (Article 24). In particular Article

[10] Joint statement issued on August 2, 1956, by the governments of France, the United Kingdom, and the United States.

4 provides that: "The duration of the Company shall be equal to the duration of the Concession." As the concession was to last for ninety-nine years from the date of the opening of the canal in 1869, the Egyptian government was under an obligation not to bring the company to an end before 1968. It is obvious that this provision must have been intended to protect the shareholders, because if Egypt had been entitled to nationalize the company the year after it had been completed, the shareholders would have been wiped out, except, perhaps, for an illusory promise to pay compensation.

A less direct recognition of Egypt's duty to respect the continued existence of the company can be found in the Treaty of 1888, which refers to "the system under which the navigation of this Canal has been placed," and in the fact, pointed out by Mr. T. T. F. Huang in his article "Some International and Legal Aspects of the Suez Canal Question," that between 1856 and 1956 the Egyptian government had concluded more than 100 agreements with the company as it would have done with a foreign power, and that many of the general laws of the country have not been applied to it.[11]

To hold that in these circumstances the Egyptian government was entitled to wipe out the company and seize all of its assets so as to "serve the purely national purposes of the Egyptian Government" is to disregard all considerations except the technical one that the company was necessarily incorporated in Egypt. In this connection it is important to note that modern international law has tended to recognize the true essence of a situation and has refused to be bound by form alone. Thus in the two world wars the prize courts held that the fact that a ship was sailing under a neutral flag did not prevent it from acquiring enemy character.

But, it has been argued, even if the existence of the company and of the concession was fixed at ninety-nine years, Egypt was entitled under the exercise of her sovereign power to bring them to an end before the expiration of that period, subject only, if at all, to a promise of compensation. If this

[11] T. T. F. Huang, "Some International and Legal Aspects of the Suez Canal Question," Amer. Jour. of International Law, LI (1957), 277-307.

is a true interpretation of sovereignty, then every agreement and concession made by a state will, in the future, depend solely on the will of the promisor. It is the negation of all legal and moral duties on the part of the state, and a repudiation of the basic principle of international law *pacta sunt servanda*. In the present case it would mean that the shareholders would be forced to accept an ephemeral promise in place of their concrete assets. But of far greater importance is the fact that there would be no guarantee that the maintenance of the canal when in Egyptian hands would not deteriorate to a disastrous degree. It is also possible that the absolute control of the canal by Egypt would lead to the demand for extortionate tolls. An appeal to the United Nations would then prove to be of little value.

This leads to the final and perhaps the most interesting question raised by the Suez dispute. As Nasser had used force to seize the property of the Suez Canal Company, could force be used to dislodge him if he refused to accept reasonable terms? It is on this point that there seems to have been a continuing difference of opinion between Great Britain and France on the one hand and the United States on the other. The former seem to have assumed that if the negotiations with Egypt broke down, then they would be entitled to use force in defense of what was a vital interest to their economic life. To meet Nasser's force with nothing more effective than legal and moral arguments was to engage in a losing battle. On the other hand, the American view seems to have been that the forcible seizure of the canal did not constitute an armed attack against a member of the United Nations, which alone would have justified the use of force under Article 51. On two occasions the United States government made it clear that it was opposed to the use of force. The first was when the Menzies mission went to Egypt on September 2 after the London Conference. It is hardly surprising that "the documents which have been published since show that the arguments of Mr. Menzies of Australia and his fellow members of the Committee made not the slightest impact upon

Colonel Nasser." [12] Similarly the Suez Canal Users' Association was stillborn when Mr. Dulles was careful to announce that the purpose of the association was not to coerce Egypt. Colonel Nasser, who is no mean card player, found for the second time that he had all the court cards in his hand.

It was this divergence of view concerning the right to use force that prevented the United States, France, and Great Britain from following a single consistent policy during the negotiations on the Egyptian seizure of the canal and later led to the fatal division between them after Israel crossed the Sinai border. The question has not been finally settled and may arise again under different circumstances. It will then be necessary to determine whether the limitation of force to self-defense against an armed attack is a reasonable and practical provision in a world in which the United Nations has not itself been able to carry out its duty to prevent threats of aggression and other breaches of the peace. There is, unfortunately, much to be said for Mr. Acheson's view that moral pressure alone may not prove adequate against those who are prepared to use physical force. It is not certain how the United Nations can continue to be effective if it insists that so impractical a doctrine is an essential part of its existence.

[12] Documents on the Suez Crisis (Royal Institute of International Affairs, London, 1957), p. 13.

Commentary

QUINCY WRIGHT
Professor Emeritus of International Law,
University of Chicago

PROFESSOR GOODHART DISCUSSES three legal issues involved in the Suez situation during the crisis of 1956: first, the legality of President Nasser's nationalization of the Suez Canal Company; second, the legality of Israel's intervention in Sinai on October 29, 1956; and third, the legality of the intervention by Great Britain and France at Suez on October 31, 1956.

Incidentally he discusses the legal issues raised by the Egyptian discrimination in the passage of Israel's ships through the Suez Canal and the Straits of Tiran. There is no disagreement between us on this. The Suez discrimination is contrary to the terms of the Treaty of 1888, to the Egyptian-Israeli armistice, and to the Security Council resolution of 1951 calling upon Egypt to stop this discrimination. The opinion of the Permanent Court of International Justice in the Wimbledon case, interpreting Germany's treaty obligation to accord free passage through the Kiel Canal, also supports Israel's position. The Aqaba discrimination is contrary to the principle of freedom of navigation of straits connecting portions of the high seas, set forth by the International Court of Justice in the Corfu Channel case. The Arabs claim that the Gulf of Aqaba is not high seas, because Israel lacks good title to the port of Elath, and the four Arab states with territory on it can close it by agreement. The Israel title, however, is supported by the armistices and has been generally recognized. Egypt's contention that these discriminations are justified by continuance of a state of war with Israel is insupportable, because the United Nations Charter prohibits a state of war initiated by a member of the United Nations. A state of war is surely incompatible with the obligation of members to "refrain in their international relations from the threat or use of force against the territorial integrity or political independence of any state" [Article 2 (4)]. Egypt's plea that these discriminations are justified by a "defensive necessity" is also inadequate to support such general discriminations, though it might justify Egypt in taking precautionary measures to assure that any Israeli vessel planning to use the canal was not intending to damage Egyptian installations while in passage.

This problem is not directly related to the issue of President Nasser's nationalization of the Suez Canal Company. The discrimination, which dates from 1949, appears to have been acquiesced in by Great Britain for five years while the Universal Suez Canal Company was administering the canal and British military forces were policing it. This discrimination, furthermore, is inadequate to justify Israel's invasion of October, 1956, because it had been a matter of controversy for seven years and could not, therefore, be considered to create such a condition of "necessity" as to justify an armed attack by Israel on Egyptian territory.

I will now make some comments on the three principal points discussed by Professor Goodhart, dealing with his last point first.

1. Nationalization of the Canal Company

Professor Goodhart questions the legality of President Nasser's nationalization of the Suez Canal Company on the basis of Article 3 and Article 4 of the statute of the company (1856) providing that although the seat of the company was in Alexandria, its administration and legal domicile should be in Paris and that "the duration of the Company shall be equal to the duration of the Concession." The statute, however, like the concession, was an act under Egyptian law and subject to subsequent Egyptian legislation. The contractual obligation of Egypt to the company in the concession is not strengthened in international law by its inclusion also in the statute, although the terms of the statute may strengthen the company's claim that the nationalization act cannot affect its assets outside of Egypt. The company's rights in Egypt, in any case, rest on a contract with Egypt under Egyptian law.

Professor Goodhart also draws attention to numerous agreements made by Egypt with the company "as it would have done with a foreign power" and of the fact that "many of the general laws of the country have not been applied" to the company. But again, it is difficult to see how the making of subsequent agreements with an Egyptian corporation, or exempting that corporation from some general laws, acts that are certainly within the legislative power of Egypt, gave the company an international personality with rights under international law.

The issue is one not of form, but of substance—was the company an Egyptian corporation or an international personality? Only in the latter case would it have rights per se under international law, unless indeed one invokes a conception of "human rights," a conception recognized in principle by the United Nations Charter, but not as yet implemented by explicit covenants. There is no analogy here to the prize court cases, which Professor Goodhart cites, holding that ships under neutral flag have an enemy character if the predominant ownership is enemy. Such cases clearly were governed by international law concerning the right of neutral states to protect the vessels of their nationality at sea against belligerent action in time of war; and the belligerent's prize courts were competent in the first instance to apply international law to determine the enemy or neutral character of the vessel. There was no question in these cases but that international law applied. In the present case, however, the issue is whether the matter is governed by Egyptian law or by international law. It seems to me that the contractual rights of the company in respect to its functioning in Egypt were governed by Egyptian, not international, law.

It has also been suggested that there was no supervening necessity that might have justified President Nasser in taking over the company in exercise of the police power. The constitutional law of most countries, however, recognizes a distinction between exercises of the police power and of the power of eminent domain. The first can be exercised only under necessity, but does not require full compensation, while the latter requires only a public purpose, but does require full compensation. This distinction appears to be recognized also in international law, which requires a state not to deny justice to aliens within its territory, but refuses to find such a denial of justice if aliens are deprived of title to property in its territory through the proper exercise of either the police power or the power of eminent domain. Professor Goodhart raises the question: "As Nasser had used force to seize the property of the Suez Canal Company, could force be used to dislodge him if he refused to accept reasonable terms?" Surely it is a prerogative of a state to use force to maintain its law *within its territory*. Such a normal exercise of sovereignty is not an armed attack against another state and cannot justify an invasion by another state.

The basic distinction in international law has been between instruments and transactions governed by that law and those governed by the municipal law of a state. The principle *pacta sunt servanda* refers, in international law, only to the former. In principle a sovereign state has full control over its municipal law and over rights under that law, subject only to its duty not to deny justice to aliens. The company's concession and statute appear to have been instruments of Egyptian municipal law. Consequently, Nasser's nationalization would not be a denial of justice to the foreign interests involved and would not, therefore, be a violation of international law if the nationalization served a public purpose and was followed by prompt and adequate compensation.

It may be that a rule of international law is developing that distinguishes between alien property within a state's territory, which is subject to eminent domain, and contracts or concessions made by the government of a state with a foreign individual or corporation, which should not be subject to that procedure. This principle, however, would not apply if the company was an Egyptian corporation and not an alien one;

and in any case, international tribunals have generally held that concessions to foreign private companies, even when foreign governments hold stock in them, as in the case of the Anglo-Iranian Oil Company, are instruments of the municipal law of the conceding company unless protected by the explicit terms of a treaty or other international instrument. This was the case, for example, in the Mavrommatis Palestine concession, which the Permanent Court of International Justice sustained because of the obligations undertaken by Great Britain in the Palestine Mandate.

The British government attempted to show that the Suez Canal Company's concession was expressly protected by the Constantinople Treaty of 1888, but the preamble of that treaty, especially when read in the light of the *travaux préparatoires*,[1] indicates that the purpose of the treaty was not to accord international status to the company, but to give international protection to the right of navigation through the canal because that right was not assured by the concession, as it would have been if the concession had been an instrument of international law. Furthermore, Article 14 of the treaty provides that the engagements of the latter "shall not be limited by the duration of the acts of concession of the Universal Suez Canal Company," thus indicating that the treaty right of navigation was not tied up with the limited duration of the concession. The treaty, therefore, supports the Egyptian claim that the company was a creature of Egyptian law.

I do not wish to be dogmatic on this question. The conflict between good faith of states in carrying out contracts and concessions and the anxiety of states not to be bound by the dead hand of the past against present public interest has been considered extensively in the United States Supreme Court with reference to the application of the constitutional provision forbidding impairment of the obligation of contracts by the states of the union (Dartmouth College, Charles River Bridge, and other cases). In spite of the explicit constitutional provision, the Supreme Court has been aware of the danger

[1] See T. T. F. Huang, "Some International and Legal Aspects of the Suez Canal Question," *Amer. Jour. of International Law*, LI (1957), 277-307.

of considering either of these claims as absolute and, while in principle maintaining the sanctity of contracts, has permitted states to construe contracts and concessions deemed contrary to public interest so strictly that their value is practically confiscated, thus applying a standard not unlike that of international law prohibiting denials of justice to aliens. On the whole, it seems to me that the only claim of the foreign shareholders of the company against Egypt is for full compensation for the fair value of their property taken over by Egypt.

2. Israel's Invasion of Sinai

Professor Goodhart seeks to justify Israel's invasion of Sinai on grounds of "necessary self-defense." Article 51 of the United Nations Charter, however, permits individual or collective self-defense only "if an armed attack occurs against a Member of the United Nations." Professor Goodhart believes that this must be read in connection with Article 1 of the Charter, which states the primary purpose of the United Nations "to take effective collective measures for the prevention and removal of threats to the peace, and for the suppression of acts of aggression or other breaches of the peace." Because the United Nations had failed to take effective measures to eliminate Egypt's "threat" to destroy Israel by building armaments and alliances, by declaring that a state of war existed only suspended by the armistice, and by tolerating or even stimulating fedayeen raids, Israel, he believes, was justified in taking protective measures. The recent arms shipments to Egypt from Czechoslovakia he cites as making the danger more critical.

As a matter of Charter interpretation, the issue concerns the imminence of Egypt's menace to Israel. Was there an immediate threat or only a long-run danger? The Charter uses a number of expressions to indicate the degree of imminence of danger to the peace (italics mine).

a. Article 51 refers to "armed attack," which is an actual

"breach of the peace" in the sense of Article 1 (1, Clause 1)
and Article 39, going beyond a "threat to the peace" and
certainly justifying military defensive measures if it also constitutes an "act of aggression" in the sense of these articles.

b. Article 2 (4) requires members to refrain from "threat
or use of force." Article 39 requires the Security Council to
determine the existence of any "threat to the peace, breach
of the peace, or act of aggression," and Article 1 (1, Clause 1)
asserts the primary purpose of the United Nations to take
measures to remove "threats to the peace" and to suppress
"acts of aggression or other breaches of the peace." The term
threat in these articles, because of its close association with
the term breach of the peace, is clearly intended to refer to
imminent dangers of attack creating "the instant and overwhelming necessity of defense" that customary international
law has held justifies military self help (the Caroline Case).
Whether such a threat may also constitute an "act of aggression" permitting "individual or collective self-defense" under
the Charter is not altogether clear, because such a threat might
be short of the "armed attack" referred to in Article 51.

c. Article 2 (3) requires the members to "settle their international disputes by peaceful means in such a manner that
international peace and security, and justice, are not endangered." Article 34 authorizes the Security Council to in-
vestigate disputes or situations, the continuance of which "is
likely to endanger the maintenance of international peace
and security." The latter phrase is repeated in other articles
of Chapter VI, and Article 1 (1, Clause 2) expresses the same
thought as the second purpose of the United Nations:

> to bring about by peaceful means, and in conformity with the
> principles of justice and international law, adjustment or settle-
> ment of international disputes or situations which might lead
> to a breach of the peace.

d. Article 14 authorizes the General Assembly to "recommend measures for the peaceful adjustment of any situation,
regardless of origin, which it deems likely to impair the general welfare or friendly relations among nations."

Thus four typical situations of decreasing gravity are recognized: first, "breach of the peace"; second, "threat to the peace"; third, situations endangering "international peace and security"; and fourth, situations "likely to impair . . . friendly relations among nations." Recommendation on the last type, in which the danger to the peace is most remote, is made a responsibility of the General Assembly, but "prompt and effective action" in the first three types of situation constitute, under Article 24, the "primary responsibility [of the Security Council] for the maintenance of international peace and security." The Charter, however, provides different procedures for these three types of situation; "breach of the peace" and "threat to the peace" are treated together in Chapter VII, although only the former would strictly constitute an "armed attack" under Article 51, while disputes and situations endangering "international peace and security" are treated in Chapter VI. As already noted, Article 1 (1) makes the same differentiation in its two clauses as does Article 2 (3, 4). This distinction, which is critical in Charter interpretation, undoubtedly places the prevention of hostilities ahead of the just settlement of disputes. The Security Council must act effectively to stop hostilities or immediate threats thereof, but it can only recommend on the settlement of disputes or situations that endanger international peace and security.

Undoubtedly the just settlement of disputes is in the long run essential if peace is to be maintained; but, on the other hand, human experience has shown that if states are free to utilize armed force to obtain what they consider justice, wars will recur and weaker states will suffer injustices. Thus, as Judge Charles DeVisscher has said: "So long as the individualistic distribution of power among states persists, with the major political tension that it engenders, peace will serve justice better than justice will serve peace." [2]

I do not think Professor Goodhart gives sufficient emphasis to this basic distinction of the Charter. He notes Israel's appeal for five years to the United Nations on the Suez and

[2] Charles DeVisscher, *Theory and Reality in Public International Law* (Princeton, 1957), p. 328.

Aqaba issues and suggests that if a state cannot resort to forceful self-help, a wrong-doer who is careful to avoid armed attack can act with impunity and suggests that ordinary state law gives its citizens powers of self protection if the police fail to give it. I do not believe, however, that any civilized legal system would accept a plea of necessary self-defense in a murder trial merely on the ground that the authorities of the state had been negligent in protecting vital interests of the defendent threatened by the victim's behavior over a considerable period. The defendent would have to show an actual attack or an immediately impending attack such as could be deduced from attempted burglary or robbery. Territorial invasion, not justified by defensive necessity, international authority, or explicit invitation of the government, is analogous to murder because it inevitably involves homicide usually on a large scale. It was so treated by the Nuremberg Tribunal. The Charter does make it possible with this interpretation for a wrong-doer who is careful to avoid armed attack to continue his wrong-doing unless the peaceful procedures provided by the Charter can induce him to mend his ways. This may be unsatisfactory, but the framers of the Charter felt that the injustices that it might permit were less than the injustices that would inevitably flow from unilateral resorts to military self-help.

Professor Goodhart assumes that the relations of Egypt and Israel constituted a threat to the peace requiring effective Security Council action in default of which Israel could engage in military self-help. But the General Assembly, which assumed competence after the British and French had vetoed a Security Council resolution, while recognizing the situation as one that endangered international peace and security, considered it one that the parties at interest were obliged to settle peacefully in accord with the armistice and the Security Council's six-point recommendation of October 13, 1956. The General Assembly did not perceive an "armed attack" or "threat to the peace" by Egypt, justifying self-help by Israel.

It is to be noted, however, that Israel was not branded as an "aggressor." According to precedent, the General Assembly merely called for a cease-fire by both sides. As this was eventually accepted, there has, as yet, been no occasion for declaring anyone an aggressor, as there was in the Hungarian case. In that case, the Soviet Union declined to accept the General Assembly's cease-fire and was denominated an aggressor. This issue might arise in the Suez case in connection with Egypt's claims for compensation for the damages it suffered from the intervention. This might require that the facts be examined to determine whether the danger to Israel from Nasser's belligerent statements and his incitement of *fedayeen* raids amounted to an "armed attack" in the sense of the Charter. It would also, however, be necessary to determine whether the massive size of the Israel invasion, Israel's long delay in withdrawing from the Gaza and Aqaba areas, and Prime Minister Ben Gurion's statement at the time of the invasion, repudiating the armistice and declaring an intent to acquire territory beyond the armistice lines, did not indicate objectives on the part of Israel other than defense. It may be that Israel could sustain a case for defense, but much could be said on the Egyptian side.

3. Anglo-French Invasion of Suez

Professor Goodhart attempts to defend the Anglo-French intervention in a similar manner. He supports the contention of those countries "that they were entitled to intervene to protect what they regarded as a vital interest of their own." With the extremely subjective character of the term "vital interest" this would seem to leave an indefinite discretion to states to resort to military self-help.

It appears that the only interests that have been considered under the Charter sufficiently "vital" to justify military self-defense are actual, or perhaps immediately threatened, attacks on the territory or armed forces of a state. Attacks on official agencies of a state in the territory of another (as the Chinese Boxer attack on the legations in 1900), attacks on resident citizens of the state tolerated by the authorities (as in the

Nanking barrage of 1927), or seizures of merchant vessels (as in the American-French hostilities of 1798) have in the past been considered justifications for armed defensive action; but under the Charter, these would probably be considered situations endangering "international peace and security" rather than "armed attacks" or "threats to the peace."

It is true that traditional international law permitted military reprisals to gain a remedy for a clear violation of international law after peaceful means had failed, provided the reprisals were no more severe than the injury complained of; but it was the purpose of the Charter to eliminate this procedure.

One can admit that freedom of navigation in the Suez Canal was in the usual sense a "vital interest" of Great Britain and other states. The Constantinople Treaty of 1888 was concluded in recognition of that fact, which was reaffirmed in the Anglo-Egyptian treaties of 1936 and 1954. Professor Goodhart says that Great Britain and France "seem to have assumed that if the negotiations with Egypt broke down, then they would be entitled to use force in defense of what was a vital interest to their economic life." He refers to the danger of "extortionate tolls" being charged and the canal deteriorating because of maladministration. These dangers, however, were speculative. Nasser declared from the first that he would respect the Convention of 1888. He administered the canal efficiently from the date of nationalization to that of intervention without raising dues and without discrimination, apart from the Israel discrimination, which the British had been acquiescing in for years. He accepted the six principles, proposed for negotiation by the Security Council on October 13, through his representative Foreign Minister Mahmoud Fawzi, who, on invitation, attended that meeting.[3] In his press conference of October 16, 1956, Secretary of State Dulles discussed the six principles agreed upon by Egypt and the Western powers and approved by the Security Council.[4]

[3] United Nations Security Council, Rec. 742nd meeting, October 13, 1956, p. 7 and United Nations Review, November, 1956, p. 48.
[4] U. S. Department of State Bulletin, XXXV (1956), 659.

Nasser's declaration concerning canal administration under Egyptian authority on April 24, 1957, after the interventions and the clearance of the canal, implemented these principles in such large measure that the Security Council acquiesced, at least for the time being.[5] This record hardly justifies Professor Goodhart's assumption that Egypt could not be trusted to observe its treaty obligations.

Referring to the Anglo-French interest in preventing injury to the canal from the Israeli-Egyptian hostilities, Professor Goodhart says that "under the common law it is not only the right, but a matter of legal duty, for a civilian to intervene in putting down breaches of the peace if the police have failed to do so." He says:

> There is therefore no reason to think that the Security Council would have been able to agree on a course of action at the time when Great Britain and France intervened at Suez.
> What steps then ought they to have taken to protect their vital interest in the canal?

The answer might well be that they ought to have refrained from vetoing the Security Council's resolution, already accepted by the Soviet Union, China, the United States, and four other members, calling upon Israel and Egypt to cease fire.[6] Surely that would have been more likely to protect the canal than the bombarding of Port Said, which was certain to induce Egyptian retaliation.

But Professor Goodhart says that this would have given "a complete victory to Colonel Nasser, which he could have exploited in the future." It should be added that he would have remained subject to his obligations under the Treaty of 1888, to the supervision of the parties to that treaty under Article 8, and to the jurisdiction of the Security Council, which had declared the principles that he should observe and to which he had agreed.

[5] Quincy Wright, "Suez and International Waterways," Foreign Policy Bulletin, XXXVI (1957), 141; U. S. Department of State Bulletin, XXXVI (1957), 775.
[6] U. S. Department of State Bulletin, XXXV (1956), 750.

What I fear some Western states can be accused of is not "colonialism" in a strict sense, but unwillingness to apply to Eastern states the principle of territorial sovereignty, limited only by international law and treaties, that they have accepted for themselves since the Peace of Westphalia. Western states also hesitate to apply in their relations with the East the Charter prohibition of military self-help, except in necessary self-defense or with the authority of the United Nations. The Eastern states are insisting, however, that the principle of the "sovereign equality of states" applies to them also and that the principle requiring members of the United Nations to "settle their international disputes by peaceful means" applies to all powers great and small. These are the principles that the Charter seeks to establish. Professor Goodhart insists that international machinery to prevent injustice is a precondition for the prohibition of military self-help. Justice, he implies, must come before peace. But this order of development is contrary both to historic experience within states and to the prescriptions of the Charter. Peace must come first. Justice is a delicate flower that does not bloom amidst the clang of arms. In England the king's courts began to develop the common law only after the king's arms had established the king's peace. The United Nations, like the League of Nations before it, seeks to organize collective security against aggression so that institutions and procedures of peaceful settlement may have the opportunity to function, and it seeks to develop international law so that nations will be confident that it embodies justice. The difficulty of this task has been illustrated often since 1920, but the world's reaction to the interventions in the fall of 1956, both in Suez and in Hungary, marks progress. With the threat of intercontinental ballistic missiles carrying hydrogen war heads, the effort must be continued if succeeding generations are to be saved from the scourge of war and a world of justice under law is to emerge.

XII

The United Nations and the Suez Crisis

CLYDE EAGLETON
*Research Professor Emeritus of International Law,
New York University*

I HAVE HAD SOME DIFFICULTY in trying to decide where to begin this essay because it has so many ramifications. I am going to begin with self-determination, mostly in the hope of intriguing your interest by making you wonder how I will get around to the subject assigned to me, which is the relation of the United Nations to the Suez Canal issue. I suspect, however, that you will not have much trouble seeing the connection!

Self-determination is a magical word today, though nobody knows what it means. It brings a sympathetic response from most Americans—naturally enough, since this nation was born in that way and its people have always been anticolonial in feeling. There is no international law that says that a group of people have a right to determine what government they want; in the past, those groups that achieved self-determination did so by their own might or with the help of someone else, as happened in the case of the United States. They did not go to a court about it, nor were they voted in by the community of nations. Yet the feeling seems prevalent everywhere in the world that when a group of people say they want to be independent, or even when someone else says it for them, they are morally and even legally entitled to have independence.

273

This attitude leaves a lot of questions unanswered. Is just any group whatever entitled to self-determination? The Confederacy in the United States? Long Island? *Ad absurdum*, each individual human being? This is not a far-fetched thought of my own, for the United Nations General Assembly put into the draft Covenant of Human Rights (not yet adopted) a right of self-determination for the human beings to whom it applies! Is a group necessarily better off independent than under the administration of some competent state? And would independence for all claimants mean more or less order and peace in the community of nations?

There are many other such questions, and I do not raise them from an *anti*-anticolonial viewpoint. I would like to find a road between colonialism and anticolonialism, for the conflict between these views has become one of the most important issues in the world today—I am inclined to say, *the* most important. Both the United States and the United Nations have become so badly entangled in it that they can not find a road out. The anticolonials have become a third force in the politics of the world, able to be a balance between Western democracy and communism, able to blackmail either side, and especially the United States.

This development became possible after the establishment of the United Nations. That institution, in the first place, enables one to think of decision by the community of nations, rather than of a unilateral struggle for independence, which has thus far been the situation. The General Assembly is a forum where the small states can be heard with their pleas and their complaints; in it, at present, these small states have equal votes and constitute a voting majority. The term *self-determination* was put into the Charter, and along with it provisions concerning trusteeship and colonies, the latter euphemistically described in Chapter XI as "Non-Self-Governing Territories." This combination of factors made possible a gradual strengthening of the anticolonial forces in the United Nations and led to a very interesting constitutional development within that body, which I shall not survey here. I remark only that the Charter is not allowed to stand in the way of what is wanted; it is interpreted as desired by majority vote, and reference to judicial interpretation is consistently denied.

Now, the anticolonial members of the General Assembly can usually make up a majority on any issue that concerns them, particularly if the United States is on their side, as has frequently been the case. We might note, too, that it is the weakest members of the United Nations that thus dominate its action. The fourteen states that pay the smallest part of the budget—.04 of 1 per cent each—are all in this bloc. Taking fifty-three states that are usually in the anticolonial bloc—and this includes the comparatively large contribution made by the Soviet bloc—all fifty-three together pay less than one-third of the budget.

The anticolonial struggle has thus become crucial for the United Nations, partly because it is so dominated, and partly because the claim is now being made that it is the authority that should decide that a group is entitled to self-determination. Actually, it is no longer self-determination, but United Nations determination, that is called for; and the United Nations was not equipped or authorized to perform such an important function. I shall return to the effect of this struggle upon the United Nations as an institution.

The above situation, so sketchily presented, constitutes the factual background under which the United Nations must try to carry out the purposes and principles of the Charter. When the state of Israel was created, the anticolonial group had not coalesced nor realized its strength; as it grew in strength and activity, the position of the Arab states was strengthened against Israel. In 1948, the Security Council could determine that a threat to the peace existed in the Middle East and impose an armistice; in 1951, it could condemn Egypt for blockading the Suez Canal, though it did nothing effective about it; by now, in the General Assembly, which has largely taken over such matters, it would be an exceptional situation in which there was a vote against any member of the anticolonial group. On the other hand, it is not at all difficult to get a majority *against* any colonial power. Indeed, self-determination, as practiced in the General Assembly, is not applied to any oppressed peoples except colonial possessions—the plight of Hyderabad, or Kashmir, or Hungary, or the Republic of the South Moluccas, arouses little or no interest among the states in the anticolonial group.

When, in 1952, Nasser ousted Farouk and sought to make himself the leader of the Arab world, the Middle Eastern conflict centered around Egypt; the withdrawal of British troops left the Suez Canal to Egypt, and the nationalization of the Suez Canal in July, 1956, in retaliation for United States refusal of aid for the Aswan Dam, focused the problem around the Suez Canal. But the point that I wish to make is that this is all part of the anticolonial movement and we are not apt to obtain a satisfactory settlement of the Suez issue, or of the situation of Israel, or more generally a satisfactory operation of the United Nations, until the anticolonial struggle is somewhat cleared up, and workable principles of self-determination are established and put into use.

This is the background, very sketchily stated, of the relation of the United Nations to the Suez Canal issue. When the canal was nationalized on July 26, 1956, the matter was not taken to the United Nations. The United Kingdom and France proposed a conference, and the United States supported this proposal; on August 16, twenty-two states, not including Egypt, met at London, where the United States suggested an international board to operate the canal. A five-man committee was sent to interview Nasser, who made no concessions; and so, on September 12, England and France brought the matter to the attention of the Security Council. On September 19, there was a second conference, at which Secretary Dulles proposed a Suez Canal Users' Association. I observe that Mr. Dulles has steadily watered down his proposals in order to meet the sovereign claims of Egypt, and to keep in favor with the anticolonialists.

On September 23, the English and French asked the Security Council to act, and this was followed next day by a similar request from Egypt, based on its own complaint. The Security Council discussed the matter at nine meetings, from

October 5 to 13, and on the last day adopted six principles, agreed to by Egypt, as follows:

1. There should be free and open transit through the Canal without discrimination, overt or covert—this covers both political and technical aspects.

2. Egypt's sovereignty should be respected.

3. The operation of the Canal should be insulated from the politics of any country.

4. The manner of fixing tolls and charges should be decided by agreement between Egypt and users.

5. A fair proportion of the dues should be allotted to development.

6. In case of disputes, unresolved affairs between the Suez Canal Company and the Egyptian Government should be settled by an arbitration with suitable terms of reference and suitable provisions for the payment of sums found to be due.

However, Egypt, Syria, and Jordan announced a unified command of their military forces, and on October 25, Israel mobilized. On the next day Israel marched against Egypt and easily defeated its forces. The United States asked the Security Council to meet to consider the situation, but it then became further complicated by the Anglo-French ultimatum that they would intervene unless the fighting was stopped. Israel was willing, but Egypt refused, and on October 31 the English and French began military action against Egypt.

The Security Council considered the matter on October 30. A resolution by the United States calling upon Israel to withdraw and upon all members to refrain from the use of force was vetoed by England and France, with Australia and Belgium abstaining; a Soviet resolution was also vetoed. Thereupon a Yugoslav resolution was adopted to "call an emergency special session of the General Assembly as provided in the General Assembly's resolution 377 (V)"—the Uniting for Peace resolution adopted in 1950. The United Kingdom and France voted against this resolution, but under the Uniting for Peace resolution, their votes did not prevent decision. So the matter was transferred to the First Emergency Special

Session of the General Assembly, in which there is no veto, but in which there is an anticolonial majority.

On November 2, Resolution 997 (E.S.-1) was adopted, calling for a cease-fire, withdrawal of forces, and refraining from acts which would obstruct implementation of the resolution. On the next day, Canada proposed a resolution, which was adopted as 998 (E.S.-1) calling upon the Secretary-General to

> submit to it within forty-eight hours a plan for the setting up, with the consent of the nations concerned, of an emergency international United Nations Force, to secure and supervise the cessation of hostilities in accordance with all the terms of the aforementioned resolution.

On November 4, Resolution 999 (E.S.-1), introduced by nineteen Afro-Asian states, authorized the Secretary-General to arrange a cease-fire and report within twelve hours; the Secretary-General tried, but it is to be doubted whether anyone expected him to succeed. On the next day, the General Assembly approved the Secretary-General's plan for an emergency force and in Resolutions 1000 and 1001 (E.S.-1) set up a United Nations Command. Resolution 1002 (E.S.-1) called upon Israel and the United Kingdom and France immediately to withdraw their forces; and the problem then was turned over to the regular session of the General Assembly, which began on November 12.

Meanwhile, the English and French had said they would stop action if Egypt and Israel would accept a United Nations force to maintain order until a permanent settlement could be reached; until the United Nations force was ready, they would stay between Israel and Egypt. Israel said she would agree to a cease-fire if Egypt would; she also said that the Armistice of 1949 was by now a fiction and that the United Nations Truce Supervision people should leave Gaza. Strong pressures from all sides concentrated upon the United Kingdom, and on November 5 a cease-fire was ordered. On December 16 the United Nations force moved in, and by December 22 the English and French forces were out, having suffered a remarkable humiliation.

I wish now to consider the United Nations Emergency Force, which some think of as the beginning of a real international police force. Perhaps it is a beginning, but at present it is far from being a police force. The report of the Secretary-General, planning the force, was based upon General Assembly resolutions; these, he said, implied that the responsible officers for such a force should be appointed by and made responsible to the General Assembly and under its instructions to the Secretary-General. The force should be recruited from members who were not permanent members of the Security Council; it should be temporary in nature, and its tasks should be determined by the General Assembly; and it should have no intent to affect the military balance. Furthermore it was clear, he continued, that since the General Assembly under the Uniting for Peace resolution did not have the authority given to the Security Council by Chapter VII of the Charter, the force could not be stationed in or operate in a country without the consent of that country. While it was true that the resolution (1000 E.S.-1) called upon the force to "secure the cessation of hostilities," this was to be done in accordance with the terms of the resolution; and since this called for a cease-fire and for the parties to withdraw, the Secretary-General concluded that the force could not operate until after the belligerent forces had withdrawn and then only by the consent of Egypt. The United Nations Emergency Force would not be a military force occupying a country; it was no more than an international patrol, inserted between the belligerents, by their kind permission.

The reasoning of the Secretary-General is impeccable; it was approved by the General Assembly, and the force has operated upon regulations drawn accordingly. Nevertheless, I could wish that the Secretary-General had stretched logic a little more in the direction of strengthening the United Nations. I am inclined to agree, in this respect, with Professor Maxwell Cohen, in the Canadian *International Journal* and with Hamilton Fish Armstrong in the July issue of *Foreign*

Affairs, that he might have claimed a little more administrative authority;[1] but I have to admit that he was faced with an anticolonial majority entirely in favor of Egypt and backed by the United States of America. An opportunity was lost here, for which the Secretary-General can not be blamed.

Now, I should like to look back more critically over the situation. It is clear that the anticolonial group has had its way. The United Nations had taken no action concerning raids by Egyptian *fedayeen* on Israel, beyond hortatory resolutions addressed to both sides. Egypt had for years blockaded the Suez Canal to Israeli shipping; this was condemned by the Security Council in 1951. Egypt asserts that she is at war with Israel and therefore has a right to blockade; yet surely such a position, condemned by the Security Council, is as illegal under the Charter as Egypt asserted the action of England and France to be illegal. The Foreign Minister of Israel put it in these words: "A comfortable division of powers has been made; the Arab states unilaterally enjoy the 'rights of war'; Israel has the responsibility for keeping the peace." [2] The United Nations did not inquire into the legality or the consequence of Egyptian seizure of the canal.

The reason for this inactivity is manifest—the anticolonial majority; and, for the same reason, strong action was taken by the United Nations against Israel, France, and England. It is not necessary to inquire as to the legality or justification for the action of these states; it made no difference whether they were right or wrong. The decision would be the same by an anticolonial majority political vote.

The condemnation of the three states was justified by President Eisenhower when he said that the "use of military force to solve international disputes could not be reconciled with the principles and purposes of the United Nations." [3]

[1] Maxwell Cohen, "The United Nations Emergency Force: A Preliminary View," *International Journal*, XII (1957), 109-127; Hamilton Fish Armstrong, "UN Experience in Gaza," *Foreign Affairs*, XXXV (July, 1957), 600-619.

[2] See Abba Eban's talks at the United Nations Security Council, Rec. 558th meeting, September 1, 1951.

[3] U. S. *Department of State Bulletin*, XXXVI (1957), 387.

Israel had asked for certain guarantees as a condition for withdrawal, and as to them, the President asked: "Should a nation which attacks and occupies foreign territory in the face of UN disapproval be allowed to impose conditions on its own withdrawal?" He replied: "I do not, myself, see how this could be reconciled with the Charter of the United Nations." [4] This is possibly a correct statement of the principles of the Charter, but one would wish that the United Nations would apply it equally. But this it can not do; it is stymied; its tiller is tied down and it can move only in one direction. It can not render justice equally between its members; it must always favor the anticolonials against the colonial powers.

This sad situation of the United Nations was assured by the attitude of the United States—if its various tergiversations can be called an attitude. The American people have always been anticolonial in their feelings; I have been myself, but now I find no solution in so feeling. The anxious desire to keep the new states on our side in the struggle against communism has reinforced the government in its anticolonial policy, though we know that the colonial powers are our chief friends and allies and also the states without which, with us, the United Nations could not survive. This is a dilemma from which we have not been able to extricate ourselves, but on the whole we have been on the anticolonial side; we have not slapped any of them down, but we have joined with them to slap down some of our best friends. Without our support it is to be doubted whether the anticolonial majority could have achieved so great a triumph for Nasser and so great a humiliation of England and France. The result has been to reduce the United Nations to impotence in any issue affecting a colonial power.

I interpolate at this point, after considering Mr. Goodhart's views and Mr. Wright's comment, that if the United Nations does not, or can not protect a member and that member is not allowed to defend itself, the aggrieved state is left with no means of redress. This would mean that law-abiding states

[4] *Ibid.*, 389.

would be left at the mercy of law-breaking states and that law breakers would have sanctuary in the United Nations and could not be touched by the use of force. As Mr. Goodhart stated, it would be dangerous then for law-abiding states to be members of the United Nations; consequently I can not agree with Mr. Wright, who says that we must put peace above law and justice. This would mean that the law-breakers would rule the world.

Mr. Eisenhower has strongly supported the principles of the United Nations in his speeches, and, I think, with sincerity; but the United States, whether under Truman or Eisenhower, has not always felt that it must be bound by these principles. The Truman Doctrine concerning Greece and Turkey and the action in Korea were undertaken without waiting for the United Nations to approve. We did not let the Suez Canal issue go before it; we used it to gain the favor of anticolonial states by condemning England and France; we abandoned it again in the Eisenhower Doctrine. True, that doctrine is said to be subordinated to the United Nations, but this is manifestly impossible. In the face of a Russian veto in the Security Council and an anticolonial majority in the General Assembly, it would not be possible to secure United Nations approval for military intervention by the United States in the affairs of the Middle East. If the Eisenhower Doctrine means anything, then, it must mean action taken independently of the United Nations—the same sort of action for which we condemned France and England.

In what I have said I have not intended to be anti-anticolonial; I still think self-determination is a noble principle. But no practical means have been provided for determining what group of people should be free, and when, and under what conditions; the United Nations has no authority beyond recommendation and no criteria for making such a determination. It is simply not reasonable to assert that any group that desires independence is entitled to have it. What a world of anarchy this would produce! Even less reasonable is it to say that all peoples under colonial rule, and *only those peoples*, are able, and should be permitted, to be independent states.

Yet this is the foundation upon which the anticolonial majority in the United Nations stands.

If you ask me what all this has to do with the Suez Canal crisis, my answer is that this crisis, or others like it, can not be properly solved until the United Nations is brought out from under the control of the anticolonial majority; and I am sure that this can not be done except through strong leadership by the United States. I do not mean that we should turn against them; not at all. There is ground for complaint over past exploitation of colonies, and there is some basis for claims to self-determination; I object only to the present extremism of the anticolonial group. The colonial powers also have some rights and some things to their credit. Indeed, it was the training given by them that stirred up in many colonies the desire for independence and modern standards of living; India is doubtless a democracy today, rather than Communist, because of British training. What we need are solutions falling between the extremes; some sort of birth control for nations.

I suggest two possibilities for consideration that might help in the restoration of the United Nations as the instrument of justice that it was intended to be. One is that the United States push for a statement of criteria upon which—rather than by political vote—the United Nations would make decisions concerning claims for independence. I mean by this, objective decision, decision according to principle and criteria. If this were done, the struggle between colonial and anticolonial would be put upon another, less emotional footing; a middle path between the contending factions could be provided.

The other suggestion is that a better voting system be provided in the General Assembly, one that would more nearly reflect the actual responsibility of each member in the institution. Weighted representation is being more seriously considered than it used to be.

Either proposal would be extremely difficult to realize; but without one or both, the chances are that for a long time the United Nations will be unable to reflect justice or make effective decisions. It has perhaps gained a little in making the smaller states have more confidence in it, but this is offset by the control that they have achieved over it, and by the loss of confidence in it on the part of the Western powers. The United Nations Emergency Force is perhaps a useful precedent for the future. But, on the whole, I think the United Nations was not able to contribute much to the settlement of the Suez or Middle East issue, and for the reasons I have mentioned. Exploitation of the principle of self-determination has led to strong nationalistic feelings, and the United Nations has had to bow to the *sacro-egoismo* of sovereignty. The Suez Canal, a passageway of concern to the whole community of nations—and I would say the same for the Panama Canal—should not be left entirely under the control of any one state. It was unfortunate that the United States should have used its great strength in the direction of national sovereignty rather than using the opportunity to build up the United Nations.

Commentary

FRANCIS O. WILCOX
*Assistant Secretary of State
for International Organization Affairs*

PROFESSOR EAGLETON'S THOUGHT-PROVOKING interpretation of the influences affecting the United Nations and its handling of the Suez crisis in particular are well designed to make us ponder again the purposes of the United Nations and the currents that direct its activities. Rather than concentrate on anticolonialism, as does Professor Eagleton, I would identify five basic forces that motivate the activities of the United Nations and that have found expression in its Charter. These forces, of course, arise from the desires of men and women everywhere and constitute world-wide political and social forces that predate the United Nations or the twentieth century. These drives are: first, the maintenance of peace and security; second, the pacific settlement of disputes; third, economic advancement and social progress; fourth, civil and political rights; and fifth, self-determination of nations and peoples. The United Nations in the General Assembly reflects these aspirations and, as in any political community, the representatives of the governments lay emphasis on one or several, depending on events and circumstances at the time.

The United Nations is a system wherein the international community may maintain order without oppression and obtain change without anarchy. We have heard the thesis, perhaps, with particular reference to the Quintuple Alliance, 1818–1821, but also with regard to the League of Nations, that international organization would always seek to maintain the status quo. Professor Eagleton, on the contrary, sees the United Nations as an instrument for fomenting political, even revolutionary, change. I am inclined, however, to take the middle road and regard the United Nations more as a means for influencing order and progress among states while guiding inevitable change in a constructive manner.

Expansion of the United Nations Community

The community of nations has grown significantly since 1945. The United Nations, its principal forum and agent, was established in 1945 with fifty-one members. From 1945 to 1955, United Nations membership increased to sixty-three. Since then, in less than two years, eighteen additional members have been admitted.

This expanded membership, coupled with the increased role of the General Assembly, in which all members are equally represented, has caused apprehension among certain statesmen and scholars. We believe this apprehension is exaggerated.

First of all, some persons conceive members of the United Nations as consistently voting in geographical blocs. This is not the case, except for one monolithic bloc, the U.S.S.R. and its satellites. The fears currently expressed are that the Afro-Asian group of nations may, as a matter of agreed policy, vote together and control General Assembly action on important matters in a manner contrary to Western interests. This, in my opinion, is more a mathematical possibility than a logical expectation or certainty. The mathematical facts are as follows.

As presently constituted, when all eighty-one members are voting, fifty-four votes are needed for the General Assembly to act on matters requiring a two-thirds majority. If all the Afro-Asian states were to combine, they would have a "blocking minority" of twenty-eight votes, sufficient to block action on matters requiring a two-thirds vote and enough to give them a major voice in deciding all important issues. By contrast, in the "new" General Assembly, the Latin American states now have but 24 per cent of the vote; non-Communist Europe 19 per cent; the Soviet bloc 11 per cent; and the old British Commonwealth countries 5 per cent.

In practice, however, the Afro-Asian group does not regularly vote as a bloc, and when it does it is apt to be on issues for which there is overwhelming support from states outside the Afro-Asian area. Again, I think we should look at the record of the last General Assembly.

Take first the vote on the principal resolutions relating to the Middle East crisis. Here, certainly, one might expect to see Afro-Asian solidarity. Yet, out of eleven important resolutions approved between November 1, 1956, and February 2, 1957, this bloc voted as an entity on only two, and in both these cases the resolutions received total votes of seventy-four in favor, two against, and two abstentions. Indeed, the general observation may be made that the Afro-Asian states displayed considerable unanimity in casting affirmative votes on the resolutions that were adopted by impressive or overwhelming majorities. In other words, they did not act as an irresponsible splinter group in opposition to the will of the majority.

The voting record on the Hungarian situation demonstrated less unanimity, although there was an increasing tendency for all United Nations members, including those from Africa and Asia, to be more sharply critical of brutal Soviet actions as they became revealed. On this issue, it might be observed, we would have welcomed a solid Afro-Asian bloc vote. But on only three out of ten resolutions were more than twenty Afro-Asian votes cast affirmatively, and these dealt with the less contentious issues of relief for the Hungarian refugees. The vote on the remaining seven resolutions reflected wide splits within the bloc. The point I want to emphasize is this: the Afro-Asian group does not constitute a solid voting bloc.

Of course, there is a tendency for states with common interests and problems to vote together when they think this will serve those interests. These tendencies, wherever they exist, present problems to all who wish to see international issues dealt with on their merits. At the same time, we should not exaggerate the extent to which such bloc voting prevails nor should we exaggerate the practical consequences.

The expansion of the United Nations from fifty-one members to eighty-one, with an increased representation of African, Arab, and Asian states, however, has encouraged in varying degree United Nations activities that reflect the motivation of the five aspirations I identified earlier. The new members will affect the voting majorities in favor of several if not all of these forces, and we would be wise to anticipate this tendency. They now share the responsibility of the United Nations Organization to promote stability and order as well as further progress. Positive leadership from us in these efforts will certainly be met by their co-operation. I shall later turn to several examples, which demonstrate that the United Nations Organization has become, as stated in Article 1(4), "a center for harmonizing the actions of nations in the attainment of [their] common ends."

Self-determination and the United Nations

When I listed the five built-in forces that motivate the United Nations and articulate the hopes of people everywhere, I placed self-determination after the other four, because, either as concept or reality, it usually is espoused as a means to the attainment of the other four: security, peaceful relations, economic and social betterment, and civil and political rights. I shall first discuss and dwell at greater length on some issues relating to self-determination, however, because Professor Eagleton has directed his remarks to this subject.

I question whether colonialism or anticolonialism is the single most important question in the world today or that it dominates all others, as Professor Eagleton contends. Man's desires for security, peaceful relations, economic and social advance, and civil and political freedom are also important, and each aspiration influences our attitudes and behavior on other questions.

Self-determination, however, is the chief method we accepted, as far back as 1648, if not earlier, for organizing our world society. The development did not arise from the establishment of the United Nations, nor is that organization of states the first to confirm by collective action the recognition of new members. The United Nations might, however take credit for providing a theoretical conception of international order and progress to its old and new members alike.

Conferences of states from the fifteenth to the seventeenth centuries, of course, conceded new memberships to their community, while the eighteenth century saw a considerable expansion of the national-state system by that method. The increasing practice was to confirm the existence of new states by treaty at a conference. In the twentieth century, the Conference of Versailles both recognized and stimulated further demands for self-determination, and the League of Nations afforded membership and implicit collective recognition to additional new states.

The United Nations could no more ignore this develop-

ment of the principle of self-determination than it could deny
its own nature and genesis. The concept of self-determination
is a psychological and political force with which we must
reckon, and the United States could not set itself against that
concept without denying its own heritage and placing itself
in opposition to a principle subscribed to by the overwhelming
majority of mankind.

The world order that the United Nations seeks to build
comprises sovereign member states; consequently, one of the
United Nation's principal tasks as well that of the older states
should be to familiarize new members with the principles and
techniques of our society. The United Nations, however, does
not concern itself solely with existing states. For example,
there is the work of the United Nations in the area of trust
territories and concerning other non-self-governing territories.
The Trusteeship Council with its balanced representation of
administering and nonadministering powers oversees ten
trust territories. The Special Committee on Non-Self-Governing Territories examines information from other dependent
areas with a total population of approximately 150,000,000
people. While it is not stipulated in the Charter that all these
people will or should achieve independence, it is agreed that
all should progress toward self-government.

Undoubtedly some dependent areas may choose to continue
indefinitely a relationship to a metropolitan power which provides them with a form of self-government, but falls short of
complete independence. This is generally acceptable to all
United Nations members, provided that the people of the
particular area have freely chosen this solution.

The United States and others do not regard the principle
of self-determination as being applicable solely to so-called
colonial areas. The General Assembly has agreed with us that
this principle is also applicable to certain areas that have
been denied this former exercise of statehood, such as Estonia,
Latvia, and Lithuania, and to other states now denied their
full exercise of self-government, such as Hungary.

I agree with Professor Eagleton as to the desirability of a
statement or a study on the meaning of self-determination

and, perhaps, a criteria for independence. The Economic and Social Council, on the initiative of the United States, has, in fact, recommended to the General Assembly the conduct of a thorough study of the concept of self-determination. This study would embrace an examination of the concept of peoples and nations; the essential attributes and applicability of the principle of equal rights and self-determination, including the rights and duties of states under international law; the relationship to other Charter principles; and the political, economic, social, and cultural conditions best suited to facilitate the application of the principle of self-determination. The General Assembly will consider this proposal this fall.

Ever since the inception of the United Nations, our government and others have given much thought to the possibility of establishing criteria under which the exercise of self-determination would result in the achievement of the goals of self-government or independence by peoples ready to assume these responsibilities, and these studies continue.

In the annual United Nations consideration of conditions in trust territories, it has become apparent that a body of precedents is being established by which a territory's political progress can be successfully measured as it advances. We have already witnessed the termination of the agreement between the United Kingdom and the United Nations whereby British Togoland, in response to a vote of its people, joined with an independent Ghana. On the other hand, the French government's efforts to secure agreement from the United Nations to terminate the trusteeship of French Togoland met with some hesitation. A Visiting Mission went to the territory this summer in connection with the French request. Its report will be examined at the General Assembly this fall. This report suggests steps to be taken prior to the termination of trusteeship that would enable the people to govern themselves in the future with confidence. However, conditions in various areas differ so widely that it is extremely doubtful whether any set of criteria could be established embodying all desirable prerequisites for independence that would be just or applicable to all.

It is clear that the members of the General Assembly can provide sizeable majorities for the principle of self-determination. On a resolution requesting administering authorities to establish target dates for the attainment of self-government or independence by several trust territories in Africa, the vote at the Eleventh General Assembly was forty-five in favor and fourteen against, with sixteen abstentions and five absences. The United States opposed the resolution and found itself in the minority on a significant vote. The majority in favor and significant abstentions came from every region of the world.

There is also evidence that the General Assembly can behave with commendable responsibility. After contentious debate on both Cyprus and Algeria, the General Assembly last year unanimously passed resolutions designed not to exacerbate the two situations in the hope that those concerned would find just and peaceful solutions.

The overwhelming votes against Israel, France, and the United Kingdom as a result of military action against Egypt, could not, in my opinion, be ascribed to the General Assembly's predilection for self-determination, as suggested by Professor Eagleton, any more than it was a vote for economic advancement and social progress. Some members, of course, might have had their memories jogged. The General Assembly reacted upon other predilections, for the maintenance of peace and security and for the peaceful settlement of disputes.

The Maintenance of Security and the Peaceful Settlement of Disputes

The United Nations Charter is very explicit in its second article that members are not to employ force in the settlement of their disputes. It reads at paragraphs 3 and 4:

All Members shall settle their international disputes by peaceful means in such a manner that international peace and security, and justice, are not endangered.

All Members shall refrain in their international relations from the threat or use of force against the territorial integrity or political independence of any state, or in any other manner inconsistent with the Purposes of the United Nations.

In my view, President Eisenhower was correct when he said that the "use of military force to solve international disputes could not be reconciled with the principles and purposes of the United Nations."

Events preceding and arising from the military action against Egypt cast further doubt as to the wisdom of that action.

On September 26, 1956, the Security Council took up the matter of the Suez Canal at the request of the disputants after initial efforts to settle the question first of all by direct negotiations came to naught. As a result of the discussions in the Security Council and in the office of Secretary-General Hammarskjold, the Security Council on October 13 adopted unanimously a resolution setting forth the six requirements for a settlement of the Suez question enumerated by Professor Eagleton. Before the Security Council adjourned, Secretary of State Dulles expressed the general understanding that it remain seized of the Suez Canal matter and that the Secretary-General might continue to encourage interchanges between the governments of Egypt, France, and the United Kingdom. During the following week, the Secretary-General pursued his discussions with the Foreign Minister of Egypt in order further to explore and clarify means of finding a solution to the Suez problem in conformity with the requirements approved by the Security Council. These exchanges of views were embodied in a letter Secretary-General Hammarskjold addressed to the Foreign Minister on October 24. From the Foreign Minister's reply, dated November 2, there was apparent a broad area of agreement between the government of Egypt and the Secretary-General. The attention of the United Nations by this time, however, was concentrated on the events flowing from the Israeli and Franco-British military operations against Egypt. As a consequence the discussions between the Secretary-General and the parties on the future operation of the Suez Canal were suspended.

A primary reason for the United Nations Charter's injunction against the use of force in the settlement of disputes is that such action may spread and involve a growing number of states. This was certainly the case arising from the military action against Egypt, where there existed most of the ingredients for a third world war.

It is pertinent to examine the votes by which the General Assembly successively called for the withdrawal of foreign forces from Egypt. This examination will show, I believe, that no anticolonial bloc acted as an irresponsible splinter group in this matter. The resolution of November 1-2, 1956, sponsored by the United States, was adopted with seventy-six in favor and five against, with six abstentions and one absence. This vote was an affirmation of the Charter's principles that unauthorized force was not to be used against a member. It had the support of all twenty Latin Americans, ten of the sixteen Europeans (with two opposed, three abstaining, and one absent), the two Africans, all the eleven Arab states, and all but one of the Asians. Even the old Commonwealth members were divided, with two abstaining and two opposed. This vote, of course, does not reflect the divided opinion within the various nations involved. The resolution of February 2, 1957, deploring Israeli noncompliance with earlier withdrawal resolutions, was adopted with even an increased majority of seventy-four in favor and two opposed, with two abstentions and two absent. These voting majorities might be compared with that at the recent General Assembly which concerned the issue of self-determination as it related to target dates for independence or self-government in certain trust territories in Africa, where the vote was forty-five to fourteen, with sixteen abstentions and five absences.

Now I conclude from this record as well as from the votes concerning the tragic situation in Hungary that the General Assembly remains adamant against the illegal use of force. I also conclude that the General Assembly has a predisposition to try to re-establish conditions conducive to the peaceful settlement of such problems. In this connection, we might contrast the condemnatory language the General Assembly

employed against the U.S.S.R. for its intervention in Hungary
with the cautious, uninflammatory language it used in requesting the withdrawal of forces from Egypt.

Other Assembly Predilections

The General Assembly's capacity to act concerning economic development and social progress as well as civil and
political rights is necessarily limited by other considerations.
Nevertheless, it has increasingly manifested its interest in
significant projects for economic development, and its activities in the social field are quite extensive. The General Assembly's work in the field of civil and political rights, however,
may have been overambitious at the first, but efforts to bring
certain states up to the standards of more politically advanced
communities through programs of information and assistance
are going forward, and significant progress has been made on
behalf of the political status of women.

The General Assembly's endeavors on behalf of economic
development are probably more intense than in the social and
human-rights fields. At the last General Assembly considerable
interest was manifested in the question of the establishment
of a Special United Nations Fund for Economic Development. A compromise resolution was unanimously adopted, requesting an *Ad Hoc* Committee to inquire further into the
matter, and its report, together with the recommendations of
the Economic and Social Council, will be considered by the
forthcoming General Assembly. I mention this matter to demonstrate again the various influences that operate in the General Assembly.

With respect to the Suez Canal dispute, however, the General Assembly never attempted to justify Nasser's seizure of
the Suez Canal as a measure contributing to economic development or the social progress of the Egyptian people. Neither
did it accept the thesis that foreign intervention in Egypt
was justified because Nasser denied the Egyptian people their
civil and political rights.

The General Assembly's concern for the legitimate exercise of civil and political rights was evident, however, in its consideration of the situation in Hungary. In its resolution of December 15, 1956, the General Assembly declared that the U.S.S.R., by using its armed force against the Hungarian people, "is violating the political independence of Hungary" and condemned "the violation of the Charter of the United Nations by the Government of the U.S.S.R. in depriving Hungary of its liberty and independence and the Hungarian people of the exercise of their fundamental rights." This resolution was adopted, fifty-five in favor, with only the U.S.S.R. and its satellites against. Thirteen members abstained and three were absent. Significantly, only four Asian members abstained, and of the eleven Arab states four voted in favor and seven (presumably desirous of Soviet support on Middle East questions) abstained. The two African members also voted in favor.

The General Assembly's Special Committee on the problem of Hungary, established by the resolution of January 10, 1957, devotes thorough attention in its report to the denial by the U.S.S.R. and its satellite regime in Hungary of the civil and political rights of the Hungarian people, and we certainly anticipate that this and other matters concerning Hungary will be considered at the forthcoming General Assembly.

Conclusion

It would seem evident that when the General Assembly considers any question, various considerations and predilections will influence the representatives. I think it would be a mistake to view one predisposition as being consistently overriding. The one exception might be the common purpose of members of the United Nations to preserve their freedom and their independence. It was unfortunate that our close allies sought to run counter to these predispositions of the United Nations members and experienced the result of the quick action of the General Assembly, operating for the first time under the Uniting For Peace resolution of 1950. Nevertheless, I believe that the United Nations is the stronger now, for the world knows that the United Nations will act, even when great powers are involved, in defense of the principles of the Charter.

The enlargement of the community of nations and concomitant increased membership of the United Nations presents both an opportunity and a challenge. The United States should and does offer both its assistance and counsel in realizing the legitimate aspirations of the peoples of the United Nations. If the United States and other members of the free world give such leadership, we have no reason to be apprehensive about the United Nations, and we shall move in the direction of making our society of nations a community where all people may live in security, prosperity, and freedom.

XIII

The Prospects of Communism in the Middle East

WALTER Z. LAQUEUR
Author and Editor

I

IT IS UNLIKELY that the subject of communism would have been included in a symposium on the Middle East ten years ago, or even five. At that time practically everybody seemed to agree that there was no such issue; western Europe had its Communist problem, but not the Middle East. Some pointed to Islam and to Moslem society, which, they said, acted as an impenetrable bulwark against all and any revolutionary ideas. Others referred to the absence of a strong industrial working class, which, they argued, precluded the emergence of a strong Communist movement. This was the time when Prime Minister Mustafa Nahas of Egypt said in the negotiations with British diplomats that he did not worry greatly about Russia, "for Russia is 4,000 miles away." Factually this was a formidable exaggeration, but the argument in itself was symptomatic and significant: *psychologically,* Russia —and communism—were indeed four thousand, and perhaps more, miles away.

All this has changed considerably over the last few years; communism in the Middle East has not only become a major regional problem, it is one of the most important issues in world politics in general. Nevertheless, there are still many people who tend to underrate the role played by communism

297

in the Middle East both as an ideology and as a political
movement. Some regard Soviet, rather than Communist, influence as the paramount factor. Others argue that the term
Communist is used far too indiscriminately nowadays in the
Middle East. According to them, the term *communism* is
applied to various groups of fellow travelers or perhaps to what
is only the anti-imperialism of the more radical Arab nationalists. There is a grain of truth in these contentions: Russia,
as a great power, and as one that has tried hard in recent years
to appear as the champion of the political aspirations of some
Arab countries, does of course enjoy a considerable measure
of influence and prestige. It is also true that, though the
slogans of Communists and radical nationalist groups in the
Middle East are similar, the ultimate political aims of these
movements are not quite identical. But this is only part of
the over-all picture and, in my opinion, the less important
part at that.

To clarify the issues at stake, a little semantic investigation
may be called for, because much depends on the meaning attached to the term *communism*. If one regards communism
in the context of the early twenties, as a revolutionary, radically left-wing movement, basically internationalist, militantly
atheist, wholeheartedly in favor of the class struggle, a party
that claims to represent and lead the industrial working class,
then it follows beyond any shadow of a doubt that there is no
communism in the Middle East today. Nor is there any reason
to assume that communism in this sense will gain any influence in the Middle East in the foreseeable future, and those
who argue that all talk about communism in the Middle East
is an invention of malevolent outsiders would appear to be
quite correct. But all these assumptions, though still widespread, are unfortunately quite fallacious. This specific brand
of early revolutionary and very radical communism no longer
exists anywhere in the world. Communism on the tactical
level has changed very much during these last thirty years and
nowhere more than in the underdeveloped countries of Asia
and Africa. The revolution from below has been replaced by
the revolution from above; the intransigent attitude towards

religion and "bourgeois nationalism" has given way not merely to toleration, but to conciliation; the class struggle has been largely superseded by the Cold War, the struggle against the West. And if there has been no radical ideological revision as far as the central role of the industrial working class is concerned, in practice Communist leaders have been perfectly content to base themselves on other social classes—on the peasants in China during the thirties and forties, on the middle class intelligentsia in the Middle East.

In the Middle East, in particular, communism has been radically purged of those elements that might be distasteful to the present generation of nationalists. It ceased to rely on slogans borrowed from Western democracy, the rights of man, and internationalism (obligatory for use in countries with a liberal tradition), and spoke instead in terms of nationalism, military power, and economic aid.

Communist ideology not only promised membership in a powerful club which gave military and political backing and apparently asked nothing in return: it taught valuable new techniques for manipulation of masses and for winning sympathies among certain well-meaning groups in the West. It produced an excellent new justification and guiding lines for bureaucratic anti-capitalism of the old style—and for expansion of the bureaucracy. In short, the new radical movement which had been in search of a programme found itself being offered one which suited its mood perfectly, yet without demanding the re-orientation of loyalties which Communism demands in the West.[1]

[1] A. V. Sherman, "Intellectual Ferment in the Middle East," *Soviet Survey*, XVI/XVII (1957), 25. Other important articles that have been of use in the preparation of the present paper are A. Bennigsen, "Le Front National dans la nouvelle stratégie Communiste au Moyen-Orient," *Politique Etrangère* (Paris), V (1956), 614 et seq., and H. Carrere d'Encausse, "Données de la Politique soviétique au Moyen-Orient," *Les Cahiers de la Republique* (Paris, 1956), p. 49 et seq.

II

The Middle Eastern Communist parties have basically much in common, but the current political problems facing each of them are not identical, varying in accordance with the different conditions in each country. A brief survey of the specific problems facing each party, therefore, should preface any discussion of the more general trends in Middle Eastern communism.

The history of Egyptian communism goes back to the early twenties, but the groups existing now were founded only during World War II. Until very recently, there were a number of Communist factions that fought each other bitterly on organizational and tactical issues and sometimes on purely personal lines. But this internecine strife did not prevent the spread of Communist ideas, especially among the intelligentsia, and the gradual Egyptianization of what had originally been, both in leadership and composition, a movement mainly of foreigners. Since the summer of 1952 the chief issue for Egyptian Communists has been their attitude towards the regime of General Naguib, and later Colonel Nasser. At first, in July and August, 1952, they were favorably disposed towards it. In their propaganda they argued that about one-third of the members of the new junta were "progressives"; among them was Colonel Nasser. But this estimate was rather optimistic or, at least, premature; in effect there was only one Communist in the executive of the Free Officers and another who might perhaps be defined as a fellow traveler.

The new regime released most of the Communists in prison, but only a few weeks later, following the Kafr Dawar incidents, the various Communist groups began to criticize the Free Officers. This gradually turned to violent opposition; the officers retaliated in kind and adopted strict anti-Communist measures. During that period, between the autumn of 1952 and the spring of 1955, there was much apprehension among the Communists that Naguib's and Nasser's government would initiate reforms on Kemalist lines in Egypt; from the Communist point of view, this would have been a very dangerous thing indeed. They, therefore, supported all the domestic foes of the junta, first the Wafd, later the Moslem Brotherhood, and in the end General Naguib in his struggle for power against Colonel Nasser.

The turning point in the Communist attitude came only in the summer of 1955 when it appeared that the danger of Kemalism had disappeared and that the Free Officers had come to regard foreign policy, not domestic reform, as their most urgent preoccupation. The Egyptian Communists assumed, quite correctly, that this policy would bring the junta into conflict with the West and that it was therefore to be encouraged. Of the two mainstreams in Egyptian communism, HADITU (the Democratic Movement for National Liberation) was the first to come around to this point of view; the other main group, the Egyptian Communist party, continued to oppose Colonel Nasser and his colleagues until early in 1956. From prison the HADITU leaders sent Nasser an open letter, which was widely publicized in the country, in which they expressed "total and unreserved support" for his policy. This provoked ironic comment on the part of some non-Communist observers, for despite their professions of loyalty, Communists continued to be arrested for some months, and the flirtation appeared to be rather one-sided at that time. Nevertheless, the new Communist approach proved to be successful in the end: the Egyptian rapprochement with the Soviet Union in the summer of 1955, the arms treaty and so on, were bound to change the attitude of the regime towards the local Communists. The Communist leaders and militants were gradually released from prison. Some of them, notably the trade-union organizers, were prevented from returning to active politics. But most of the intellectuals were given positions of influence; it is probably no exaggeration to say that most of the writers in the influential Egyptian dailies and weeklies are Communists who were arrested and imprisoned at one time or another between 1950 and 1955. They have, to a large extent, created today's political climate in Egypt. One seasoned observer, sympathetic to them, has gone on record as saying that he found more enthusiasm for "socialist realism" in Egypt than in Russia's eastern European satellites.

The Communist movement in Egypt, split since its early days, reunited only in June, 1957. A new executive was elected, or appointed, at a conference held in Rome under the sponsorship of the Italian Communists. We do not know, however, whether all factions inside Egypt have indeed joined the united party; it may well be that a few continue their separate activities. The united Communist party (like all political parties) is still illegal in Egypt; from time to time through their spokesmen and fellow-traveling publicists, the Communists have demanded more democratic freedom and a return to partial parliamentary democracy, especially in connection with the elections that took place in Egypt in July, 1957. But, for obvious reasons, they have not made a major issue of this demand; for even if the party is illegal, communism in Egypt has now ample scope for its activities through other channels. The main "front organization," the "Partisans of Peace," is legal, which amounts to a near monopoly, for no other semipolitical organization is permitted to exist. As things are, the Communists are quite content to work from inside the existing legal organizations such as the state party, the Liberation Movement, and National Union. Their assumption is that they will be able to provide leadership and infiltrate part or all of their program and, through these means, gradually divert the regime in the desired direction. An outside observer favorably disposed towards both Colonel Nasser and the Egyptian Left has thus described their attitude:

> The junta is a coming force, they say. But it has no sense of direction. There is a vacuum and we will fill it; it has no ideology, no cadres, no political know-how. We will give it its orientation. . . . And thus the Communists and "progressives" have taken the place of the American advisers who between 1952 and 1954 were trying to channel the regime towards a prudent reformism.[2]

[2] Jean et Simonne Lacouture, L'Egypte en Mouvement (Paris, Editions du Seuil, 1956), p. 269.

Egyptian communism, in contrast to the party in other countries, has not so far produced any outstanding leaders, nor has it achieved any spectacular organizational or political achievements. Nevertheless, with conditions so propitious during the last few years, it could not fail to have a tremendous impact on Egyptian politics and especially on public opinion. A clash at some future date between them and the present government is not excluded, though both sides are clearly not interested at present, and probably for a good time to come, in a trial of strength. For the moment there is a wide community of interest. And if this should change one day, the Communists' chances will be considerable, for they have the only political organization in Egypt with several thousands of "cadres."

This may not sound very impressive with regard to a country of more than twenty million inhabitants, but the main criterion is that they have no rival in the field, since the old parties, dissolved years ago, could not adapt themselves to conditions of illegality. Let me emphasize again that such a clash is not at all likely in the foreseeable future; the Communists in any case greatly prefer gradual domination to any sudden take-over at a time of crisis, which may or may not succeed.

That a period of illegality, even a comparatively short one, may propel a Communist party into a position of considerable importance was shown in Syria after Colonel Shishakli's fall, early in 1954; since then communism has become one of the main factors in that country. The Syrian experience is also highly instructive in showing to what lengths a Communist party will go to cover up its real aims and intentions and to appear "respectable," part and parcel of the national movement. The present leadership of the Syrian Communists dates from the middle and late thirties; in contrast to the other Arab parties, the turnover at the top has been small. Since 1942 the party has been in a state of semilegality most of the time, but this has not seriously hampered its activities. The romantic underground atmosphere attracted many people, especially among the younger generation, whereas police arrests and searches never seriously interfered with party activities. On paper, their strength is not really impressive even now; the Syrian Communists have only one official representative in parliament, their leader, Khalid Bakhdash. But a closer inspection shows that parliamentary representation is not really a true measure of their influence. For the Communists in Syria do not only dominate all three sections of the trade-union movement; they have been instrumental in organizing and guiding many other professional, cultural, and social groups, such as writers, lawyers, and various youth associations, and through these they exert very considerable influence on public opinion and the political life of the country. They have collaborated closely with the Socialist Baath party and that group of young army officers that now exerts so much influence in Syria. In recent by-elections they have invariably collaborated with the Baath, and it is of some interest to note that, as far as domestic policies are concerned, the Communists are now a less "radical" party than the Baath. According to their present propaganda they are part of the general national movement, not a party with distinct and separate aims. When Khalid Bakhdash visited Cairo some time ago and was interviewed by an Egyptian weekly, he said that there was nothing very remarkable in his autobiography—it was identical with the life story of the average Arab patriot. In the Syrian parliament Bakhdash declared that his party stood for "Arab nationalism and nothing else." On another occasion he stated (incredibile auditu): "Syria is not communist; it is nationalist and Arab, and will remain so." What is perhaps most significant is that the Syrian party has dropped from its program the demand for agrarian reform that had been one of their main planks during the previous decade. They have reprimanded the Baath more than once in recent years for being too "anti-clerical"(!) and have stressed time and again that these domestic issues should be subordinated for the time being to the common struggle against imperialism—in other words, against the West. They have tried in every possible way to play down and even discard those traditional Communist demands that were liable to arouse suspicion and opposition in other circles.

This self-effacement is, however, not an unmixed blessing as far as the Communists are concerned. For people may come to inquire about the *raison d'etre* of this party; if the Communist party is really indistinguishable from the other nationalist parties, why should it lead a separate existence? Why should anybody join the Communists if there is no difference between them and, say, the Baath? The answer is that the Communists have, of course, a very specific and distinct political program of their own, though it is now being played down. But if it is a cause of embarrassment at present, in the long run it will undoubtedly prove a great advantage, for nationalist slogans, however effective and however justified, are not enough to feed people or to clothe them, or, generally speaking, to run a modern society. The Communists have a practical program for modernization and industrial development; their rivals at present have none, apart from some vague talk about "no capitalism, no communism, but co-operation," which simply is not good enough.

Communism in Lebanon has made a good deal of noise in recent years, but it is not really a major political force in that country. The Communist party in Syria and Lebanon originally had a united high command, but after 1945 it was decided to break this up and to establish a separate and autonomous Lebanese party. This was done in order to allay the fear and suspicion of Syrian domination prevalent in many sections of the Lebanese population. Recently, however, a united high command for the two parties has been re-established after it was found that the previous set-up had not really improved the chances of communism in Lebanon. As in Syria and the other Arab countries, the Lebanese Communists do not at present appear as militant radicals, but concentrate their propaganda on generally accepted slogans against the West and in support of Arab unity and the Cairo-Damascus axis.

In contrast to the situation in Lebanon, communism in Jordan has made great headway during the past three or four

years. At present the Communist and all other political parties are suppressed, but it is unlikely that the seeds sown in
the early fifties, especially among the intelligentsia, have been
really lost. Communism continues to be a very potent force.
From the tactical point of view, the Jordan experience is of
some interest; in Amman (as in Baghdad during an earlier
period) the Communists used the "double front" stratagem.
This means that the Communists were not satisfied with
covering up their activities by working through a popular
front. Their representation within that popular front, the national bloc, was Communist guided and inspired, but it was
not identical with the Communist party. These tactics were
dictated in part, of course, by the need to evade police re-
pression, but in addition there was the realization that the
Communist party would be the more successful the better it
concealed its real identity. In the parliament elected in October, 1956, this Communist national bloc had a sizeable representation—and one representative in the cabinet. Following
the clash between King Hussein and the Nabulsi government
in April, 1957, parliament and the political parties were dissolved. The Communist party leaders such as Fuad Nasser,
Yakub Ziaddin, and M. Shuqair have fled to Syria. (There is
a preponderance of intellectuals—lawyers, physicians, and
teachers—in the Jordan party leadership as in all other Arab
parties.) But the Communist party, better adapted than the
other political forces in Jordan to underground activities, continues to function, and it may well emerge as the leading
factor, should the present regime suffer a serious setback or be
overthrown. In Jordan, as in Syria and other Arab countries,
one of the reasons for the success of communism is the personal attraction of the party leadership. These comparatively
young men and women have a far stronger appeal than the
politicians of the old school because of their broader intellectual outlook and greater political integrity. Never having been
in office, they are generally believed to be more honest than
those who represent the *ancien régime*, more willing and more
able to give their countries efficient government.

That this personal factor is of considerable importance is

shown by the Iraqi and Persian example. As far as social conditions are concerned, both these countries offer a very favorable breeding ground for Communist activities. (Economic development alone, even had it been more striking, is no panacea against the growth of communism.) Nevertheless, communism, which used to be a factor of some importance in Iraq during 1944–1945 and in Persia during 1942–1947, and again under Dr. Mossadegh, has apparently not made much headway in these two countries in the last two years. In Persia, the Tudeh party was apparently mainly interested in infiltrating the state administration and the army, whereas in Iraq the Communist party concentrated its activities on the intelligentsia. But both parties have failed to produce any outstanding leaders during the last ten or fifteen years, while ideological and personal rivalries at the top have had a detrimental effect on the work of the party.

Nevertheless, communism still stands a fair chance in both Iraq and Persia. Economic development, paradoxically enough, may in the short run improve their prospects, for material progress will generate a growing demand for a larger measure of political freedom. The present regimes have not been able to give the new and growing forces in society that feeling of having a stake in the country that is really the basic characteristic of an integrated nation. On the contrary, even mild reformers have frequently been dubbed "Communistic" by the rulers. Only a broadening of the basis of political power and social reforms rather than economic development schemes (however desirable in themselves and however efficient on paper or in reality) may one day bring about a radical change in these countries.

The Turkish example shows that this is not impossible. The Turkish Communist party was the earliest in the Middle East and at first it was the strongest and most influential. But the Kemalist reforms have effectively limited the appeal of communism in Turkey, and the attempts to revive the party during World War II were not very successful. There is of course, the traditional fear of Russia as an aggressive imperialist power to make communism in Turkey appear as political activity on behalf of a hostile power and thus tantamount to treason. But this alone would perhaps not have prevented the spread of communism. What ultimately diminished its chances was the experience that progress in the political, social, and economic fields could be achieved without the assistance of foreign ideologies and organizations. In these circumstances, communism in Turkey has preferred during the last decade to act through various front organizations, but even these have been illegal and not very successful. As things are, the only hope for Turkish communism would be a grave and prolonged internal political crisis, and even then it is not certain that the party possesses the necessary cadres to exploit such a situation.

Until very recently communism had not been an issue in the outlying Arab countries such as Saudia, Kuwait, Yemen, and Libya. The situation in the Sudan has been different; the Sudanese party has been active as an offshoot of the Egyptian HADITU for the last decade and has on the whole been not unsuccessful in its propaganda among the local trade unions, peasant organizations, and especially the Khartoum intelligentsia. Nevertheless its progress during the last two or three years, since Sudan gained independence, has been slower than expected.

Both Western and Eastern interest in Libya remains limited for the time being. Yemen continues to be cut off from the outside world; its flirtation with the Soviet Union cannot possibly be of much consequence domestically in view of the general backwardness of the country and its autocratic regime. Conditions in Saudia, Kuwait, and Bahrein are quite different as the result of the influx of foreign workers, technicians, teachers, etc. Communism in these countries is already a political factor and will probably continue to grow; it is behind the incipient trade-union activities and supports the struggle of the new middle class for more freedom.

The appeal of communism in Israel has been limited from the very beginning as a result of Comintern opposition to Zionism, and, subsequently of the anti-Israeli line taken by the Soviet Union. Nevertheless, there has been a Communist party in Palestine for the last thirty-seven years, which has polled with almost uncanny consistency 4 per cent of the vote at elections. At present the Israeli party bases itself mainly on immigrants whose experience in their new homeland has fallen short of their expectations and on the Arab minority. At one time, six or seven years ago, the Communist position in such Arab-populated areas of Israel as Nazareth was really unassailable. Since then they have suffered some setbacks, but they are probably still the strongest organized force in the Arab sector.

III

This short and very sketchy survey of the present state of Middle Eastern communism raises a number of important questions. But perhaps the most baffling riddle is the apparent contradiction between the numerical weakness and inconspicuousness of the Communist parties and their tremendous political influence. The number of Communist deputies in the parliaments of the Middle East is completely insignificant, and they are not represented at present in any Middle East government. All Arab rulers, including Colonel Nasser and Shukri Kuwatly, have declared their implacable opposition to communism as an ideology. How, then, can one explain the fact that Arab political life, and especially public opinion, as expressed in the press and radio, has been so thoroughly permeated by Communist ideas and slogans? How can one explain the enormous Communist successes within every possible framework outside the party proper—national movements, socialist parties, sundry intellectual, professional, women's, and youth organizations?

Some observers attempt to explain these extremely complicated problems in very simple terms. Those sympathetic to the cause of Arab nationalism say that the Arabs have legitimate national aspirations for which they have found little sympathy in the West, whereas Russia has given them, in recent years at least, substantial support. Others, less sympathetic, point to the seemingly irresistible fascination that the dynamic great powers have always exerted on large sections of the politically articulate in the Middle East. Germany and Italy had many well-wishers in their time in Arab lands; now that Russia is surf-riding on the wave of the future these sympathies have been directed eastwards from the Berlin-Rome axis. These explanations suffer, as I have said, from the oversimplification of a complex issue; they tend very much to underrate the impact of communism as an ideology in underdeveloped countries.[3] Communism offers, or in any case claims to offer, a systematic method to modernize Middle Eastern society, to develop the various countries, to catch up with the advanced West. It also offers a coherent Weltanschauung that may be crude and quite false on essential points, but that is consistent, superficially plausible, and emotionally suited to the elites of underdeveloped countries. The sad truth about the Middle East is that it is not merely a power vacuum, but a vacuum in a much deeper sense, reflecting the breakdown of traditional beliefs and values. As one observer recently put it:

> The West, meaning the North Atlantic region, is the home of the only civilization that is alive today. Clichés about a meeting between East and West, between eastern spiritual values and western technology are meaningless and seen as meaningless by the people who matter in the Middle East today. Islamic civilization can be studied: it can no longer be lived—and even the study is carried on in the West or directed from it.[4]

[3] For amplification of this very important point the reader is referred to Morris Watnick, "The Appeal of Communism to the Underdeveloped Peoples," in Bert F. Hoselitz, ed., The Progress of Underdeveloped Areas (Chicago, 1952), p. 152 et seq.; John H. Kautsky, Moscow and the Communist Party of India, (Cambridge, 1956); J. Kautsky, "From Marx to Mao," Soviet Survey, XVI/XVII (1957), p. 35; Bernard S. Morris and Morris Watnick, "Current Communist Strategy in Non-industrialised Countries," Problems of Communism, IV, No. 5 (September-October, 1955), 1.

[4] Andrew J. A. Mango, "Turkey and the Middle East," Political Quarterly, April-June, 1957, p. 154.

I believe these things should be stated bluntly and uncompromisingly, for they are essential to a realistic appraisal of developments in the Middle East in our day.

But what about Arab nationalism as a rival of communism in the Middle East? Arab nationalism certainly is a much more potent political force than Islam, and it evokes profound emotions among many people throughout the Middle East. Many of its spokesmen maintain that its appeal is so much stronger than that of any other political group that it can well afford a temporary alliance with Russia and even with communism—in the end it will swallow all its foes and rivals.

For this commendable optimism there is, however, little objective justification. In the eyes of the Communists, bourgeois nationalism, including lower-middle-class nationalism or Nasserism, is not a rival force. Never since Adolf Hitler has communism tended to underrate the impact of nationalist movements. It has adopted nationalist slogans, and in the Middle East in our day the Communists appear as impeccable patriots, second to none in the intensity of their nationalist beliefs. This is possible because nationalist propaganda in the Middle East is concentrated on the negative aspects of national independence, i.e., opposition to outside enemies, who threaten, or are believed to threaten, the Arab countries.

There is no competition at present between communism and Nasserism on the nationalist level for the simple reason that there is no divergence of opinion; as for other aspects, communism has everything Nasserism possesses plus a practical social and economic program. This should not be interpreted as a disparaging observation vis-à-vis Arab nationalism, for most national movements in history have lacked a precise social and economic content. National movements are called upon to solve national questions, not social issues. But it so happens that in the Middle East the national movement, if it is to be successful, has to be at the same time a movement of radical social reform, in view of the weak social structure of the area. As things are in the Middle East, integral nationalism, despite momentary successes, does not really stand much chance, and it is in this context that there is room for grave misgivings about the ability of Arab national socialism to compete successfully with communism. In comparison with the social and economic ideas advanced by the spokesmen of Arab national socialism, Marxism-Leninism is both highly sophisticated and very practical.

All this does not mean that there will at some future date be a mass exodus from the national movement into the Communist parties. Such a dramatic development appears improbable and a less spectacular, but nonetheless very effective, process seems far more likely, namely, the gradual acceptance of Communist ideas and techniques, not as an alternative to Arab nationalism, but through the medium of the nationalist movement itself. This indeed is a process that has already begun. Is it reversible? The identity of interests between Colonel Nasser and the Communists is, after all, only a partial and temporary one, and it is not unthinkable that he may one day turn against his erstwhile allies, as Chiang Kai-shek did in 1927. But the big difference is that in Syria things have already developed beyond that stage, and that Chiang could, after all, rely on a mass party, the Kuomintang, for which there is no equivalent in the Arab world. And, finally, there is the danger that by the time any such split between Communists and nationalists is likely to occur, the country in question will be so firmly within the Soviet orbit that the non-Communist forces will stand little better chance than Dr. Benes in 1948.

Communism in some Middle Eastern countries, then, is moving towards a specific form of popular democracy, much less Communist in content than the eastern European version, in which the main stress is on political collaboration with Russia in the foreign political field. In a sense, communism in the Middle East is moving perhaps too fast for Moscow, which would presumably be quite satisfied with its neutralization on the lines of Nasser's "positive neutralism." The social structure and domestic politics of the various countries are of little interest in this context. Afghanistan, with its medieval political regime and social structure, has been moving closer to the Soviet orbit. But communism in the Middle East, with its many internal weaknesses, has a momentum of its own and tends to progress faster than planned. At present the main danger, from the Communist view, is that communism may make too much headway in one specific country (say Syria) and that as a result other countries will become alarmed and antagonized. Lenin believed himself to have discovered the "law" about the uneven development of developed countries, which he thought was the cause of inevitable conflicts and wars between capitalist nations. But there may also be a Laqueur law of the uneven development of underdeveloped countries. The way King Hussein of Jordan and others have reacted to recent developments in Syria tends to prove it. Communism, which has tried for several years to make an alliance with the whole Arab national movement, may be compelled to differentiate and to be satisfied with a working alliance with only part of it.

If the Communists should come to power in one or more Middle Eastern countries, it will undoubtedly be as part of a national alliance or popular front. The Communists would be in power, in a sense, but they would be unable to carry out most of their program. Nor could they count on direct Soviet support. For this reason, such a development, though fraught with grave dangers, ought not perhaps to be regarded as a major disaster. It might not be an irreversible process, and counterforces against communism might develop among that elite and the intelligentsia, which at present are only too ready to give communism a try. But here we pass from known facts to the realm of political speculation, which, however fascinating in its implications, is beyond the scope of this study.

Commentary

R. N. CAREW HUNT
Lecturer, St. Antony's College, Oxford University

MR. LAQUEUR BEGAN by telling us that it was unlikely that ten or even five years ago the subject of communism would have been included in a consideration of the Middle East. This is true enough. But what should be added is how much it is due to his labors that it has become possible to discuss the subject adequately at all. He has been a pioneer in this field, and all students of the history of the Communist movement have reason to be grateful to him. He has given us an illuminating account of the rise of communism in this area. My object, however, is not so much to comment on this essay as to deal with the part played by the Soviet Union. This requires some reference to historical background.

Marx's obsessive preoccupation with economic factors led him to underestimate seriously the force of nationalism, which he held to be a bourgeois phenomenon, destined to disappear with socialism. Lenin, while so far concurring, believed nonetheless that nationalism could be made to serve the cause of revolution. His analysis of imperialism had led him to the conclusion that when industrialized countries reach a certain stage of development, they can no longer exist without colonial markets to which they can offload their surplus products in exchange for cheap raw materials and, with the "super profits" thus obtained, bribe their own proletariats with higher wages. This would inevitably give rise to demands for national independence on the part of the backward peoples thus exploited, and the best way of injuring the capitalist countries was therefore to attack them through these overseas dependencies and so cut the taproots of their prosperity. Hence, Communist parties must support national liberation movements. This doctrine was set out in the Theses on the

National and Colonial Question approved by the Second
Comintern Congress, of 1920, and was elaborated in the
Theses of the Sixth Comintern Congress, of 1928, which represented the party line until it was changed after Stalin's
death.

Nonetheless, little was done in the interwar years to apply
this doctrine to the Middle East, nor was much attention paid
to building up Communist parties there. Hostility to religion,
and particularly to Islam, and the dogma that revolutionary
movements must be based on the urban proletariat gave the
Soviet Union, which directed Comintern policy, little room
for maneuver. Moreover, in these early years, the hopes of
Moscow were fastened upon the West, where it was assumed
that revolution would quickly spread. Then, by 1925, it had
become apparent that it would not, and a new target had to
be found. The British were firmly entrenched in large sectors
of the Middle East, and there was as yet no nationalist movement other than Wafdism in Egypt that could be exploited.
But in China they were less committed, and an organized
movement existed in the Kuomintang. Hence that country
was chosen as the most suitable field of operations. But the
Chinese Communist-Kuomintang alliance led to disaster and
did not dispose Stalin to enter into similar collaboration with
the national bourgeoisie elsewhere. In the thirties the rise of
nazism created a new situation. To have stirred up trouble in
the Middle East, even had there been the machinery for so
doing, would have antagonized the mandatory powers, to
which Russia now looked as potential allies. After World
War II Soviet policy followed much the same pattern. Up
to 1950–1951 its main concern was with western Europe.
Then it was directed to the Far East with the Korean War
and the fomenting of trouble in Southeast Asia until by 1954–
1955 it had become clear that no further advantage was to be
gained from interference in that quarter. Thus it was from
about that time that the Soviet Union began to interest itself
actively in the Middle East, where conditions for intervention
had become exceptionally favorable.

The two non-Arab countries of the Middle East, Turkey

and Iran, know their Russians and have no illusions about them. In the post-World War II years the Russians had unsuccessfully tried to reach conclusions with them both. To achieve their long-cherished objective of obtaining control of the Turkish Straits, they had engaged in a war of nerves that had caused such tension as to lead the American government in 1947 to give financial assistance to Turkey—the United States' first major commitment in the Middle East. Thus emboldened, the Turkish government threw in its lot unreservedly with the West, and in 1950 rejected finally and conclusively the Soviet demand that the Turkish Straits should be placed under joint control. In Iran the Russians met with an even more serious diplomatic reverse. With the assistance of the Communist Tudeh party, they had set up an autonomous republic in Azerbaijan under an old Comintern agent, Jafar Pishevari; they had refused to evacuate their armed forces on the date line of March 2d, 1946, as they were pledged to do; and they had extorted agreement to the establishment of a Soviet-Iranian oil company. Having so far succeeded, they withdrew their troops, whereupon the Iranian government crushed the rebel regime in Azerbaijan, and the Majlis refused to ratify the oil agreement. The Russians were thus outwitted, but could do nothing about it.

Yet it is from events in Iran that we may, for the sake of convenience, date the sequence of events that was to lead to the Russian intervention in the Arab world. The assassination in March, 1951, of the Prime Minister, General Razmara, was followed by the rise to power of the xenophobe Dr. Mossadegh, and at the end of April the Anglo-Iranian Oil Company was nationalized. The result was to plunge the country into insolvency, from which it was rescued in 1953 by a military coup d'état, engineered by General Zahedi. Mossadegh was imprisoned, and in the following year, the Majlis, now weary of melodrama, approved an agreement with a consortium of oil companies. But, in the meantime, the British, who had failed to secure United Nations support, had been compelled to evacuate Abadan. Iran had thus set the fashion of nationalizing the assets of the West and had proved that this could be done without retribution.

This blow to British prestige coincided with a deadlock in Egypt. The country had been given independence under King Fuad in 1922, the British Government, whose main concern was to safeguard its communications with the East, reserving to itself the right to defend it. This had failed to satisfy the nationalists, and the position had been revised by the 1936 treaty. British military operations conducted during World War II on the basis of this treaty had preserved the Suez Canal and had saved Egypt from enemy occupation. The war, however, had left Britain exhausted, whereas Egypt had been little affected. Hence the Egyptian government now demanded the evacuation of all British troops. The British Labour government was inclined to accede to this on the principle that however desirable it might be to retain forces in a country, they could not operate effectively if that country was hostile; and to ease the situation the British forces were withdrawn in 1947 from Cairo and the Delta and were concentrated in the canal area. It was felt, however, that if the 1936 treaty was to be so revised as to provide for the withdrawal of the British, it must also provide for their return in the event of an international emergency, and it was because Egyptian public opinion rejected this that the agreement reached in the autumn of 1947 between the Sidki Pasha and Mr. Ernest Bevin came to nothing.

This abortive agreement coincided with the setting up of the Cominform and the adoption by the Russians of an aggressive policy designed to obstruct the recovery of Europe. The result was to increase the importance of the Middle East upon which the European economy was largely dependent for its supplies of oil. The vulnerability of the area in the event of war began to occasion anxiety, and the withdrawal of the British from their bases, and particularly from the canal zone, had now to be regarded in the wider context of the Cold War.

A union of the Arab states for the purpose of mutual defense had for some time been encouraged by the British government. The first steps had been taken in 1943 by the Iraqi

Prime Minister, Nuri es-Said, who had proposed the formation of a league to be brought about by unifying Syria, Lebanon, Palestine, and Jordan in a greater Syria and its merger with Iraq. This, however, was frowned upon by Egypt, which did not want to see the balance of power transferred from the empire of the Nile to that of the Euphrates, and by King Saud, who was opposed to a strengthening of the Hashimite dynasty. The initiative was then taken by the Egyptian Prime Minister, Mustafa Nahas, and resulted in the Pact of the Arab League of March, 1945, of which the weakness and disunity were revealed in the Arab-Israeli war of 1948. In consequence of the Arab defeat, the Inter-Arab Joint Defense Alliance was constituted in April, 1950, by Egypt, Syria, Lebanon, and Saudi Arabia and was joined with some reluctance by Iraq and Jordan. It was, however, no more effective than the Arab League, which had set it up, and provided no answer to the problem of collective security.

On October 15, 1950, the Egyptian parliament unilaterally abrogated the 1936 treaty and rejected a proposal made two days earlier by Britain, the United States, France, and Turkey that Egypt should join them on a basis of equality and partnership in a Middle East Defense Organization (MEDO) to which the British military base in the canal zone would be transferred, an approach that was interpreted in Cairo as a device for enabling the British to remain and for preventing Egypt from renewing her attack on Israel to avenge the humiliation she had so recently suffered. There followed a period of undeclared war on the canal zone, culminating in the Cairo riots of January, 1952. King Farouk thereupon dismissed the Wafdist government and imposed martial law. Soon after, however, a military junta, of which the nominal leader was General Naguib, carried out a coup d'état. In June a republic was proclaimed; in July King Farouk abdicated.

Naguib was a popular figure. But he had never been admitted to the inner counsels of the junta, and when he showed a disposition to return to parliamentary government and introduce much needed social reforms, he was replaced by Colonel Nasser, who could be trusted not to attempt either.

Thus it was with Nasser that in July, 1954, an agreement was finally concluded under which the British government, yielding to pressures, including American, undertook total evacuation of the canal zone within twenty months, with the right of re-entry in the event of an attack by any country except Israel on any member of the Arab League or Turkey. That Nasser had agreed to the inclusion of Turkey raised hopes that he might now be willing to co-operate in some larger scheme for the security of the Middle East, but this he showed no inclination to do.

In the autumn of 1954 the Turkish Prime Minister had been invited to Cairo, but when it became clear that the Revolutionary Council (as the new Egyptian regime styled itself) was not prepared to make alliances outside the Arab League, the Turkish government signed in Baghdad in February, 1955, a Pact of Mutual Co-operation with Iraq, then alarmed at Russian intrigues with the Kurds. In April the British government adhered to the pact, which was joined in September by Pakistan and in October by Iran. Thus the Middle Eastern countries constituting the northern tier were now bound in alliance, much to the indignation of Egypt, which professed to see in the pact a challenge to her position as the leader of the Arab world and an imperialist plot for bolstering up Israel. Syria, at least as violently nationalist as Egypt, took the same line, as did also Saudi Arabia until King Saud began to be concerned at Nasser's increasing influence.

The Middle Eastern countries that had signed the Baghdad Pact were not formidable either individually or collectively. But the pact itself was an attempt to extend the NATO organization to the Middle East, and Britain had adhered to it in order to retain bases that the Russians were determined to see removed, as they have been. For the Soviet government now decided that the time had come to intervene. Mr. Laqueur sees the first intimation of this intention in a statement published on April 17, 1955, in *Izvestia*, the organ of the Soviet Foreign Ministry, to the effect that "the situation in the Middle East had seriously deteriorated of late," and that "in the interest of peace"—always an ominous phrase when the Russians use it—the Soviet Union would do everything in its power to develop closer relations with the countries of that area.

The establishment of such relations was facilitated by a change that had recently come over Soviet policy towards the underdeveloped countries. The famous *Theses of the Sixth Comintern Congress*, to which reference has been made above, had been drafted when the Comintern was still smarting over its reverse in China. They had thus laid down unequivocally that only under the leadership of the Communist party could any country free itself from imperialist oppression and achieve independence; and that although liberation movements in such countries would be spearheaded by the national bourgeoisie, the Communists must treat this class as an enemy, even if, in the initial stages, it was necessary to co-operate with it. Unfortunately for the pundits, no successful revolution conducted on these lines was on record, whereas in the years following World War II a number of Asian countries had won their independence and had set up bourgeois nationalist governments, which all the efforts of the local Communist parties had failed to overthrow. As long as Stalin had lived, the independence of these countries had been declared to be fictitious, and their rulers had been attacked as "lackeys of the imperialists"; but the Malenkov government adopted a more flexible approach and made gestures of friendship towards them, accompanied by offers of practical assistance. To this new line Communist theory had to be adjusted, and rulers like Nehru and U Nu, hitherto denounced as reactionaries who had deceived their peoples, were rehabilitated.

Nasser had come in for his fair share of abuse. But the Soviet government had noted with approval his attitude at the Bandung Conference of April 1955, and his refusal to be drawn into any Western-sponsored defense scheme. With the exception of Iraq, none of the Arab states had any particular reason to fear the Soviet Union, which had never interfered with them and had supported their nationalist aspirations; whereas they regarded Israel not only with hatred as a puppet

that the West had created at their expense in order to secure
a foothold in the Middle East, but also with alarm for fear
the rapid increase of her population might well lead her to
seek to extend a frontier already embracing territory not assigned to her under the Partition Plan of 1947. The large-
scale Israeli raid of February 25, 1955, this time directed
against the Egyptian army, had led to a recrudescence of
border trouble and to pressure on the part of the Egyptian
military authorities for increased armaments. Negotiations
with Washington and London failed to obtain them in sufficient quantities, because of the Tripartite Declaration of
1950, and thus the way was opened for a deal with the Russians, who agreed to supply armaments through Czechoslovakia against payment in cotton, with which the Egyptian
market was then glutted. According to the accepted version,
the deal was concluded when D. T. Shepilov, then editor of
Pravda, later Foreign Minister, and now disgraced, visited
Cairo in July, so that it coincided with the Geneva summit
conference, which had raised such hopes in the West.

The events that followed the Czech arms deal call for only
the briefest recapitulation. Pressure on Israel increased in the
form of *fedayeen* raids. Jordan was detached from its British
connection. The struggle of the French against the Algerian
nationalists, who were abetted by Egypt, assumed the character of a large-scale civil war. Then came the affair of the
Aswan Dam. The American government had promised financial assistance for this project provided the Egyptian government bore an agreed share of the cost. But not only did the
arms deal raise doubts as to whether Egypt would be able to
meet her obligations, but Nasser was acquiring the reputation
of a trouble-maker and had recently recognized the Peking
government. The State Department had second thoughts,
and in July the American offer, which had never been accepted, was withdrawn. On July 26 Nasser nationalized the
canal and declared his intention of using its revenues to
finance the Aswan Dam. After conferences in London and
abortive negotiations in Cairo, the issue went to the United
Nations, where an Anglo-French resolution demanding in-

ternational control of the canal was defeated by the Russian
veto.

Meanwhile a joint Egyptian-Syrian-Jordan army command
had been formed for the scarcely concealed purpose of liqui-
dating Israel. On October 29 the Israeli government fore-
stalled this by invading the Sinai Peninsula, and by November
2 the Egyptian forces had been defeated. On October 30
Britain and France vetoed a Security Council's resolution calling for a cease-fire, and on November 5 they landed troops in
Egypt, which they agreed on the next day to withdraw in
deference to the ruling of the United Nations and on the
understanding that that body would set up an expeditionary
force to implement its decisions. The Arabs, however, gave
full credit for the withdrawal to the Soviet Union, by this
time a major power in the Middle East, which, whether bluff-
ing or not, had threatened armed intervention. Thus, the already considerable prestige of the Soviet Union was greatly
increased. The reply to this has been the Eisenhower Doctrine, which promises military and financial assistance to any
Middle Eastern nation requesting such aid against overt aggression by any country controlled by international communism. The doctrine, assisted by certain Egyptian excesses,
succeeded at first beyond expectation. The Baghdad Pact was
revitalized; Saudi Arabia and Jordan were detached from the
Cairo orbit; and in the Lebanese elections of May the pro-
Western coalition was maintained in power.

Recent events—the Moscow agreement under which the
Soviet government has made a loan to Syria at a low rate of
interest, "to fulfill the country's military requirements," followed by the discovery of an alleged American plot in Damas-
cus, and the rise to power of a military faction consisting of
a group of young officers of markedly leftist sympathies—may
mean that the Soviet Union is now counterattacking. So far,
the key to its policy in the Middle East has been its alliance
with the national bourgeoisie. As long as such men as Nasser
could be trusted to embarrass the Western powers, refuse
to be drawn into any commitments sponsored by them, and
thus insure that the Middle East would be a neutral glacis

in the event of war, the main objectives of Soviet policy appeared to be satisfied. But Nasser has recently shown an inclination to reinsure with the West and does not appear disposed to go beyond an attitude of "neutralism" toward the two world blocs.

It may therefore be that the Russians are no longer content with this and now want to force the pace, in which case their choice of Syria as a protégé is intelligible enough in view of the country's geographical position vis-à-vis the northern tier and the fact that it is at loggerheads with all its neighbors. But while the situation there holds dangerous possibilities, it would seem premature to say at the present stage that Syria has taken a decisive step on the road to Moscow, and still less that she is now reduced to the position of a Russian satellite.

In conclusion, it has to be recognized that the disappearance of Western imperialism offers in itself no guarantee against the extension of Soviet influence, in particular through the Communist movement, if the colonial powers are replaced by native autocracies. The governments of the Middle East have tended, perhaps inevitably, to be narrow oligarchies without an adequate sense of responsibility towards those whom they govern. Thus the nationalist of yesterday who had believed that his lot would improve once his country was rid of the "imperialist oppressor," to whom he had been taught to attribute all his misfortunes, has now found that he was mistaken. As Mr. Laqueur has pointed out, the local Communist parties, under Moscow-trained leaders, have gained greatly in strength since World War II. They are recruited almost exclusively from what is by courtesy called an intelligentsia, whose emotional acceptance of something resembling a Communist ideology, though one in which xenophobic nationalism has replaced those elements that communism originally borrowed from the liberal tradition of internationalism, is filling the vacuum created by the rejection of the political norms of the West. So far, these parties have lacked mass support, but should they appeal for it, it might well be forthcoming.

What in fact has been restraining the spread of communism
in this area is, once again, Moscow's alliance with the national
bourgeoisie, as this class is opposed to any far-reaching change
in the social and economic structure and thus a fortiori to
communism. As long as the Russians believe that their interests can be served best by supporting bourgeois nationalist
leaders, the Communists will have to soft-pedal. Yet such alliances may not endure. The sympathy that these national
bourgeois governments feel towards the Soviet Union is,
under the circumstances, natural enough. Yet it is not un-
tinged with suspicion, and in spite of all that their propaganda
asserts, none of them can afford a complete break with the
West. The Soviet theoretical journals have recently been at-
tacking the iniquities of bourgeois nationalism with an un-
usual asperity, while continuing to make an exception of the
underdeveloped Asian countries which are represented as
seeking to complement their political independence by
achieving economic independence. If, however, it should be
decided that the policies adopted by the governments of
these countries no longer justify the exception made in their
favor, the Russians may be expected to return to their former
hostility and throw their full weight behind the nascent Communist movement in the Middle Eastern countries. This
movement will have fertile soil on which to work until genuine efforts are made to deal with the problems of poverty and
disease, put an end to corruption, and create a social order
more consonant with the needs and dignity of the common
man.

XIV

Concluding Comments

ERNEST K. LINDLEY
Director, Washington Bureau of Newsweek Magazine

WE HAVE HAD a bountiful feast. The menu, I think you will agree, has been excellent—varied and well-balanced, packed with proteins and vitamins and containing very little fat, superbly prepared by a battery of master chefs, and delightfully served with piquant sauces and seasoning. But after thirteen or fourteen courses, each qualifying as a *pièce de résistance*, I feel stuffed to capacity and in need of a quiet period for digestion.

I shall not attempt a well-ordered recapitulation. My remarks will be selective, falling for the most part under the first topic, "The United States and the Middle East." My interest in that subject is, of course, not that of someone with any responsibility for formulating and conducting American policy, but that of one of the breed of commentators and columnists who coach those who have the responsibility. We not only tell them where they have been, or are presently, wrong—or occasionally right. Sometimes we are also venturesome enough to tell them how to do better in the future. We are never discouraged when, as so often is the case, our pupils disregard our advice. We continue to give it freely and in generous quantities. Nor are we ever deterred by the discovery that we have read the future no more clearly than did a president or a secretary of state or a Middle East expert. Senators and Cabinet members and cabinetmakers come and go. But columnists and commentators endure—not only as an institution, but as individuals—to the envy at times, I suspect, of public officials who have to suffer for their mistakes or the whims of fate or the electorate.

It is probably unnecessary for me to emphasize that I speak neither as a public official nor as an expert on the Middle East. Some of the observations I am about to make may seem to take unfair advantage of that dual freedom. Perhaps others may seem too obvious to require mention, but in this, as in so many other matters, it is easy to lose sight of the fundamentals. Among them seem to me to be these:

1. It is *vital* that the Middle East remain part of the free world. Its loss to communism would alter the world balance of power drastically, perhaps catastrophically. I do not believe that it is necessary to elaborate this point.

2. The Soviet interest in the Middle East—in those parts not already incorporated into the Soviet Union—is short of vital. Control of the Middle East is, of course, an old Russian ambition and essential to eventual Communist domination of the world. It is a prize that Moscow must be expected to keep on seeking. But the Soviet Union does not need the Middle East in order to survive or to continue its industrial growth. Nor does the "socialist camp" as a whole need the Middle East in order to survive in its present dimensions. At least the Soviets say they do not need the oil—and this is a case in which we should be content to take them at their word.

The Soviets have, in fact, recoiled every time they have encountered determined opposition in the Middle East. They withdrew from Iran in 1946—and that was under Stalin, who was supposed to be tough. They did not venture military intercession in support of the later Communist effort to take control of Iran from within. They took heed when we went to the aid of Greece and Turkey. At the time of the Suez crisis, there was no indication that they intended to intervene—at least not before they saw that we opposed the Israeli-British-French initiative and that the British and French were faltering. Indeed, they at first seemed to assume that Nasser would fall and apparently were prepared to write him off.

It follows that the so-called Eisenhower Doctrine was not a risky step. On the contrary, it probably reduces somewhat the risk of a major war in or over the Middle East. It could usefully have been set forth a decade earlier. One may say it was implicit in our support of Iran and our aid to Greece and Turkey, and that the danger of deliberate overt Soviet military action in the Middle East has never been very great. However, it is well to remove—not only in Moscow, but in the capitals of the Middle East—all doubt that such action would be met with force by us. A clear warning became all the more advisable as a result of the impression—poorly founded, I believe—that Soviet hints of military intervention or retaliation caused Britain and France to halt and abandon their Suez venture.

The question now arises whether the Soviets may not become more definitely committed in the Middle East, through a Communist or at least a pro-Communist regime in Syria or through alliances, secret if not open, with Syria and Egypt. There has not yet arisen in the Middle East any regime that Moscow has acclaimed as a member of the "socialist camp." Communist prestige is thus not committed. And for various reasons, including the effect on other Middle Eastern nations, one would think that Moscow would be reluctant to give such a blessing even to a regime that was in fact truly Communist. It is much better for their purposes to continue to pose as supporters of nationalism. And, unless we mislead them by fogginess and irresolution, it is hard to believe that the Soviets would shoulder the risks of a definite military alliance with any nation, at least any small one, at a distance from their borders.

As soon as the arms deal with Egypt was announced, it began to be said in some quarters that, as the Soviets now had a base in the Middle East, we should sit down and negotiate with them. That would be pleasing to them. But it is a counsel of defeatism. Generally—one thinks of limited possible exceptions arising chiefly from existing treaty rights—it seems to me that we should not concede that there is anything in the Middle East about which we should negotiate with the Kremlin.

3. The Middle East and the West are economically interdependent—or at least the oil-producing nations and western Europe and Britain are economically interdependent. They have direct, substantial interests in achieving or restoring and preserving harmonious relations. We should do what we can to improve these relations on the basis of equality and partner-

ship. Under present circumstances, the oil-producing nations and their Western customers have a common interest in reducing the power of the oil-transit countries to cause trouble. Alternative means of shipping oil should be vigorously developed—long-range tankers, a pipeline through Turkey, a pipeline and possibly a canal through Israel. Oil from the Sahara, if found in sufficient quantities and rapidly exploited, might be extremely helpful. If the hopes of the oil geologists for Libya should materialize, a number of Middle East problems, actual or potential, might become more manageable.

4. Communism and anti-Western nationalism: There appears to be some difference of opinion as to the relative weights of these two influences. Elsewhere in the world it has sometimes been difficult to distinguish between a Communist who *talks* like a non-Communist nationalist and a non-Communist nationalist who *acts* like a Communist. Up to a point the practical difference may be unimportant—and after that point the non-Communist nationalist who chose to play with the Communists may be dead or in jail. Abroad, as at home, we should eschew a finding of guilt based on mere association. We should be slow to give up any man as hopelessly lost—even genuine Communists have changed their minds. But that does not mean that we should ignore mischievous or foolish policies and actions or fail to support and to give preferential treatment to regimes and individuals who understand the dangers of entanglement with Moscow.

5. Neutralism: We should press no nation to join a military alliance with us. I agree with Mr. Minor in applauding what the President said a year ago last June, and on other occasions, about our relations with nations that have chosen not to join the military alliances in either the free or Communist worlds. But there are a number of varieties of neutrality or neutralism. There are the imposed unarmed neutrality of Austria and Finland, the professional neutrality of Switzerland, and the technical neutrality of Sweden. No one questions where the sympathies of these governments and an overwhelming majority of their peoples lie. There is the national Communist neutralism of Tito. In Asia there is the relatively passive neutralism of

such small countries as Burma and Cambodia. There is the groping neutralism of Indonesia. There is the active neutralism of India, well intended on the whole, although not so high minded as it purports to be and sometimes injurious to the free world and the cause of peace. There are the policies of Saudi Arabia and Jordan, and of Lebanon. All of these forms of nonalignment, neutrality, or neutralism differ significantly, even profoundly, from the recent policies and propaganda of Syria and Egypt. Hostile acts and words are not made less objectionable by labeling them "positive neutralism."

6. Economic and technical aid (I touch on only a few points): It is widely, if not universally, understood that we do not seek to buy, and indeed can not buy, friendship. We have a vital interest in the survival of new nations. And most of them cannot hope to achieve the economic growth necessary to survival without outside technical and economic aid. We should stand ready to help them all. But obviously those who are contributing to the common defense should receive preferential consideration.

The suggestion that more aid be funneled through the United Nations may not be wholly without merit. But the argument that the recipients of aid would prefer that channel is not, I think, very appealing to the people who have to put up the money. As a matter of fact, there is no visible tendency among the more or less neutralist countries to shun aid from us—most of them seem quite eager to get it. Even the Burmese, who once decided that receiving more aid from us would be unneutral, have changed their minds. Nor, it seems to me, should we be disconcerted by Soviet competition in this field. The Burmese do not seem to be very happy with the results of their big trade deal with the Soviet Union. Perhaps, as Mr. Carew Hunt suggested, Syria may eventually serve as a salutary example.

7. Our support of nationalism: Our opposition to imperialism and our support of self-government have been too steadfast and active to be misunderstood by any informed person. In reality I do not think our position on this question is misunderstood by many, if any, of the leaders of any of the new or emerging free nations. A few of them have been reluctant to give us

public credit and particularly to challenge Communist propaganda against us. But they know our record, not only our traditions and the example we set in the Philippines, but the pressures that we have exerted on our closest allies. They cannot help knowing also what the British have done during the last decade, beginning with the relinquishment of their Indian empire. The Sudan, Ghana, the West Indian Federation, the Federation of Malaya—it should be plain that the general policy of Britain is actively to promote the conversion of its wards into self-governing nations.

The French have been slower to yield to the inevitable, but the French empire also is well on the way to liquidation. In fairness we cannot forget, or let others forget, that the problem of converting colonies into commonwealths or independent nations is in some instances greatly complicated by the presence of substantial minorities of European settlers. Totally to disregard their interests and welfare, especially when they are rooted in the land, often for generations, would be flagrantly unjust.

Furthermore, some of the problems that are put under the heading of "colonialism" by Communists and crusading nationalists are not really colonial questions. We do not hold our position in Okinawa because we are imperialistic; we hold it, at very considerable expense to ourselves, for the common defense of the free world. We hold a number of island groups in the central Pacific for the same reason. (The United Nations Charter draws a distinction between ordinary and strategic trusteeship.) A number of other positions in the world must be similarly regarded. Cyprus is one. The suggestion that it be put under the control of NATO appeals to me. The Suez Canal area, even more emphatically, is another—not only because it embraces an important international waterway, but because it lies at the threshold of Africa and is also a highly suitable site for a base to support the defense of the Middle East. My nomination for the worst blunder in Western policy in the Middle East since the second world war is the surrender of physical control of this area. The British could not comfortably have remained there much longer and might well have withdrawn even if we had not pressed them to do so. The wise alternative was to internationalize the force along the canal. That, it seems to me, should have been a prime objective of American policy starting eight or nine years ago. If tenaciously pursued, it might —despite the obvious difficulties—have been crowned with success.

We missed the opportunity again last fall. I cannot agree that our policy in the Suez crisis, or our wavering course in the months just before the crisis, flowed from either a plain moral dictate or a sound appraisal of the realities. Probably in all the circumstances it was advisable for us to take a stand against Israel, Britain, and France—although each of them, it seemed to me, had considerable justification for resort to force. But it is most regrettable that the British and French did not take the entire canal and hold it until the United Nations or some other appropriate international agency was prepared to take full and permanent responsibility for its operation and defense. Our efforts in the United Nations, it seems to me, should have been directed toward that and related constructive solutions.

8. Israel: Undeniably our policy was often made, or at least voiced, with a sharp eye for the next election. That does not mean that it was wrong in substance. In any event, what has been done will not be undone. Israel's Arab neighbors will have to adjust themselves to the fact that Israel is there to stay. Let us hope that they understand just as clearly that we oppose the expansion of Israel by force. We have demonstrated (1) that Israel has no unrestricted claim on our support and (2) that our influence on Israel contributes tangibly to the security of her Arab neighbors. Only the United States could have prevailed upon Israel to yield what it took last fall—and perhaps considerably more. Neither we nor the United Nations can compel Israel and her neighbors to make peace. But we can prevent them from fighting each other.

9. The long pull: It seems to me that we should do much more than we are doing to promote cultural and intellectual associations with the Arab nations and others in the Middle East—and indeed with all the new and emerging nations of Asia and Africa. We should offer more help in the training of

teachers, administrators, scientists, and technicians. I should like to see the number of Asian and African students in the United States trebled and quadrupled and a comparable increase in visits or exchanges of scholars and other leaders. For the long pull, we could make no wiser investment.

As I stated in the beginning, the observations just made do not pretend in any way to be a summary or recapitulation of the essays that have been presented here. They merely record certain impressions resulting from their treatment of matters connected with the policy of our own country in the perennially troubled regions of the Middle East.

Index

[Proper names beginning with al- are alphabetized
under the second part of the name.]

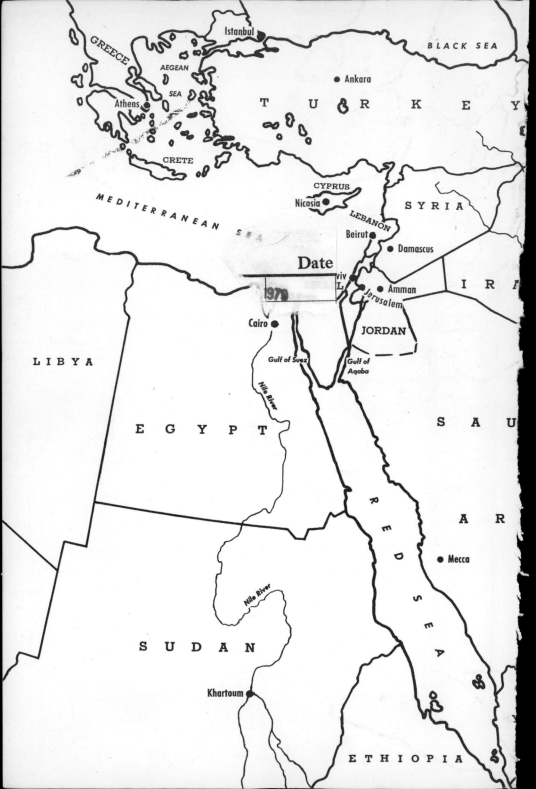